PENGUIN BOOKS

GOOD ARGUMENTS

Bo Seo is a two-time world champion debater and a former coach of the Australian national debating team and the Harvard College Debating Union. One of the most recognized figures in the global debate community, he has won both the World Schools Debating Championships and the World Universities Debating Championship. Bo has written for *The New York Times*, *The Atlantic*, CNN, and many other publications. He has worked as a national reporter for *The Australian Financial Review* and has been a regular panelist on the prime-time Australian debate program *The Drum*. Bo graduated from Harvard University and received a master's degree in public policy from Tsinghua University. He is currently a Juris Doctor candidate at Harvard Law School.

PRAISE FOR *GOOD ARGUMENTS*

"[An] enlightening introduction to the style, function, and variety of formal debate . . . Full of intriguing historical snapshots and practical advice, this is an inspiring study of how good-faith arguments can bring people together rather than tear them apart."
—*Publishers Weekly*

"Bo Seo pulls off the hat trick of persuasion, combining crisp logic, a compelling story, and a likable, trustworthy narrator. While his book will turn the shyest introvert into a wannabe debater, it makes a compelling argument of its own: that civil disagreement can save our troubled civilization."
—Jay Heinrichs, *New York Times* bestselling author of *Thank You for Arguing*

"At a time of polarization and rage, we all need to learn how to disagree well—and this important, compelling, and wise book should be at the heart of how we do so."

—Johann Hari, *New York Times* bestselling author of
Stolen Focus and *Lost Connections*

"This is not just the electrifying tale of how Bo Seo won two world debate championships. It's also a user manual for our polarized world. I can't think of a more vital resource for learning to sharpen your critical thinking, accelerate your rethinking, and hone your ability to open other people's minds. *Good Arguments* is the rare book that has the potential to make you smarter—and everyone around you wiser."

—Adam Grant, #1 *New York Times* bestselling author of
Think Again and host of the podcast *WorkLife*

"*Good Arguments* is a book so timely and needed in this fractioning world we are living in. It assumes that a quarrel is something you first have with yourself, get it out of the way, and start to respect and listen to the person across the room from you. Seo has written a book that forces us to think and then speak as the philosopher he knows is right on the tip of every tongue. This book is brilliant and a pleasure to read; in the end, he instructs us not to win but to convince, and unexpectedly, he teaches how to persuade, for words are deployed as weapons of love."

—Jamaica Kincaid, author of *See Now Then*, *Mr. Potter*,
and *The Autobiography of My Mother*

"In a world increasingly rent by division within and between nations, Bo Seo's lucid and humane search for 'better ways to disagree' could not be more timely or valuable."

—Kevin Rudd, former prime minister of Australia
and author of *The Case for Courage*

"I adore this beautiful story of a young person's journey from fear of conflict and altercation to embrace of wonderful disagreement and argument. In this touching memoir, debate is not a mere activity but a way of life that offers hope of a cure for a diseased society. *Good Arguments* is essential reading!"

—Jeannie Suk Gersen, John H. Watson Jr. Professor of Law
at Harvard Law School and author of *A Light Inside*

"From two-time world champion debater Bo Seo, a thoughtful, instructive, and eloquent meditation on the art of debate and why its central pillars—fact-finding, reason, persuasion, and listening to opponents—are so valuable in today's alarming ecosystem of misinformation and extreme emotion. When Bo Seo's family immigrated from South Korea to Australia, he was a shy, conflict-averse eight-year-old who worried about being an outsider, and in *Good Arguments*, he recounts how debate not only helped him to cross language lines but also gave him confidence and a voice of his own."

—Michiko Kakutani, *New York Times* bestselling author of
Ex Libris and *The Death of Truth*

"I had lots of conversations about political and social issues with Bo Seo when he was a student at Harvard, and I never felt, even for a second, that he was being disputatious or even argumentative. On the contrary, they were delightfully agreeable. Now I understand why: it was because Bo Seo is a debater, in fact, one of the best debaters in the world. If you want to learn how debating can help you become a more engaging conversationalist, a more broad-minded thinker, or even, maybe, just a better human being, you must read *Good Arguments*."

—Louis Menand, Pulitzer Prize–winning author of
The Metaphysical Club and *The Free World*

"Today, more than ever, we see the importance of navigating disagreements constructively. In his new book, *Good Arguments*, Bo Seo offers some tips we can all use in doing so, drawing on his deep experience as a champion debater."

—Stephen A. Schwarzman, *New York Times* bestselling author of
What It Takes: Lessons in the Pursuit of Excellence

Good Arguments

HOW DEBATE TEACHES US TO
LISTEN AND BE HEARD

Bo Seo

PENGUIN BOOKS

PENGUIN BOOKS
An imprint of Penguin Random House LLC
penguinrandomhouse.com

First published in the United States of America by Penguin Press,
an imprint of Penguin Random House LLC, 2022
Published in Penguin Books 2023

ISBN 9780593299531 (paperback)

THE LIBRARY OF CONGRESS HAS CATALOGED THE HARDCOVER EDITION AS FOLLOWS:
Names: Seo, Bo, author.
Title: Good arguments : how debate teaches us to listen and be heard / Bo Seo.
Description: New York : Penguin Press, 2022. | Includes bibliographical references and index.
Identifiers: LCCN 2021058137 (print) | LCCN 2021058138 (ebook) |
ISBN 9780593299517 (hardcover) | ISBN 9780593299524 (ebook)
Subjects: LCSH: Debates and debating. Classification: LCC PN4181 .S34 2022 (print) |
LCC PN4181 (ebook) | DDC 808.53—dc23/eng/20220318
LC record available at https://lccn.loc.gov/2021058137
LC ebook record available at https://lccn.loc.gov/2021058138

Printed in the United States of America
3 5 7 9 10 8 6 4

DESIGNED BY MEIGHAN CAVANAUGH

Some names and identifying characteristics have been changed
to protect the privacy of the individuals involved.

Bo Seo is available for select speaking engagements. To inquire about
a possible appearance, please contact Penguin Random House
Speakers Bureau at speakers@penguinrandomhouse.com
or visit prhspeakers.com.

For Jin Kyung Park
and Won Kyo Seo

CONTENTS

INTRODUCTION

Before my ninth birthday, I lost the ability to disagree. I experienced the loss as a kind of erosion: there was no disabling moment, only a slow and steady fade. In the beginning, I resisted. Though the words caught in my throat, I found ways to spit out my objections. But then I tired of the effort, risk, and self-disclosure that arguments entail. So I began to linger in the silences between speech and, once there, told myself I could find a way to live in this safe and hidden place.

It was July 2003 and my parents and I had just moved to Australia from South Korea. The decision to immigrate—in pursuit of fresh opportunities in life, work, and education—had excited me in the beginning, but now in Wahroonga, this quiet, wealthy suburb in the north of Sydney, I could see that it was a folly. We had left behind good friends, food made with actual spices, and 48 million people who spoke our language. And for what? The alienation I felt—in the refrigerated aisles of Woolworths or atop the jungle gym at the local park—had the irritating quality of being boldly chosen.

In response to my complaints, Mum and Dad were sympathetic but unmoved. I got the sense from how they repeated the word *transition* that discomfort and confusion had been accounted for in some grand arithmetic.

My parents were somewhat dissimilar to each other. Dad grew up as part of a sprawling, conservative family in a country town on the easternmost point of the Korean Peninsula. Mum was raised by urbane progressives in Seoul. He eschewed material comforts; she had an instinct for glamour. He loved people; she prized ideas. However, the stages of immigration brought to the fore qualities they shared: a fierce independence and a determination to realize their dreams.

I spent these early weeks in Sydney in the back seat of a rental car as my parents zipped around town working through a list of tasks. Furniture purchases, tax file number registration, an apartment lease—each tied us more closely to this city but none inspired a sense of attachment. When I asked if there was anything I could do, my parents said I had only one job: "Find your feet at school, okay?"

The locals in Wahroonga knew the elementary school in their suburb as the Bush School. Surrounded by a wildlife reserve, the school campus was always on the verge of being overrun by plant life. Thickets of bush clawed against classroom windows and ear-sized mushrooms bloomed on the seats of the abandoned amphitheater. In the summer, the place was lush and green. But on this wintry Monday morning in August, my first day of third grade, the leaves shimmered pale silver and the boundaries of the campus were covered in shadows.

At the blackboard in class 3H, Miss Hall, a young woman dressed in powder blue, wore an expression so soft that it seemed to dissolve every edge on her face. She gestured for me to come through the door and, as I shuffled to the front of the room, wrote on the board in perfect cursive: "Bo Seo, South Korea." In front of me, some thirty pairs of eyes widened at this unlikely combination of words.

For the rest of the week, I found myself at the center of the class's attention. On the playground, I learned that the shtick that played for the most laughs was mock argument. One of my classmates would praise some achievement of Western civilization—"How good is white bread?"—and I would respond, using the dozens of English words within my reach, "No, rice is better!" The other kids shook their heads but could not disguise their exhilaration at the hint of conflict.

However, over the course of the month, as the novelty of my presence subsided, disagreements between me and my peers took on a different tone. When conflict arose on the sports field or in a group project, my halting attempts to express myself caused exasperation and flashes of anger. In these zero-sum situations, I learned that the distance between being odd and being at odds was short, and a gesture or some words, misinterpreted or misconstrued, could push one over the line.

The worst part of crossing language lines is adjusting to live conversation—to its rapid, layered rhythms and many about-faces. In an argument, these difficulties compound. Language becomes less precise, and the pressure squeezes one's faculties. Tripping over loose words and broken sentences—the detritus of broken speech—I never got far.

Some kids, inspired less by malice than by a savage instinct for power, pressed their advantage. They scrunched up their faces and asked whether anyone could understand what I was saying. Others strained to make accommodations, then faltered in their goodness and walked away with a sheepish "Never mind." For months, I tried to hold my own. The fighting self, the bargaining self, the pleading self—each one attempted his work.

Then, sometime before the end of the school year in November 2003, I found myself unwilling to keep arguing. No issue or principle could seem to justify the costs of disagreement. If I tried to override that judgment, some combination of my legs, stomach, and throat would revolt.

So I learned to wear a distant smile. In the classroom, I rushed to admit ignorance, while on the playground, I conceded fault. Even as my language skills improved, the range of words on which I relied most narrowed to *yes* and *okay*. In the early days of my compromise, I committed to memory the disagreements that I did not voice but might one day wish to revisit. Then, in time, even these memories faded away.

By the time I entered the fifth grade in January 2005, I had found ways to make the most of my agreeableness. School reports praised my sunny disposition and ability to follow instructions. Among friends, I mediated conflicts and steered conversations toward consensus. My parents reported to family back in South Korea that I was adjusting magnificently.

And I was. Whereas I had once been embarrassed by my inability to hold my own in an argument, I could now see that the real embarrassment lay in choosing to argue at all—in the red faces, in the flying spittle, in the uselessness of the exercise. I felt I had found the groove in which I could ride out my childhood.

Then on a spring afternoon in March 2005, something changed and a habit of life almost two years in the making came undone.

. ° .

Walking into the assembly hall after lunchtime, I cursed myself for the act of self-betrayal. Three days earlier, my fifth grade teacher, Ms. Wright, had called for volunteers to join a new activity at the school: "Debate is a structured argument in which two teams vie for the hearts and minds of the audience; a battle of the wits!" Almost everyone declined the offer, but when the teacher flagged me down on my way out of the classroom, I found myself nodding at her request. To avoid an argument, I opted into debate.

The rules were simple. A neutral third party assigned a topic ("That we should ban all zoos") and assigned one team of three people to argue in favor and another team to argue against, without regard to the speakers' actual beliefs. The first affirmative speaker opened the debate, which then toggled back and forth between the two sides until all the speakers had spoken for their allotted time (in our case, four minutes).

At the end of the round, the adjudicator—another neutral party, often experienced in debate—delivered a judgment on which side had won. They evaluated individual debaters on three measures: the *manner* of speech, the *matter* of their arguments, and the *method* or strategy behind their contributions. Yet for their ultimate adjudication they needed only to consult their consciences on one question: Which side had convinced them?

I had not slept well the previous night. Though in a regular debate teams had limited time to prepare their cases (anywhere between fifteen minutes and one hour), we had been given several days. This felt like a mercy. The difficulty of everyday disagreements lay for me in their immediacy. How I had wished in these altercations to be able to pause time, if only for a moment, to gather my thoughts and summon the right language. Now, as the first affirmative speaker, I could plan most everything in advance, and so I had, researching and writing into the wee hours.

The assembly hall had been simply arranged. Onstage were two tables, each with three seats, that looked out from a modest height into the crowd of sixty-odd kids seated in snaking rows. Avoiding the gaze of the audience members, I walked behind my two team-mates: Isabella, an athlete with a striding gait, and Tim, a neurotic kid whose legs squirmed to their destination. Overhead, the rain drummed on the metal roof an ominous percussion.

Our opponents from 5J, the other fifth-grade class, had already taken their seats, and as we climbed the stairs to meet their level, they flashed us looks of derision. The two girls on their team soon resumed chatting between themselves and waving at friends in the audience. But the third member, Arthur, a model student in wire-rimmed glasses, kept staring in our direction. I had had trouble with Arthur on the playground, where he used his smarts to demonstrate his superior command of subjects ranging from botany to World War II and left opponents speechless with rapid-fire arguments and constant interruptions.

However, on this stage, where we had been promised equal time and consideration, Arthur somehow seemed less untouchable. Whereas before I had noticed only his arched eyebrows and perfectly shined shoes, I now spied the small stain on his shirt and the mole on his right cheek.

At the center of the stage, Ms. Wright pulled back her mane of hair and opened the debate in a roaring voice: "Good afternoon, everyone, and welcome! What you are about to watch is a debate. In a debate, when someone—anyone—is delivering a speech, everyone else has to listen in silence." She placed one finger across her lips and led the group in a twenty-second-long "shhhhhhh."

Then with her other hand, Ms. Wright picked up a notebook. "Turn your book sideways and draw six columns down the page, one for each speaker. I want you to write in the columns all the points raised by each person. The rule in debate is that every argument requires a response, simply for having been raised." The audience rushed to follow her instructions. Some kids used rulers to draw perfect, measured lines; others went freehand. "When the round is done, this is how we will decide who has won: not on the basis of which position we hold or who the speakers are, but on the quality of the arguments. Any questions?"

The next thing I heard was the topic—"That we should ban all zoos"—followed by my name. I felt the weight of the room's attention shift toward me. To scattered applause, I gathered my index cards and approached the center of the stage.

What I saw from the edge of the platform was unlike anything I had seen before. Every pair of eyes in the audience stared at me, blinking. Every mouth hung open but silent. The adjudicator, a sixth-grade teacher, held his pen against a blank notepad, ready to write down my ideas. For the first time since I moved to Australia, I felt that I might be heard.

I had spent years avoiding arguments. Had my mistake been not to run toward them?

• • •

Some seventeen years after that fateful day in 2005, I am still running toward good disagreements. On this path, I have reached several milestones but no finish line. I have twice won the world championships for competitive debate, and I have coached two of the most successful debate teams in the world: the Australian Schools Debating Team and the Harvard College Debating Union. I have moved around the world—from South Korea to Australia, to the United States and China—and searched in each place for better ways to disagree.

This book, the sum of a short lifetime's reflection, is about two forms of debate.

One is competitive debate, a formal game in which rival sides argue their case on an assigned topic before an impartial adjudicator. The origins of this contest stretch back to antiquity—to ancient Greek rhetorical education, to early Buddhist religious practice—and its evolution is intertwined with the development of parliamentary democracy. Today, competitive debate thrives in high schools and universities across the world and counts a disproportionate number of former presidents and prime ministers, Supreme Court justices, captains of industry, prize-winning journalists, prominent artists, and civil society leaders as alums. The activity is dead easy to learn but impossible to master. For this reason, it makes room for children and presidential candidates. (What does this say about each?)

The other form of debate is the everyday disagreements we encounter in our lives. Few people join a debate team, but everyone argues, in some form, most days. Since we disagree not only about the way things ought to be but also about the way things are, the mere act of perceiving can spark conflict. In the resulting arguments, we seek to persuade others, find solutions, test our beliefs, and defend our pride. We judge, correctly, that our personal, professional, and political interests rest on our ability not only to win these arguments but also to prevail in the right way.

My argument is that competitive debate can teach us how to disagree better in our everyday lives. Disagreeing well can mean many things—getting one's way, reducing future conflict, preserving the relationship with one's opponent—and this book will have something to say about each of these. However, I define the aim in more modest terms: we should disagree in such a way that the outcome of having the disagreement is better than not having it at all.

To this end, I offer in this book a tool kit and a testament.

In the first half of the book, I present five basic pieces of competitive debate—topic, argument, rebuttal, rhetoric, quiet—as well as the skills and strategies needed to wield them. I believe that these elements reveal a physics that underlies our everyday arguments and, in sum, form a body of knowledge that is more accessible than formal logic and more broadly applicable than negotiation.

The second half of the book applies the lessons of competitive debate to four areas of life—bad disagreements, relationships, education, technology—and builds the case for how good arguments can improve our private and public lives. Here, I suggest that the millennia-old tradition of competitive debate provides a testament for how a community built *around*, not *despite*, arguments might work. As with any true testament, the conclusions are not always clear-cut. The history of debate is replete with instances of domination, manipulation, glibness, and exclusion. However, I argue that debate *also* creates the possibility for something altogether more wonderful: lives and societies enriched by exciting, loving, revelatory disagreement.

I admit this is a weird time to be writing a book about good arguments. These days, few of us are shipping off to fight a war against our political opponents, but the suspicion, contempt, and hatred that disagreements stir in us seem as vast as they have ever been. In the resulting arguments, we assume bad intentions and talk past one another. Precisely at a time when the will to debate seems ascendant, the values and skills required to sustain such conversations have sunk to a nadir. This is what we mean by the term *polarization*—not that we disagree, or even that we disagree too much or too often, but that we disagree badly: our arguments are painful and useless.

Amid all the shouting, some people have abandoned hope for disagreements. In 2012, the Republican candidate for the U.S. presidency, Mitt Romney, told a private gathering that some 47 percent of people would always side with the Democrats and that these people were chronic dependents who paid no income tax. Four years later, the Democratic candidate, Hillary Clinton, described half of her opponent's supporters as "deplorables." Both politicians apologized, but the notion that some people are beyond the pale of persuasion and rational argument is a taboo that is nonetheless built into the prevailing logic of electoral politics.

However, the worst consequences of such loss of faith may land closer to home—in the silences that emerge between lovers, friends, and family. University of California researchers found that, weeks after the U.S. presidential election in 2016, Thanksgiving dinners attended by people from precincts with opposing politics were curtailed by thirty to fifty minutes. "Nationwide, 34 million hours of cross-partisan Thanksgiving dinner discourse were lost."

The tragedy is that there has never been a better time to debate. Ours is a period of unprecedented personal freedom, political suffrage, and global connection. The public square is more diverse, and the public conversation more contested, than ever before. Acknowledging the ways in which our disagreements are deficient need not detract from these important achievements. Nor does it mean we should romanticize the past. Never have we embraced such pluralism and better managed our disagreements. So we need to forge a new path.

In such unsettled times, we may be tempted to pine for consensus—to dwell on our commonalities at the exclusion of our differences. As a naturally shy person, I feel the pull of this instinct most days. But I also know firsthand the bitter fruits of this aspiration.

For several years of my childhood in Sydney, I purged arguments from my days and structured them, instead, around the pursuit of agreement. The experience left me with the conviction that there is a paucity about an agreeable life. Sustaining one requires too many compromises and self-betrayals. It saps one's relationships of their most worthwhile qualities—among them candor, challenge, and vulnerability.

My travels around the world have convinced me that a political life without disagreement is also impoverished. Nations are, at their best, evolving arguments. No other view of community affords so much respect to human diversity and the open-endedness of our future. Meanwhile, its opposite, a singular insistence on unity, has tended in history toward despotism and crude majoritarianism. In a liberal democracy, good arguments are not what societies should *do* but also what they should *be*.

. . .

In those early and unhappy years in Australia, I knew the origin of my troubles. I had learned in Sunday school that the existence of multiple languages owed to an altercation in a city named Babel. At one time, the people of the world spoke one language, and in their arrogance they resolved to build a tower tall enough to reach the heavens. But as the edifice pierced the sky, an enraged God intervened. He confounded people's speech so that they could no longer understand one another. Then he dispersed them around the world.

It took me many years to see the story in a different light. The collapse of the edifice unleashed chaos into the world in the form of new cultures and dialects—a point eloquently made by writer Toni Morrison in her Nobel lecture. Banished from the tower, we took up residence in the square and began the hard work of travel and translation.

The destruction of the tower made it necessary for us to debate, but it gave us a bigger life.

People often ask me how I managed to find my voice in argument—not in the company of friends but, rather, in the heat of competition. I puzzled over the answer for many years. These days, I wonder how it could have been any other way. Disagreement is not always the best response to conflict, but it may be the most revealing one. Arguments require us to disclose ourselves in a way that physical brawls or simple forbearance do not. In conflict with the world, we discover the boundaries of who we are and what we believe.

Now we are used to seeing arguments either as the symptom of some malaise in our society or as a cause of our discontent. Indeed, they are both. However, my ultimate hope is to convince readers that arguments can also be a cure—an instrument to remake the world.

I knew none of these things and had none of these words on that spring afternoon in March 2005 when I first discovered debate. But

I had a feeling that I had been given a life raft, one that might not only save me but also take me to a brighter future, if only I could hold on. Staring out into the crowd from the edge of the stage, I felt something else sprout inside me: ambition, green and insistent.

My breath slowed. As I recalled the first few lines of my speech, I felt the ground beneath my feet regain its solidity. I guessed that once I began, I might never again stop. For that's the thing about unleashing a voice: you never know what it might say next.

1

How to find
the debate

On a Monday morning in January 2007, a couple of months after my graduation from elementary school, the green gates at the entrance to my secondary school, Barker College, served as a portal to a new world. For me and the other twelve-year-olds on the first day of middle school, the contrast between where we had been and where we were now felt stark. My former classmates had galumphed around the playground in loose interpretations of the school uniform, but the students on this campus, in their starched white shirts, seemed to be facsimiles of the children on the admissions brochures. Whereas the grounds at the Bush School had sprawled and tangled, the manicured campus of this all-boys middle school intimated an order of things—one I had good reason to learn, and fast.

By lunchtime, I had realized this would be no easy feat. In a school with a couple thousand kids, it made less sense to speak of one order than of multiple. The classroom conformed to one set of expectations—students referred to teachers as "sir" and "miss" and politely raised their hands to speak—while outside, on the playground, jungle rules prevailed. One carried on a certain way in the light-filled atrium of the music building and another way in the mildewy locker rooms next to the gymnasium. The place was a kaleidoscope of expectations.

Over my three and a half years in Australia, I had grown into a fine code-switcher. I had learned to toggle between the intimate language of home and the cheerful, shallow vernacular that school seemed to reward. However, the problem at Barker was that its rules and codes were illegible to me. What jokes were appropriate and when? How much should one reveal about oneself and to whom? I gleaned answers to these questions only by tripping over them.

In these first weeks of school, I never regressed to silence, but I found my comforts where I could. I fell in with a group of laconic, easygoing Aussie kids named—for neat alliterative effect—Jim, Jon, and Jake. Whereas the most ambitious kids in our class shook and fizzed and used every conversation to prove their virtues, the Js seemed to take things in their stride. In the afternoons, we shared a box of hot chips from the kebab shop—a staple of Australian takeout food—and not more than a handful of words.

What I never told them was that I had come to the school with a goal of my own: to join the debate team. Since my first competitive round in the fifth grade, I'd had only fleeting opportunities to revisit the activity. But I knew that the culture of debate was well-entrenched in Sydney's middle and high schools, most of whom maintained a team that competed, weekly, in a league. Debate occupied an odd place in the life of these schools. Like chess or Quiz Bowl, it provided a competitive outlet for unathletic kids but, unlike these other indoor activities, enjoyed a certain credibility on account of the reputation that its alums went on to do big things.

At Barker, anyone could attend debate training on Wednesday afternoons, but only one team of four students in each year group could represent the school at our local league on Friday evenings. To join the team, one had to audition. Ahead of trials in the first week of February, I sussed out the competition—"So this debate thing . . . ?"—but few people seemed interested. Perhaps this was going to be a piece of cake, I thought. Thank goodness for sports and other distractions.

But I was mistaken: the first round of trials, set to begin at four o'clock on a Thursday afternoon, attracted more than thirty kids. The white-paneled room on the top floor of the English building felt like the inside of a refrigerator; as the students arrived, alone or in pairs, dressed for the outside heat, they shuddered. Presiding over the auditions was the year coordinator, Miss Tillman, a history teacher with a stoic air.

Miss Tillman explained that we would not do a full debate for the audition. Instead, each student would be given a topic, a side (affirmative or negative), and thirty minutes in which to write a speech that covered two arguments for their position. In elementary school, we had prepared our cases over the span of weeks, often with the aid of teachers and the internet, but now we had to go solo against a strict time limit. "This audition format won't show me and the other judges everything," Miss Tillman said, "but it should reveal your . . . responsiveness."

In the waiting room, I stumbled on another discovery: some trialists seemed confident about their chances. The students who had attended Barker since the third grade made it known in the subtle way of twelve-year-olds that they had been successful debaters on the junior circuit and that they expected to continue their run. "We were successful on the junior circuit and expect to continue our run," one of the trialists said, before scanning the room for signs of comprehension.

Out of nowhere, I heard Miss Tillman call my name. I wondered whether she would give me some additional instructions or words of encouragement. Instead, she handed me a white envelope that contained a scrap of paper with a few handwritten words: "That we should have compulsory military service. Affirmative."

After I read that last word, things began to move fast. Everything before the envelope had been potential energy—a mind in search of an object, tension in need of release—but now the setting, a windowless nook next to the main waiting room, crackled with consequence. I found the experience of prep to be oddly liberating. The topic transported me to a new environment and assigned me a new identity. I went from being a twelve-year-old, uncertain of his beliefs and others' expectations of him, to an advocate in some chamber of deliberation.

The fact that I had no say in what I had to argue added, paradoxically, to this sense of freedom. I felt at ease to flirt with ideas, unencumbered by expectations of consistency or deep conviction (I didn't choose the side), and to explore every dark corner of contentious issues (I didn't choose the topic). In debate, the other word for *topic* is *motion* and, for these thirty minutes, that was exactly what I experienced.

Then, as Miss Tillman knocked on the door, I fell down to earth. In the audition room, a panel of three teachers sat behind a long desk. One of them, a rotund biology teacher whom I had met during orientation, managed a sympathetic look, but the others looked ashen-faced, worn down by the waves of children.

I found my place at the center of the room and focused my gaze in the gap between two panelists' faces—an ersatz form of eye contact that I hoped would pass for engagement. Then I began: "Everyone has a duty to ensure a country's safety. When we fulfill that duty through national service, we get more united societies, better armies, and happier lives." The combination of nerves and an eagerness to get noticed increased, with each word, my pitch and volume. I reached a near shout and spent the next minute adjusting down.

My speech had two points: that every citizen had a responsibility to serve and that this would result in a safer nation. In truth, the material resembled less a proper debate speech (whatever that was) than a rambling and passionate plea. "Look in your hearts and ask what you owe your fellow citizens," I implored in one of the more cringeworthy moments. However, I felt that some of my points on the effect of mandatory military service on national security had landed with the judges. As I spoke about the importance of giving political leaders a more direct stake in the fate of military operations, one of the exhausted judges seemed to briefly rouse from her stupor. The other speakers in my time slot were good but not unimaginably so. I felt I had a shot.

The next day at school, shortly after the start of recess, a notice appeared on the bulletin board near the canteen: DEBATING TEAM—YEAR SEVEN. Mine was the last name on the list, above the instruction to attend the first training session with the coach at four o'clock on Wednesday afternoon. Like the topic itself, the notice felt like a ticket made out to someplace new.

• • •

That the seventh-grade coach, a lanky college student named Simon, had been one of the most successful debaters of his year group at Barker seemed an improbable fact about him. Standing at the front of the room, Simon was the shade of pomegranate seeds—wine-dark and uneven. The edges of his voice crackled with self-doubt.

It was 4:00 p.m. on a Wednesday afternoon, nearly one week after the trials, and around a dozen students had gathered in the same air-conditioned room where auditions had been held. The four of us who had been selected for the team—Stuart, Max, Nathan, and I—sat near one another but exchanged little more than pleasantries. Of the group, I gravitated toward Nathan, a sensitive kid who reminded me of a naturalist. None of us acknowledged the chilling fact that only two weeks remained until the start of the league.

Then the session began and I witnessed a transformation. As Simon stood at the whiteboard and spoke about debate, he seemed to become a different person. Some internal force filled out his posture and rounded out his words. The color remained in his face but now took on a more vital, reddish hue. He uncapped a marker, then, turning to the board, wrote one word: *topic*.

"Cast your mind back to the last argument you had," Simon said. "Recall as much as you possibly can about the encounter: the setting at the particular time of day, the specific arguments, claims, and even insults.

"Now answer this question: What was the disagreement about?"

I thought about a series of tiffs with an old friend from the Bush School who now attended a middle school in a distant part of the city. The conversations were vivid in my mind, but I found Simon's question hard to answer. For some arguments, I could not remember the instigating dispute at all. As with bad dreams, the contents disappeared even as their effects lingered. For others, I could remember too much. These disagreements began with some trivial dispute and accumulated more points of contention—other disputes, perceived slights, past baggage—any one of which could be described as what the arguments were about.

"This is a problem. If you don't know the subject of the argument, how can you decide what or what not to say, which points to pursue or let go, and whether you want to have the argument at all?"

Simon referred to research from sociologists and linguists that posited that people are better at "talking topically" than actually staying on topic. That is, we give the impression of being relevant—often through a series of verbal cues such as "on that point"—while subtly changing the subject. Since most of us enjoy breezy, free-flowing conversation, we rarely take the time to consciously reflect on what we are talking about. "So we tend to drift, covering lots of ground but moving further from resolution," Simon said.

"However, debaters do the opposite. Every round begins with a topic. That's the first thing we debaters write—on our legal pads, on the whiteboard in the prep room. Consider it an act of naming: we name our disagreement and, with it, the purpose for our gathering."

Over the next two hours, Simon taught us more about topics than I had imagined possible—or healthy.

According to Simon, the topic is a statement of the main point on which two or more people disagree:

> That Jane is an unreliable friend.

> That the government should not bail out the big banks.

An easy test for whether a proposition is an appropriate topic is to write it in the opposite form:

That Jane is an unreliable friend.	That Jane is not an unreliable friend.
That the government should not bail out the big banks.	That the government should bail out the big banks.

Both sides of the disagreement should be able to say that the statements fairly describe what they and their opponents believe.

The defining characteristic of a debate topic was that it allowed for two sides. So a general subject area such as "the economy" or "health care" could not be one because it did not identify the particular debate in question. Nor could a topic be a purely subjective opinion, such as "I am cold," since the other person could not argue that "no, you are not cold."

Broadly speaking, people disagreed about three sorts of things—facts, judgments, prescriptions—and each one gave rise to its own type of debate.

Factual disagreements center on claims about the way things are. They take the form "X is Y," where both X and Y are empirically observable features of the world.

Lagos is a megacity.

The crime rate in Paris was lower in 2014 than in 2016.

Normative disagreements concern our subjective judgments about the world—the way things are or ought to be, in our view. They take the form "A should be considered B" or "We have good reason to believe that A is B."

Lying is (should be considered) immoral.

(We have reason to believe that) tomorrow will be better.

Prescriptive disagreements relate to what we should do. These usually take the form "C should D," where C is the actor and D is an action.

Our family should get a gym membership.

The government should not impose limits on freedom of speech.

I found all this plenty interesting, but as the training session drew to a close, I also felt pangs of disappointment. Instead of secret strategies and killer moves, we had been given taxonomies; rather than sharpening our skills, we had taken a bunch of notes. I wondered whether competitive debate, like other high-skill games such as chess, tended toward esoterica until it could no longer sustain an analogy to real life.

However, later that same night, I stumbled on a reason to revisit my concern.

For the first couple of years of our life in Australia, my parents had seldom argued with each other or with me. Disagreements of opinion abounded, but Mum and Dad took the view that fighting about them was an indulgence we could not afford, not while so much work lay ahead of us. Though we had started to argue more openly in the past year or so, we still tended to elide points of conflict. This worked fine most of the time, but when one of us snapped, the resulting arguments were tangled and endless.

At this time, in the spring of 2007, almost four years after our arrival in Sydney, our family had begun to consider naturalizing as Australian citizens. In some respects, this was a bureaucratic decision that came down to such secular concerns as taxation. However, for my dad, the choice took on symbolic magnitude. Dad had been the consistent voice in our family for the importance of maintaining our cultural roots and, for him, the word *citizenship* carried real weight.

That night, in the quiet hours after dinner, Dad called for me to come downstairs and speak on the phone to our relatives in Korea. Occupied with computer games and instant messenger, I rebuffed his requests and remained at my desk. After Dad hung up the phone, he hurried upstairs to my room. The sound of his breath, shallow and irregular, gave me pause.

"How dare you ignore me? Your aunts stayed up to take the call and you couldn't even spare five minutes? You *never* talk to our relatives."

This last claim seemed to me untrue and, therefore, unfair. In the past month alone I had exchanged multiple messages with our extended family. Granted, I had been distracted tonight, but that hardly seemed to justify this kind of reprimand.

So I defended myself: "What are you saying? I'm constantly talking to our relatives." I began in Korean but switched halfway through to English—a move of convenience that carried other baggage. "Don't you *want* me to hang out with my friends? Wasn't the whole point that you wanted me to assimilate?" I saw my dad's face, a squarer, surer version of my own, take on more color and start to tremble at the edges.

Then, before I pressed the point, I found myself asking a different question: "Wait, what are we arguing about?" Certainly we had no dispute on prescription: everyone agreed we should call our relatives. We had a minor factual disagreement about the number of times I had done that, but somehow this seemed beside the point.

Over the next few minutes, the two of us worked out that our dispute had stemmed from a judgment. Dad had formed the view that I was too blasé about maintaining my connection to Korea and that missed phone calls were one symptom of this general disregard.

Once our disagreement had been named, our conversation seemed to gain a new focus and clarity. Though we only got through arguing around midnight and, even then, with a commitment to revisit the conversation, each of us walked away from the dispute with an understanding of its terrain. "Do I really have to spell it out?" Dad had asked at one point. The answer, I realized, had been "yes."

Debate had made this small corner of the world legible to me, and as I settled into bed for the night, I wondered about the other places it could help illuminate.

. . .

Meanwhile, at school, I was discovering the ways of competition. Barker encouraged some internal jostling for rank but, for the most part, redirected its students' competitive energy outward, at long-standing rivalries with other schools. Though the collective ego of the student body resided with the rugby and cricket teams, we were game to celebrate any win for the home side. In middle school assemblies, the crowd made idols of victorious mathletes and oboists.

I read into these displays all manner of promises. Whereas the overriding goal of my early years in Sydney had been to win others' acceptance, competitive success held out a grander prospect: approval and even admiration. This heaped pressure on the upcoming start to the debate season and inflamed my concerns about our level of preparation.

One person who did not seem so worried was Simon. At our second training session, he stood at a gawky angle by the whiteboard and waited for us to take our seats. His voice, as placid as his expression, betrayed no sense of urgency.

"Last week we talked about three kinds of topics—factual, normative, prescriptive—and the disagreements they create. But you probably noticed this is too tidy and simple.

"In reality, we disagree about many things at one time. We clash on facts, judgments, *and* prescriptions, sometimes in the course of a single sentence. So our job is not as easy as identifying what we are arguing about. It is instead to disentangle the multiple threads of disagreement and to chart a course for resolving some of them."

He went up to the board and wrote up a topic.

We, as parents, should send our children to the local
public school.

"Now, circle what words could be contentious—that is, could spark a disagreement between the two sides—and spell out the argument."

I copied the sentence into my book and circled the word *send*.

The answer seemed obvious: this was a dispute about what ought to be done—a prescriptive disagreement.

> We, as parents, should **send** our children to the local
> public school.

Everyone in the room arrived at the same answer, but Simon appeared unimpressed. "What else could the two sides disagree about? Try to picture the two sides looking at this sentence. Their perspectives will differ on some words. Which ones?"

The next minute passed in silence. Then something clicked and people began shouting out answers. The two sides could disagree about "local public school." They might have different factual information about what the schools are like (e.g., the number of teachers) and conflicting judgments about the purpose of school (e.g., the importance of academic achievement versus belonging to a local community). They might also disagree about the needs, personalities, and wishes of "children," as well as the responsibilities and obligations of "parents."

> We, as **parents**, should **send** our **children** to the **local**
> **public school**

Simon said the exercise, known as topic analysis, revealed the layeredness of arguments. What seemed to be one disagreement could, in fact, be several, and a failure to recognize this multiplicity led people to speak past one another. "How can we hope to make progress if the two sides are not even having the same discussion?"

Topic analysis, as a tool for revealing the layers of our disagreements, helped us in two ways.

First, topic analysis enabled us to find the heart of an argument, the fundamental clash from which other disputes stem. For example, the main issue in the dispute over school enrollment may be how we understand the obligations of parents to their children and community. If we agreed on this point, we could break the impasse. So what appeared to be an argument over prescription was, in fact, a disagreement over a judgment.

Second, topic analysis helped us to pick our battles—to distinguish the arguments we had to win from those we could afford to lose. Suppose that one of the parents believes that the schools have all the basic facilities (fact), that the parents have an obligation to improve the public school system (judgment), and that they should send the kids there (prescription). The other parent may be in complete agreement or complete disagreement. But more likely they are somewhere in the middle. We could map out some of this gray zone:

MERE DIFFERENCE ON DETAILS	MERE DIFFERENCE OF REASONING	MERE DIFFERENCE OF APPROACH
Disagree on fact	Agree on fact	Agree on fact
Agree on judgment	Disagree on judgment	Agree on judgment
Agree on prescription	Agree on prescription	Disagree on prescription
"The school does not have some basic facilities. But we have an obligation to improve it, so we should send our kids there."	"The school has the basic facilities. We have no obligation to improve it, but we should send our kids there anyway because it will be good for them."	"The school has the basic facilities. We have an obligation to improve it. But we can find other ways of doing that without sending our children there."

MERE AGREEMENT ON DETAILS	MERE AGREEMENT ON JUDGMENT	MERE AGREEMENT ON OUTCOME
Agree on fact	Disagree on fact	Disagree on fact
Disagree on judgment	Agree on judgment	Disagree on judgment
Disagree on prescription	Disagree on prescription	Agree on prescription
"The school has the basic facilities. We have no obligation to improve it, and we shouldn't send our kids there."	"The school does not have some basic facilities. We have an obligation to improve it, but we still shouldn't send our kids there."	"The school does not have some basic facilities. We have no obligation to improve it, but we should send our kids there because it will be good for them."

Since our aim in most arguments was not to eliminate our differences with the other side but rather to reach a more acceptable level of disagreement, we rarely needed to wage all-out war. For the competitive debater, whose main goal was to sell the audience on their prescription, a mere agreement on approach could be as good as full agreement. For a parent, whose main interest was doing his or her part as a citizen, a mere difference of approach could be acceptable, so long as there were other ways to serve the community. Topic analysis gave us new opportunities for compromise—found not in agreement or disagreement but in gradations of both.

For the rest of the afternoon, we worked through a long list of past topics on the board. I tried asking a couple of pointed questions about rebuttal—"So how are we going to beat these guys?"—but Simon gave brisk answers and brought us back to the exercise. Then, at six o'clock, our time lapsed and Simon sent us on our way: "See you on Friday for the big debate!"

. . .

The last class on Friday, a chemistry lesson in a sterile lab, stretched to its dull conclusion. At the demonstration bench, our teacher stained pink some liquid in a beaker while mouthing, "Titration." I could barely feign interest in the alchemy, for my attention was elsewhere. All afternoon, my phone had been vibrating with messages from the debate team: "Let's gooo, boys!" We made an odd quartet—tall and short, loud and quiet—but we were starting to think of ourselves as a team and were searching for the words to sustain the idea.

As soon as the bell rang at 3:15 p.m., I rushed out to meet the team at the kebab shop. None of us were hungry but we figured we had to eat before the start of the round in less than two hours. Looking around the table, I began to notice the undercurrents of similarity that ran beneath the more obvious differences between me and my teammates. Stuart perched on the edge of his chair and spat contentious ideas in a rat-a-tat rhythm, but he delighted when others challenged him, as Max often did in his sober and implacably reasonable way. Nathan projected agreeableness and wore a gentle smile, but he, too, never shied away from making a point. Though I still considered the Js my closest friends, I could not shake the feeling that I had found my people.

In Australia, debate night is an institution. Different leagues of middle and high schools arrange their competitions in different ways, but most hold weekly rounds between the hours of 5:00 p.m. and 9:00 p.m. Our league in Sydney paired two schools together every Friday night, so that every one of their teams from the twelfth grade down to the seventh grade faced off against each other.

As the four of us sat around the common room waiting for topic release, a parade of older debaters came to offer advice. One burly eleventh grader, the rare crossover between the rugby and debate teams, pulled me to his breast and told me to go for the jugular. Our opponents for the evening, students from a nearby Catholic girls' school called Brigidine, milled around the water fountains, some fifty meters away. Dressed in tartan skirts and maroon blazers—a typical private school uniform in Sydney—the girls seemed impossibly polished, and I found myself wishing that I had worn the cleaner of my two shirts.

Our year coordinator, Miss Tillman, and her counterpart at Brigidine oversaw the topic release. As our respective debate families, the Montagues and the Capulets, looked on, the Brigidine team and the four of us stepped to the center of the room. There we faced each other for a moment, with not a prop or costume between us. On the face of the girl nearest to me, I saw fear and determination in equal measure.

Miss Tillman handed us our envelopes, then brandished her stopwatch in the air. "Time starts . . . now!" I read the topic out loud as our team rushed to the prep room: "That developing countries should prioritize environmental sustainability over economic development. Affirmative: Brigidine. Negative: Barker." Flying up the stairs with my teammates, as the sound of our steps cleared the path ahead, I experienced again a sense of motion.

In the prep room, a dusty space used for storage, our momentum came to a sudden stop. The first twenty minutes of our allocated hour passed in unproductive chaos. We turned the whiteboard black with ideas but failed to surface one usable argument. Each of us complained, not without reason, that we had no idea what we were doing. The climate change documentary *An Inconvenient Truth* had been released months earlier, and I could not shake the mental image of Al Gore looking disappointed in our work.

Then Max, who had been oddly quiet for the duration of prep, had a brain wave. He strode to the whiteboard and wiped clean a small section at its center. Then he wrote:

> That developing countries should prioritize environmental sustainability over economic development.

"Let's do the topic analysis thing," he said. "What is this debate actually about?"

The four of us converged on an answer. Of course, the main dispute was about prescription—what to "prioritize." However, the two teams could also disagree on the descriptive meaning and the normative value of "sustainability" and "development." They could disagree, too, about the conditions in "developing countries," as well as their rights and obligations.

> That **developing countries** should **prioritize** environmental **sustainability** over economic **development.**

Seeing these threads of disagreement, we chose to focus on the last set of questions, about the rights and responsibilities of developing countries, and to argue that these nations should not be expected to shoulder the costs of climate action. Inasmuch as the global north could help reduce the trade-off between sustainability and development, that would be welcome, but where there was a choice, developing countries had a right to choose the latter. The strategy seemed fraught and open to challenge, but as my teammates and I walked out of the prep room with our half-written speeches, I felt overwhelming relief at the fact that we had found a path at all.

In the debate room, a newer classroom saturated with fluorescent light, an audience of our parents had gathered. Mum and Dad had dressed for the occasion and, from their seats in the second row, waved until I waved back. The Brigidine team had arrived before us. As I sat down, I noticed that the hour of prep had not dislodged a single fold on our opponents' uniforms.

The next words I heard came from the chairperson: "Welcome to the first round of the grade-seven competition. I remind the audience to please silence mobile phones, and now welcome the first affirmative speaker to open the debate."

For more than a minute, the first speaker from Brigidine, an austere-looking girl who had managed to hide any evidence of nervousness, stood in silence at the center of the room. As the audience began to edge forward, nervous in their wait, she began to deliver her speech in long and flowing sentences.

"Climate change is the greatest danger facing our species, one that threatens everything about the way we live today. Developing countries not only account for a huge amount of global emissions, they also bear the worst effects of environmental catastrophe."

If not for my assigned position, I might have been convinced. She spoke with unusual eloquence and passion. Her two points—that we should prefer sustainability to profitability and that developing countries could, in fact, help curb the worst effects of climate change—seemed unimpeachable. However, I also sensed an opportunity: our team had no intention of contesting either of these claims to win the debate.

Our first speaker, Nathan, bumped into the table on his way to the center of the room. As the audience studied his movements for signs of injury, Nathan regained his balance and, once in position, got his breath back, too. Then he began in a quiet voice: "I think there has been a misunderstanding here. We know climate change is a problem and that developing countries contribute to emissions. We agree with most of what the previous speaker said. But the question our team wants to ask is a bit different: Who should bear the considerable economic and human costs of transitioning to a more green world?" During the brief silence that Nathan left after this question, I sensed in the audience a small revelation.

The rest of Nathan's speech was far from perfect. None of us knew how to make proper arguments or advance a line of rebuttal. Our training in debate had not advanced past the topic. However, I could not shake the feeling that we had pulled ahead. Across the room our opponents appeared at sea. In the second row of the audience, my parents turned to each other, then to Simon, who flashed us a brief and knowing smile.

. . .

From that night, I was hooked. The win felt plenty rewarding, and so did its recognition—a healthy round of applause at middle school assembly the following week. However, in the week after the round,

I remembered more vividly the prep-room epiphanies, the communion with the audience, the animal thrill of chasing and being chased. In these early days, I knew only that my passion for debate had many and overlapping sources.

Then, as the months passed and my teammates and I progressed through the league, I gained a clearer view of what I valued most about our activity: debate made our disagreements understandable and, in so doing, revealed the world to us. In our league, we discussed the Olympics one week and reforms to the tax code the next, inhabiting at each station the persona of those who had strong opinions on these subjects. Along thought lines, we traveled the world without ever leaving the suburbs.

The only analogy I could muster was to a television show I came to like around this same time: *The View*. Created in 1997 by the network anchor Barbara Walters, the show comprised a regular group of four or five women arguing about the issues of the day ("hot topics") and interviewing guests. The show promised a diversity of opinion, and its approach was to assemble a panel that spanned the generations, as well as personal and professional backgrounds.

To my ears, the cohosts were almost unbelievably eloquent. Sure, we had read the Gettysburg Address and heard tapes of Nelson Mandela in history class, and the ladies of *The View* did not sound like that. However, their achievement seemed astonishing in its own way: to disagree, in real time, about issues ranging from politics to celebrity gossip in a way that made people want to tune in every single day.

Plus, the basic situation of *The View*'s cohosts seemed similar to my own as a debater. These women were experienced broadcasters, granted, with teams of staff behind them. Nonetheless, they filmed year-round from the same studio in New York: ABC Television Studio 23. Inasmuch as they could hope to travel the world and to illuminate its hidden corners, they could rely only on research, skills of conversation, and a judicious selection of "hot topics."

The rest of my middle school years, 2007 to 2009, passed to the rhythms of the debate calendar. Though my parents and teachers instructed me to be "well-rounded" and signed me up for school bands and low-ranking sports teams, they could not override my stubborn desires. I simply felt that I lived most fully in the fifty-hour period between debate training on Wednesday afternoon and competition on Friday evening.

Throughout these three years, our middle school debate team never enjoyed overwhelming success. In debate, "good" had many definitions but "success" had only one: you had to beat the other side. More often than not, my teammates and I did that, but our luck tended to expire around the quarterfinals. Despite the disappointments, quitting never seemed to me an option. In our league, every debater knew their counterparts at the other schools and monitored who was up, down, and out. The shame of belonging to this last group—those who could not handle the heat—would have been unbearable.

Inhabiting this middle zone of success messed with our fifteen-year-old egos. On the one hand, we had the argumentative skills to prevail in most rounds, but on the other hand, we were not quite good enough to confidently back our own instincts in the debate room. So we spent an inordinate amount of time second-guessing ourselves and devising schemes to blindside the other team. This came to a head in a round near the end of the competitive season in 2009, when we found ourselves in prep asking a dangerous question: What if we could not only analyze a topic but also manipulate it in our favor?

This round, in August against our school's main rival, Knox Grammar, stood out because it attracted a notable guest. Mr. Hood, the head of Barker's debating program, was a gentle and Solomonic man, an English teacher with encyclopedic range. He had been around debate for years. Whereas our coaches led us through individual rounds, Mr. Hood spoke about trends, fundamentals, and the long arcs of debate careers.

Besides his work at Barker, Mr. Hood sat on the league's motion committee, a group of senior teachers and officials who wrote the topics for each season. Earlier in the year, I had been mesmerized as he explained how the process worked.

Mr. Hood told me there were competing schools of thought on what made a good debate topic. However, most people agreed on a few basic elements: a topic had to be balanced (favoring neither side), deep (able to support at least three or four arguments), accessible (not requiring specialist knowledge), and interesting (new enough to be challenging). "That sounds easy enough, but the devil is in the execution," Mr. Hood said.

"Imagine you want to organize a debate about overwork in the economy. What's the topic? 'That we believe people work too hard' is an obvious first gambit but is too broad and poorly defined. You might adjust to 'That we believe a culture that celebrates overwork does more harm than good,' then realize this doesn't make room for the policy dimension you want to include. The temptation to make the debate about everything—'That we believe capitalism is broken'—has to be assiduously avoided. The eventual solution is the result of more thought, multiple revisions, and a dash of inspiration: 'That we should implement a four-day workweek.'

"The process can take a whole day because a lot hangs on getting this right," Mr. Hood said. "Debaters and their coaches have been known to refuse the results of a tournament on the basis that the motion was 'rigged.' So we need the topics to hold up."

I found this explanation moving. In our everyday lives, we charged into arguments wantonly, without regard for what the topic of a disagreement *was,* let alone whether it could support a fair and productive conversation. However, in the world of competitive debate, this class of master topic setters poured hours of their time into ensuring that our disputes took place on solid ground.

On that Friday evening, our troubles began with the topic release. In the glass-paneled atrium of a building at Knox, I stood across from one of our opponents, a boy named Franklin, who wore a large watch and his dad's haircut, as we awaited the motion release. These one-on-one encounters were akin to the face-off in boxing: a chance to get inside the other person's head. For whatever reason, on this night, I blinked first and averted my gaze from Franklin's. The envelope containing the topic felt rough against my hand, and its content—"That we should legalize recreational drugs. Affirmative: Barker. Negative: Knox"—made my stomach turn.

The timing of this motion was bad. In ninth-grade health class, we had just completed a unit on illicit drugs. An ex-con on the motivational speaking circuit came to middle school assembly and told—or warned—us to stay on the straight and narrow; our final exam involved matching the names of drugs with graphic images of mangled body parts. Around the prep room, a cavernous space that made our voices echo, my teammates and I sat in poses of dejection.

After half an hour or so, the four of us agreed that we could not win the debate. The state health department's public service announcements played in our minds like a soundtrack, disabling libertarian impulses. Then, around the forty-minute mark, I had a brain wave: "What if instead of legalizing all recreational drugs, we legalized some of them—the least dangerous ones?" My teammates looked skeptical, but I reminded them we had no better alternatives. So we resolved to define "recreational drugs" as prescription drugs and cannabis, excluding any substance with more serious side effects, such as LSD and ecstasy.

In the debate room, our first speaker, Stuart, delivered the team line with impressive conviction: "Our definition strikes the right line between liberty and public health. It is consistent with expert thinking on the subject." As he presented our definition of "recreational drugs," the opposition bench squirmed and let out yelps of protest. The audience initially seemed confused by our opponents' reaction, but as the implications of our strategy dawned on them, they, too, began to turn on us. The Knox parents snarled and tsked. In the front row, Mr. Hood took off his rimless glasses, adjusted his wool sweater, then stared past us at the plain brick wall.

The one person who did not seem to comprehend our treachery was the adjudicator. From the beginning of Stuart's speech, this baby-faced college student with wide and naive eyes wrote down our claims without a hint of resistance. He winced at our opponents' histrionics— "Barker has totally botched their definition of this debate. This should be grounds for disqualification!"—and shot sympathetic looks in our direction. By the time our third speaker, Max, concluded our case, I had come to grips with the sickening truth: we were going to win the debate.

After the round, which our team won, we approached Mr. Hood

for feedback. I felt a good deal of trepidation, but from up close, the man seemed less upset than tired, subject to some gravitational force that pulled on his shoulders and the skin around his cheeks. He told us in a firm and quiet voice that we had squirreled the debate. "That is, you misdefined or misinterpreted the topic in order to gain an unfair advantage in the round."

Mr. Hood explained that the squirrel and the motion setter were archenemies. Squirrels could be funny: in a debate about whether the U.S. government should intervene in Iraq, one team had defined "intervention" as a strongly worded rebuke. He also said squirrels mostly got their comeuppance in the end: "They contort themselves into knots, and adjudicators tend to bring the hammer down."

However, squirrels occasionally ran away with the debate, as we had done. So motion setters put a lot of thought into squirrel-proofing their topics. They sharpened the wording to eliminate ambiguity and issued additional clarifications. However, there was a limit to what they could do. "As much as anyone else, we rely on good faith," Mr. Hood sighed.

As Mr. Hood packed his old leather bag and wished us a good night, I added a couple of notes in my notebook: The squirrel is within us. The squirrel is scared.

. . .

What I did not know then was that squirrels were everywhere in the public square, if only we cared to look. For students at Barker, the transition between the ninth and tenth grades was momentous. The school comprised an all-boys middle school and a mixed-gender high school, and so the first days of tenth grade—for us, in January 2010—

marked the period of "crossing over." To a group of pubescent fifteen-year-olds, the change seemed a terrifying prospect. Everyone started wearing Old Spice deodorant in fervent preparation.

The morning of our first day of high school, straining under its heat and humidity, passed in awkward silence. Aside from a handful of extroverts and other show-offs, most of the year group self-segregated along gender lines and stared, blinking, past one another. Our French teacher, Madame Berton, could not contain her delight as she pointed to the left side of the room, then to the right. "Les garçons. Les filles. Les garçons. Les filles!"

Then, in the afternoon, the sun's heat crested and something else seemed to break, too. In snaking lines to the cafeteria, and on the green benches near the main oval, people started to have conversations. They exchanged jokes and personal details—each one a tether, a fact that one could never unhear. The campus soon gained a raucous sound. As of Friday afternoon, six people were in relationships.

The arrival of the girls changed the culture of the place. Whereas the middle school had prized a gruff and monosyllabic Aussie male, the high school esteemed sensitive and verbal kids who could hold their own in "heart-to-heart" conversations. The playground, once the realm of atavistic competition, now tended toward self-disclosure. I watched the Js and the athletes make halting adjustments and marveled at the turning tides.

This cultural change, along with our maturation, brought politics onto the playground. As a year group, we were still impressionable—once, we held a vigil for orangutans because a handful of our class-mates campaigned for us to do so. However, over the course of the year, people began to express more and more forceful views about politics, culture, and religion. The most vocal kids spoke with envi-able confidence about what was "unjust" and "unfair."

One of the broader cultural debates in Australia in 2010 was whether "political correctness" had gone too far. The term referred disparagingly to measures aimed at curtailing offensive speech. Since these measures ran the gamut from formal censorship to social sanc-tion, the people most concerned about PC culture were never short of fodder to fuel their outrage. The debate filtered down from television panels and op-ed boards, through family drives and dinner tables, to our school playground.

For me, the person who gave this abstract discussion a concrete form was my friend Jim. Brusque and shrewd, a leader in the army cadets, Jim had prospered in middle school, which had been a haven for edgy jokes about race and sex with little room for earnest avow-als of hurt feelings. I preferred his sense of humor—terse, ironic, lacerating—to those found on workmanlike American sitcoms and the too-clever-by-half specials on the BBC. Yet I found that being in on the joke required internal compromises.

Nowadays, Jim found himself more isolated. Members of our own friend group chided his speech as offensive and told him, "You can't say that." In response, Jim straightened his back, faced his accusers, and landed on the same response: "Mate, that's just political cor-rectness."

In Australia, those two words carried a lot of baggage. The term had been invoked by the far-right politician Pauline Hanson in her maiden speech to Parliament in 1996, alongside the claim that the country was "in danger of being swamped by Asians." It had then become integral to the history wars of the early 2000s over how the country should remember its colonial past. During the course of this history, the phrase had gathered layers of meaning, and it now contained claims about fact, judgment, and prescription: it asserted the existence of efforts to limit free speech, denounced these measures as illiberal, *and* proposed that they ought to be countered.

Amid long arguments in our friend group, I wondered why we had structured our disagreement around such a clunky and divisive term. The mere mention of "political correctness," like an incantation, divided opinion and raised the ire in people's voices. Then the answer occurred to me: the term *political correctness* was never supposed to be neutral. Those who worried most about "PC culture" used the term because it came with the built-in assumption that such a culture was real and bad. Such people relied on the term to gain an unfair advantage— in short, to squirrel the debate.

The strategy seemed to me diabolical, but in Jim's use of the term, I saw no malice. Instead, I sensed a lack of confidence, as well as a corresponding logic: if you did not believe that you could change someone's mind, or that they would engage in good faith, you had an incentive to fix the parameters of the discussion in your favor. In the strident, hectoring tone of Jim's critics, I could also see good reasons for this defensive posture.

However, in the end, efforts to squirrel the debate were almost always self-defeating. After a while, the other side tended to reclaim the term to their advantage. The people who defended political correctness redefined the concept to mean "kindness," which put their opponents in the preposterous position of being antikindness. In 2002, the Labor politician Mark Latham had coined the phrase "new political correctness"—describing it as "the hypocritical demand of the conservative establishment in this country for civility in political debate." In sum, the term *political correctness* itself became polarized and polarizing.

Then, one afternoon in April, near the end of the first term of tenth grade, we had a breakthrough. At lunch, Jim was sounding off about the latest escapades of the PC brigade when our friend Ellie, a no-nonsense brunette known for her blunt manner, interrupted him. I took a sharp breath. However, Ellie did not deliver a denunciation or a cutting riposte. Instead, she posed a couple of questions: "What do you mean by 'political correctness'? Like, what are we fighting about?" Jim looked taken aback but he stumbled to answer: "It's shaming people for telling jokes when they mean no harm."

Over the next ten minutes or so, the two of them found the heart of their dispute. They agreed, for example, that most legal prohibitions of speech were undesirable and that a greater concern for building an inclusive school was welcome. Where they disagreed was on the subject of jokes—and whether the intention of the speaker or the experience of the listener should guide our view of them. Setting up the disagreement in a way that both sides could accept, while avoiding the temptation to manipulate the terms of the debate in one's favor, did not eliminate the underlying tension. But it made the resulting argument more legible and navigable.

Listening to Ellie and Jim, I wondered if the greatest vice of squirreling lay in its impulse to avoid the disagreement at hand—to fix the outcome in advance by giving the opposition no room to stand. Such an approach could yield short-term wins, but it also foreclosed the possibility of genuine exchange.

During World War II, the British Parliament had debated the design of a new chamber for the Commons. Whereas Winston Churchill favored a small, rectangular room to cultivate an adversarial mood, Nancy Astor, the first woman to sit in the Parliament, advocated a circular chamber suited to a more reasonable age: "I have often felt that it might be better if ministers and ex-ministers did not have to sit and look at each other, almost like dogs on a leash, and that controversy would not be so violent." What the pair agreed on was that the setting of disagreements mattered. In the words of Churchill, "We shape our buildings and afterward our buildings shape us."

The architecture of our everyday arguments had less to do with physical buildings than with topics of conversation. However, Astor's idea of a more reasonable design—one that did not elide our disagreements but sought instead to give them better expression—seemed a worthy aspiration. The roots of the term *topic* trace back to the ancient Greek word *topos*, or place. Whether we conceived of this place as shared and open, to be discovered together, or as a narrow battleground, hostile and booby-trapped, seemed to be our choice.

On one of the last days of the term, Mr. Hood called me into his office and handed me a flyer. The sheet of paper, pristine and cool, reminded me of the envelopes we received at topic release. "This is an invitation to audition for the state debating team, the one that competes every year at the national championships," he said. "You should give it a go."

2

ARGUMENT

How to make a point

In a darkened classroom on the musty first floor of Sydney Girls High School, I counted five others slumped in poses of contemplation. I recognized only one person: Debra. Though she was only seventeen, and hence a couple of years older than me, Debra had developed a reputation on our local circuit as a fierce competitor. Coaches devised strategies to mitigate her effect, but her trail of destruction ran long. On this crisp autumn morning in May 2010, Debra, in her chair by the window, was enlarged by the sun; its rays shone through her fuzzy hair and caught in the braces on her teeth when she yawned.

The trial process for the New South Wales state debating team followed a simple arithmetic. One hundred trialists, minus most, left twelve people to form the state debating squad. This dozen people trained together for a couple of months, receiving intense feedback from some of the best coaches in the country, then were whittled down, again, by half. The remaining six—four team members and two reserves—got to represent New South Wales, Australia's most populous state, at the national championships in the spring.

No one in the waiting room asked why I wanted to subject myself to such odds. This was fortunate because I had no good answer to the question. For the past five years, I had known debate as a tool of survival—one that gave me a voice and a way to make sense of a confusing world. I had even developed a passion for the activity. However, in this small and frigid room of unsmiling faces, I felt in the grip of another kind of desire.

Prior to my life in Australia, I had neither possessed real ambitions nor been possessed by them. I received good, if unremarkable, grades at school and chose extracurricular activities that prized participation over excellence. In the third grade at my elementary school in Seoul, in early 2003, I took myself out of consideration for the class presidency and opted instead to handle admin as the class secretary. The move to Sydney later in that same year came as my parents, who had been superstars in their school days, began to worry that ambitious zeal had been lost somewhere along the chain of genetic succession.

However, in Australia, something changed, or I did. In the fourth grade, at age ten, I began to apply myself at school—to grammar rules, times tables, local geography—because I saw this knowledge as a necessary component of my integration. I stayed up nights and skipped weekends. Then, in the fifth grade, I received the top grade for the first time in one of my subjects. I heard in that moment a nagging voice inside my head. "Why not the whole grade?" it seemed to say. "The entire school?"

Nowadays, in the middle of tenth grade, I remembered to hide my aspirations behind self-deprecating jokes and other smoke screens, knowing that tall poppies—an Australian term for people whose ambitions or achievements offend others' expectations of parity—were fated to be cut. This morning, as I focused my mind for the audition, I wondered if the mask was beginning to slip.

Twenty minutes past the scheduled start time of 10:00 a.m., people began to unravel under the strain of waiting. One of the kids, Dyson, a slight and twitchy boy in a waistcoat, launched into a diatribe about the inconvenience of the delay, while in the back of the room Sienna, a tall girl in a flowing boho dress, circled her corner in a trance. Only Debra and I sat perfectly still—but I guessed she was not frozen in place by fear.

As Dyson raised his finger in anticipation of a crescendo, the door behind him opened and a university student, dressed all in black, came into the room in a gust of cold air. The woman introduced herself as one of the assistant coaches. Though she could not have been much older than us, perhaps in her early twenties, she carried herself in a full and unforced posture of authority. "The speaking order for this morning's debate will be as follows," she began. "First affirmative: Bo Seo. First negative: Debra Freeman. Second affirmative . . ."

Once the assistant coach had read the lineup, she gave us the topic: "That the death penalty is never justified."

. . .

In high school parliamentary debate, the typical prep lasts sixty minutes. The primary objective is to devise a case: a set of four or five arguments in favor of one's assigned position. These arguments are delivered in the debate by the first and second speakers, while the third speaker focuses on rebuttal. Teams tend to follow a run sheet:

Run Sheet (in minutes)

0–5	Brainstorm	Each member of the team writes down their own ideas about the topic.
5–15	Upload	Each member presents their ideas to the group.
15–40	Case Development	The group selects the four or five strongest arguments from the upload and fleshes them out.
40–55	Speech Writing	Each member writes their own speech.
55–60	Huddle	The group discusses any final points of strategy before the debate.

Prep rooms tend to follow the second law of thermodynamics: entropy in a closed system increases over time. The virtues of committee work do not shine under a time limit. Plus, the requirement that every debater uphold his or her team's line adds another dimension of pressure. Since technology and external materials are not allowed in the prep room, people have to make do with primitive tools: first principles, rough heuristics, half-recalled facts. The result is a hotbox environment in which tempers run high and occasionally ignite.

However, this particular prep room in Sydney Girls High School, a capacious and drafty teachers' lounge, suffered from the opposite problem. Around an enormous table in the center of the room, the three of us—Dyson, a gentle rugby player named Ben, and I—eyed one another in icy apprehension. For every one idea shared, five others were held in reserve. Sentences began—"I think we should . . . ," "Maybe the best point is . . ."—then died in the throat. Prep relied on the collaboration of groups, but auditions rewarded individuals. No benevolent impulse could correct this mismatch.

Ben and I exchanged a couple of ideas while Dyson scribbled reams of notes in his book. The group discussion sputtered to a stop at the fifteen-minute mark and the three of us dispersed to the edges of the room to write our speeches. This was fine by me. I actually believed in our side of the topic and knew something about the issue—a rare combination in debate. So I knew what I wanted to say.

At 11:30 a.m., the end of the hour, we three collected our notes in silence, then climbed the stairs to the main debate room. In the second-floor hallway, I heard the overlapping sound of a crowd. Placing weight on my inner heels, a trick my parents had taught me for reining in shaky legs, I walked toward the noise until it surrounded me completely. The large classroom, carpeted in forest green, contained a dozen selectors—the coaches, plus former members of the team, now in their twenties and thirties—spread across two rows of seats. When we walked into the room, they stared at us, exhaling.

I moved toward a seat in the front row but one of the selectors, a burly, red-bearded man in a leather jacket, gestured for me to go straight to the center of the room. At this moment, the audience began to drum the desks in front of them—an insistent, asynchronous percussion—until the edges of the room shook. I felt tendrils of heat climb up my spine. The smell of lard and fennel seeds from someone's half-eaten bread product made me want to retch.

Looking out into the room, I searched for a friendly patch on which to rest my eyes. Not the stylish young couple in matching jean jackets. Not the quiet, gimlet-eyed woman whom I recognized as a former world champion debater. I settled on a patch of discolored carpet between the heads of two people in the first row. Then I took a deep breath and found the words to start.

"The death penalty is murder carried out by the state. It allows the worst aspects of the criminal justice system—its arbitrariness, ineptitude, hostility to the poor—to exact an irreversible cost."

This moment, when a speaker first breaks the silence, is revealing. For the speaker, it marks a bracing encounter with the undertow of resistance and fascination that lie beneath still surfaces. Though the experience involves perception—subtle movements in the listeners' eyebrows, the gyrations of their pens on paper—it relies more on intuition: a primordial sense for the answer to the question "Am I getting through?"

"My first argument is that the death penalty is cruel and unusual. Here is how the most humane forms of capital punishment work in practice: inmates, some of them innocent of their crimes, spend upward of a decade in constant fear of their impending death. Then they are subject to what may be the most gruesome experience imaginable: the slow, stepwise administration of one's own death."

I sensed some members of the audience yield to my arguments. The nods, perfunctory at first, began to sink deeper, and the eyes, once reptilian in appraisal, softened with sympathy. So encouraged,

I heard my voice grow louder and more certain. I locked eyes with listeners and tried, through my gaze, to convey the depth of my conviction. Though I ran long on my first argument after indulging in too many rhetorical flourishes, and thus had to rush through my second point on the risk of wrongful convictions, I managed to reach my conclusion with twenty seconds left on the clock.

"Such an inhumane practice has no place in a just society. Each of us is diminished so long as it persists. Please pass this motion."

As the audience began to clap, I glanced at the opposition bench. Between two speakers who, on account of their nerves, were as stiff and pale as a pair of marble columns, Debra tied her hair into a loose bun. She produced from her bag a pair of wire-rimmed glasses that sharpened each of her features. No sooner had I reached my seat than Debra took over the spot where I had stood. From the beginning, her voice rang sharper and clearer than mine.

"What you heard from the previous speaker were not arguments. Those were assertions. He never gave you any reasons to believe what he said. He just told you what he believed and used a lot of emotive words. Well, I'm sorry, but that doesn't cut it in a debate.

"Look back on your notes, ladies and gentlemen. Ask yourself— even if you agree with the opposition, especially if you agree with the opposition—did they present a convincing case for their conclusions?"

A spurt of color flooded my cheeks. I reacted, at first, with incomprehension and outrage: What was she talking about and, in any case, who did she think she was? Then I heard a quieter voice venture a more troubling question: Could she be right? I reached for my speech notes, but then, noticing the crowd's gaze oscillating between Debra and me, I froze in place and tried to turn my face to stone. Debra turned to the results of her vivisection, a taxonomy of my errors.

"A claim made without reasons or evidence ('The death penalty is simply abhorrent') was an assertion; a claim made without evidence ('Logic dictates that the death penalty should deter crime') was speculation; and a claim reliant only on evidence ('This botched procedure in Georgia shows that the death penalty is completely unreliable') was a generalization."

I knew each of these terms. They had been among the first concepts we had learned as middle school debaters, as part of a unit on the fundamentals of argument. Since then, I had made hundreds of arguments at tournaments and in everyday life. Could it be possible that I had missed something?

Debra tended to overemphasize the *s* sound in *assertion* and *generalization*, so that these academic terms took on the edge of cuss words. I felt as though I were caught in her braces—bruised by the dull blow of the molars and scratched by the metal. So this was what it meant to be chewed out.

. . .

Later in the evening, my parents and I went out for dinner at the local Vietnamese restaurant. The cramped dining room, where families ate shoulder to shoulder around creaky tables, smelled of broth and oil. With the results of the state team trials due in less than one hour, I was grateful for the noise and the humidity and the strong scents—distractions, all, from intruding thoughts.

At our table near the kitchen, I struggled to explain to my parents how I had screwed up the trials. "Sounds like you were correct," shrugged Mum. "The selectors must have seen the truth," Dad said, nodding and unshelling a boiled prawn. "That's what counts in the end." The unimpeachable sincerity of my parents' voices inspired in me small paroxysms of frustration and rage.

Few subjects coaxed more aphorisms from Mum and Dad than "the truth." My parents raised me on the belief that "truth conquers all," a maxim that dovetailed their Christian faith and general distaste for bullshit. In their view, attempts to obscure reality were not only suspect but also doomed to failure. As the sun rises in the morning, so, too, would the truth surely dawn.

One of our favorite movies as a family is the 1992 film *Scent of a Woman*, in which Al Pacino plays an aging veteran at the end of his rope. His character, Frank Slade, is blind, drunk, and irascible. This prompts his family to hire Charlie Simms, a student who attends the exclusive Baird School on a scholarship, to look after him over Thanksgiving weekend.

The movie unfolds as a buddy film. Slade teaches Charlie to be a man; Charlie persuades Slade to give life another chance. In New York City they dine at the Oak Room, dance tango, and drive a fast car. But there hangs over the boy a dark cloud. He is in trouble at school for refusing to snitch on some classmates who were responsible for a bad prank and is set to face a disciplinary committee that is considering his expulsion.

At the hearing, Charlie is cornered. The other witness has lied to save his own skin, but Charlie refuses to do the same, prompting an irate headmaster to recommend immediate expulsion. Then Slade shows up. He launches into a five-minute tirade on courage, leadership, and masculinity. What the speech lacks in structure and sustained reasoning it makes up with pathos: "I'm not a judge or jury, but I can tell you this: he won't sell anybody out to buy his future!

And that, my friends, is called integrity." Slade and Charlie emerge victorious and leave the school to the rapturous applause of the entire student body.

The movie reflected my parents' view that truth spoke in the voice of Al Pacino: gruff, terse, unpolished, and, precisely for these reasons, pure. Even in a setting as compromised as a New England prep school, such a voice could not be ignored. Placed in competition with falsehood, the truth prevailed every time. As a child I had taken great solace from the movie, but after more recent viewings, I had found myself asking how alcoholic veterans really fared in courtroom settings in the American Northeast.

Besides, at this moment in mid-2010, the world seemed to be undergoing a change. The United States had been contending for a couple of years with "birtherism," a loose movement of media figures, controversialists, and social media users who falsely asserted that President Barack Obama had been born in Kenya. Conspiracy theories were not unprecedented, but the reach of this one was remarkable. Birtherism received regular coverage in the mainstream media. According to one poll from March, as many as a quarter of respondents agreed that Obama was born outside the U.S. and was therefore ineligible to be president.

Even on the playground at my high school, halfway around the world from Washington, DC, a classmate had professed to have seen some material on Facebook about the birther issue. We managed to laugh him off the subject, but I was troubled by the way he described these theories as "interesting," neither committing to the claims nor disavowing them.

In an interview with NBC News, the U.S. president seemed as flummoxed as anyone. He acknowledged that "there is a mechanism, a network of misinformation, that in a new media era can get churned out there constantly." Then he insisted that the American people had the wisdom to see through the nonsense. "I'm not going to be worrying too much about whatever rumors are floating on—out there." But the most honest response seemed to be the one he snapped: "I would say that I can't spend all my time with my birth certificate plastered on my forehead. The facts are the facts." Every single one of these lines was true and they were ever so slightly at odds.

At the dinner table, over a steaming bowl of pho, I thought back to the round against Debra. My situation in that round—being in possession of what I believed to be the truth and still lacking persuasive arguments—seemed apposite for our times. In a moment when truth was contested and easily obscured, one could not count on its inherent, conquering power. I wondered if, in such an era, we had to shift our attention from the mere acquisition of truth to the skills, craft, and plain old work of conveying it to others.

News came alongside dessert. As I turned a spoon in a pool of tapioca pearls, I felt my phone buzz in my pocket. The email took a few seconds to load. Mum took a sip of her tea and made out like her attention was elsewhere. Dad all but took the phone out of my hands as he leaned toward me. The message began: "We are delighted to let you know that you have been selected for the NSW state squad."

•   •   •

In the week leading up to the first squad meeting, scheduled for the last Saturday in May, I tried to play it cool. News of my selection caused a small but noticeable ripple at school. Friends and teachers, unsure, in truth, about the meaning of the state debating squad, marveled at it in vague terms: "The state squad! How about that?" I found these encounters uncomfortable because the fact of my selection changed nothing about my actual abilities: I was the same fifteen-year-old who had walked into trials one week earlier and had his ass whupped. Meanwhile, the expectations of parents and teachers and peers ran further from the truth every day. On the Friday night, I lay in bed for hours unable to sleep, considering the gulf between where I was and where I was expected to be.

An outside observer would have been hard-pressed to name what brought the twelve of us together at the entrance of Sydney Girls High School at nine o'clock on a dry and overcast Saturday morning. I could hardly pick it out myself. Among us were: the soccer captain who had come running from a game, the affable nerd with a penchant for the classics and musical theater, the extrovert who seemed to know everyone's business, Debra, and me. Then the coaches opened the door and provided some kind of answer: "State squad. Welcome!"

The adults led us upstairs to the second-floor classroom where auditions had been the previous week. In the cavernous room, lit by fluorescent tubes, we twelve sat in green plastic chairs that bent at ninety degrees. Things felt awkward at first. I had known debate only as a group activity that pitted team against team and school against school. However, eavesdropping on the gossipy conversations around me, I learned that success at this higher level was more individuated. Each of the squad members seemed to have a reputation and rivals with whom they had histories. The coaches referred to us as all-stars, but the image that came to mind was a constellation: a loose association of bright things, grouped together from the outside.

After a few minutes, the imposing, red-bearded man from my audition, now in an oversized flannel shirt, strode to the blackboard. He introduced himself as Bruce, a law student at the University of Sydney and one of the two main coaches for the state team, then gestured at his co-coach, a trimmer and older man named Mark. What impressed me about Bruce was that he made no concession to the relaxed, carefree presentation that, in Australia, was something of a national trademark. His voice thrummed with latent force and added to the general impression of a person in motion.

"Let me start with some feedback. Too many of you have either not learned or forgotten how to make a proper argument. Since you guys are debaters, I'd say this is a pretty big problem. An argument is not a list or a slogan or a pep talk or an honest expression of your feelings. It is not whatever vaguely supports your point of view. So what is it? An argument is a conclusion about the way things are, or ought to be, that is justified by a main claim and a set of supporting reasons and evidence."

Bruce turned to the blackboard and began to write out the basic steps:

First, to come up with an argument, start with a conclusion—the fact, judgment, or prescription that one wants the listener to accept.

Bob is not a nice person.
CONCLUSION

Second, take the conclusion, add the word *because*, and fill in the sentence. This is the main claim, or the point that the argument will have to prove.

Bob is not a nice person
CONCLUSION

because he is inconsiderate of other people's feelings.
MAIN CLAIM

Third, take the main claim, add the word *because*, and fill in the sentence. This is the reason—a consideration in favor of a claim.

Bob is inconsiderate
MAIN CLAIM

because he is often cruel to others, including to his friends.
REASON

Fourth, support the reason with evidence—a piece of information or fact from the real world.

At dinner last Friday, he made hurtful comments about
Sheryl's job.
EVIDENCE

An argument contains nearly infinite space for improvement. A speaker could always come up with more reasons and evidence, as well as better versions of each. Then he or she could devise more and better arguments to form a case. However, the point was that an argument is incomplete without these elements.

"So is that it?" Bruce asked. "A conclusion that is justified by a main claim and a set of supporting reasons and evidence?" Just as I started to nod my head he exclaimed, "No!"

"What are we missing? We haven't yet shown that the main claim justifies the conclusion. So, yes, we have shown that Bob is inconsiderate of other people's feelings, but who's to say this is enough to conclude that he is not a nice guy and not, say, an oblivious person?"

Bruce turned back to the board and wrote the final step:

Fifth, link the main claim to the conclusion with another reason.

> The fact that Bob is inconsiderate means he is not a nice person because, regardless of his intent, he causes people a great deal of pain.
> LINK

This last step revealed what Bruce described as an argument's "two burdens of proof"—that is, the two things that an argument has to prove before it can have a chance of convincing a listener. These burdens apply to almost every argument we encounter daily and are known as the "truth" and "importance" conditions:

> **Truth:** The main claim is factually correct or otherwise believable.

> **Importance:** The main claim supports its conclusion.

For the argument above—Bob is not a nice person because he is inconsiderate of other people's feelings—these burdens are:

> **Truth:** Bob is, in fact, inconsiderate of other people's feelings.

> **Importance:** If Bob is inconsiderate, we should conclude he is not nice.

The argument needed both legs to stand. If the speaker could not show that the main claim was true, the whole point was moot. If he or she could not show that it was important, the listener was within their rights to respond with a big shrug: ¯_(ツ)_/¯.

Between the two burdens, the one more easily forgotten was importance. In a rush to stack the argument with more reasons and evidence, speakers ran out of time to explain why any of that mattered. This was a problem because a true and unimportant argument could seldom persuade listeners to act or change their minds.

Speakers who met both burdens of proof were not guaranteed to change a listener's mind, but those who failed to meet either burden were certain to flop. They came to resemble Cassandra from the Greek epics: correct and unpersuasive.

All this sounded somewhat abstract, but as Bruce reviewed more examples on the board, I found myself thinking back to an argument I'd had at school. A couple of months ago, Joanna, the most socially conscious person in our friend group, had tried to persuade all of us to go vegetarian. For any meat or dairy product she could spin the most harrowing tales of abuse, supported with statistics and audiovisual evidence. "What do you have there?" she would ask over lunch. I knew enough to keep my answers vague—"Oh, a sandwich"—but Joanna had a keen nose for deli meats, and soon we would be deep into the many atrocities of the turkey trade.

Her intervention had worked. I found myself in these arguments running out of things to say and eventually decided to try going vegetarian. Mum humored me for a few days with inventive preparations of tofu, then defaulted to hard-boiled eggs as the substitute protein. I barely made it through two cartons of free-range eggs before calling time on the experiment.

Bruce's theory of the two burdens gave me a new perspective on what had happened. Joanna had argued that I should stop eating meat because industrial farming imposed great suffering on animals. She had provided reasons and evidence to believe the argument was true, and I had accepted them. However, a part of me remained unconvinced that such suffering required me to become vegetarian, as opposed to a more discerning or infrequent meat eater. I had been convinced of the truth of Joanna's argument but not of its importance.

In the classroom at Sydney Girls, the time neared 11:00 a.m. and Bruce brought the lecture to a close. "An argument is the fundamental building block of debate. It is, in some deep sense, what all this is for: debaters are in the business of making and breaking arguments." Bruce wished us good luck for the next eight weeks, then sent us back outside, where in the last remaining hour of morning, the sun had begun to break through.

• • •

One month into the squad process, the luck had not materialized and the indignities were beginning to pile up. The debate on free trade in which a benevolent year-twelve student had to dictate to me every word of an argument on "comparative advantage." The round on media monopolies in which an opponent produced no fewer than three interpretations of "what Bo could have meant by that rather messy point," then proceeded to demolish them. Such memories, on a loop, made for a dispiriting jukebox.

I was getting better, but the gap in experience between me and the other speakers, all of whom were one or two years older than me, proved to be insurmountable. If a debater made, on average, four arguments in a week, he or she could expect to get through 160 arguments in a school year. I now understood the basic theory of argumentation as well as anyone, but I could not replicate experience—the dumb, hard grind of doing and doing again.

In the beginning, the composition of teams in the squad process had been more or less random, but now that the coaches were starting to develop ideas about the ultimate four-person lineup, I found myself debating less often with the strongest prospects than with the people who had already missed several practice sessions. I had reached a dead end.

Then, one day, the answer came to me in an unexpected place.

As a student, I had always found ancient history class to be pretty dull. The societies we studied seemed impossibly remote, and besides, all vases looked the same to me. However, on this winter's afternoon of the last Friday in June, a lesson on boys' education in ancient Greece struck me with unusual force.

The sons of free citizens knew it as the progymnasmata, or "preliminary exercises": a set of fourteen rhetorical drills ranging from vivid description (ekphrasis) to the formal expression of praise (encomium). These written exercises were designed to prepare students to be able to deliver full-length orations, an important skill for pepaideumenos, or "learned men."

Our history teacher, a brilliant and caustic Englishman named Mr. Gregory, passed around the structure for the encomium—taken from a website named Silva Rhetoricae, or "The Forest of Rhetoric":

> Describe the stock a person comes from (people, country, ancestors, parents).

> Describe the person's upbringing (education, instruction in arts).

Describe the person's deeds, which should be described as the results of his or her excellencies of mind, body, or fortune.

Make a favorable comparison to someone else to escalate your praise.

Conclude with an epilogue, including either an exhortation to your hearers to emulate this person or a prayer.

The class groaned with boredom. Sometimes these ancient history classes unearthed a spot of exotic wisdom, and progymnasmata, with its many consonants, had seemed a promising candidate. But even the most ardent students had to concede that the drills were tedious and formulaic—less revelations than archaic exercises in box-checking.

However, Mr. Gregory seemed undeterred. He put his hands on his waist and told us with a sly smile that the progymnasmata were supposed to be boring: "These are not extraordinary secrets for extraordinary people on extraordinary occasions. Think of them as musical scales. Their effects manifest slowly through repetition."

The ancient Greeks had provided their own analogies. Some rhetoricians compared the progymnasmata to the endeavors of Milo of Croton, the wrestler who lifted a growing calf daily and thus managed to eventually lift a full-grown bull. One textbook from the period urged:

Just as it is no help to those wanting to paint to
look at the works of Apelles and Protogenes and
Antiphilus unless they themselves put their hand to

painting, so neither the words of older writers nor
the multitude of their thoughts nor their purity of
language . . . are useful to those who are going to engage
in rhetoric unless each student exercises himself every
day in writing.

The message? Citizenship was hard work. The platform from which
to address other people had to be earned, and so, too, the qualification
to judge others' contributions. To earn such a standing one needed less
inspiration and genius than perseverance.

Mr. Gregory explained that such labor gave rise to a certain art-
istry. In the Renaissance, a thousand years after the end of antiquity,
the Italian publisher Aldus Manutius gave the progymnasmata a second life. His editions of ancient Greek rhetoric textbooks spread
throughout Europe and, according to some scholars, helped under-
gird some of the most seminal works of John Milton and William
Shakespeare.

As Mr. Gregory unspooled this history, I recognized in the progymnasmata a glimmer of promise. I began to wonder if its essential
bargain—arduous, repetitive work in exchange for mastery—could
give me an advantage in the state squad. If my problem was a deficit
of experience, could I make up for lost time with exertion?

In the back of the classroom, a narrow room where every stray
sound echoed, I ripped out a sheet of paper from my notebook with
what discretion I could manage. Then I began to write down a design for a rhetorical exercise of my own. I reduced the debate argument to its most basic form and arrived at a structure centered around
the four Ws: what, why, when, and who cares?

What is the point?

Why is it true?

When has it happened before?

Who cares?

The structure was simple, but it contained the most essential features of a good argument. For example, on the affirmative for the topic "That we should abolish jury trials," I might have written:

What? We should abolish jury trials because they result in an unacceptable number of wrong verdicts.

Why? Juries do not understand legal evidence. They are unduly swayed by the media and also reflect the inherent biases of their societies.

When? Lawyers in the U.S. attest in overwhelming numbers to the "*CSI* effect," a term used to describe the distortionary effect of television shows on juries' understanding of forensic evidence.

Who cares? A wrong verdict is a miscarriage of justice for the victim, the accused, and the society at large. It also reduces confidence in the criminal justice system.

The four Ws also applied to arguments we made in our everyday lives. Though we could not plan our points in advance, we could easily reach midstream for the other elements. For example, if the eldest daughter in a family of five opposed her parents' plan to adopt a dog, she could strengthen her position with an argument that answered the four Ws:

> **What?** We should not adopt a dog because we will never go for walks.
>
> **Why?** Everyone is too busy. On Wednesdays, we don't get home until 8:00 p.m.
>
> **When?** The last goldfish we brought home from the store died due to neglect.
>
> **Who cares?** The dog will be unhappy without regular walks, and members of the family will fight over this added chore.

I sensed the temperature in the room begin to rise, though the gas heater in the corner appeared as inactive as ever. In the grip of this heat, I resolved to write a hundred arguments over four weeks—a number round and ridiculous enough to plausibly suggest magic.

· · ·

For the first days of living out my new resolution, I worked through the four Ws at my desk at home in private sessions that I hid from even my parents. However, I soon realized the scale of the task was such that I would have to work around the clock. So I began to write on the train to school in the morning and at the library during recess. I wrote two arguments in favor of the motion "That we should impose a 100% inheritance tax." And I wrote one point on either side of the topic "That we should make vaccination for infectious disease compulsory." So the hours passed.

My school friends looked at me askance. The Js poured scorn on the effort when they assumed I was doing schoolwork and, once I corrected them, switched to a posture of confusion and general concern: "Are you all right?" Even the debaters asked whether I was not taking this too seriously: "You said the state squad was random and weird and that you didn't give a crap. Remember?"

I relished the progymnasmata because, in the rest of my life, I seldom got to make arguments. Few adults asked teenagers serious questions and waited for the response. Some of the better subjects at school—such as English and history—required students to write essays, but most others rewarded cramming and rote learning. Beside classrooms, the jungle of the school playground adhered less to the authority of reason than to the laws of power and reputation.

This drought of arguments seemed to extend beyond the teenage years. In the one realm of life that treated us as adults, commerce, few questions were asked and fewer reasons given. On television, large companies used images of swimwear and abs to sell us carbonated drinks and life insurance. Older friends on internships described days of following instructions and checking boxes.

Then there was politics. Australia, in mid-2010, was in the foothills of a very bad federal election campaign. The contest between Prime Minister Julia Gillard of the center-left Labor Party and her opponent Tony Abbott, the leader of the conservative Liberal Party, managed to combine intense personal animus and a near absence of substantive debate. Each side stuck to a short list of talking points that smacked of focus groups and committee work, including their slogans, "Moving Forward" and "Standing Up for Australia."

Pundits sought to apportion blame for this present malaise. One obvious target was myopic, careerist politicians; another was a political culture that empowered pollsters and apparatchiks over elected officials. But as media figures piled on, their hypocrisy began to show. In a twenty-four-hour news cycle powered by access-based journalism and immoderate commentary, what room remained for genuine debate and argument in print and on the airwaves?

For citizens, this unedifying game of chicken-and-egg seemed to overlook a more urgent problem: we had egg on our faces. Somehow, we had managed to create this commonwealth of nonreasons where one subsisted on a diet of assertions, innuendo, and slogans.

The world of competitive debate offered an escape from all that, but it also made onerous demands. Whereas assertions gave voice to inchoate ideas on the surface of my mind, no questions asked, proper arguments asked me to interrogate old beliefs and form new ones. As I struggled to answer the four Ws and meet both burdens of proof, I began to create from the soupy mess of the mind something more coherent. Often I saw the finished argument on the page and thought, "Oh, that's what I believe."

The best part? It worked.

I started to achieve stronger performances in the squad debates. The extra practice placed in my reach a catalog of ideas and gave me the confidence to do more within any given minute. In debate, the reward for self-improvement was instant gratification. Whereas artists toiled for years in pursuit of lofty ideals, we debaters chased, weekly, more sensuous thrills: the stunned silence of opponents, a nod from the coach, a few seconds of unbroken applause.

This reward cycle contained a trace of poison. Debate fashioned a sport out of two faculties—speech and thought—that made out-size claims to who we were as people. As a consequence, we debaters found it all too easy to equate our success as competitors with our worth as human beings.

At Saturday morning training sessions, I noticed the other squad members begin to treat me with greater affection, including me in their conversations and plans. Part of me balked at the implication of hierarchy but a more forceful part of me wanted to climb, eyes closed to the height and steepness of the fall.

. . .

The final squad debate was set to begin at six o'clock on a serene winter's evening near the end of July. Gathered in the same airless room where we had awaited our first squad audition, six of us stood in a loose circle and carried on a distracted conversation. Though people tried to disguise their nerves behind jokes and bravado, their voices, sharp and atonal, betrayed signs of strain. Even Debra, who stood apart from the crowd, tapped the ground in a jagged rhythm with her feet.

Around five o'clock, Bruce entered the room. With his hair ruffled and arms tightly folded, he seemed a man in the grip of a hard decision. "I want you to know that to have made it this far in the squad process is a big achievement," he began. "Each of you could represent the state with distinction at the national championships. However, we cannot take all of you."

Bruce reached into the left pocket of his dark jeans and took out a piece of folded paper. "I suppose we better start." The speaking order that Bruce read placed me at first affirmative on a team with

Debra and a skittish year-twelve student named Micah, who would speak second and third, respectively. As the three of us inched closer together, Bruce read the topic: "That ecotage is morally justified."

This grim combination of words sent a surge of panic down my spine. I knew nothing about ecotage and I was not sure that Micah, who stood motionless beside me, softly hyperventilating, had a strong grasp on the concept, either. I looked around the room to find Debra, then, realizing she had already left, dragged my bag and Micah down the hall to meet our fate.

In the prep room, a space with the proportions and ambience of a broom closet, Debra had already taken her seat at the head of the table. As Micah and I stumbled to our chairs, she leaned forward at the angle of a wartime general. "You guys know what ecotage is, right?" I swallowed and looked over at Micah, who was rapidly losing the last trace of color in his face. Debra rolled her eyes. "The use of vandalism, property damage, and sabotage to delay or shut down environmentally harmful projects."

For the next ten minutes, Debra answered our questions about ecotage: "Examples include the planting of spikes on trees to damage chainsaws and other deforesting equipment." "The actions are not intended to hurt people but the possibility cannot be excluded." Then, as our confusion began to dissipate, Micah and I shared ideas for potential arguments and strategies. Though each of us guarded our feelings of competitiveness, we could not help addressing one another as teammates.

At the forty-minute mark, we dispersed to separate corners of the room to write our speeches. I had been assigned two arguments: that ecotage benefits the environment and that no feasible alternatives to ecotage exist. For each point, I stated the two burdens of proof, then raced to prove each one with several reasons and examples. In the first argument, I outlined six reasons why ecotage was, in fact, likely to shut down environmentally harmful projects, then gave three reasons why conservation was a more urgent priority than the protection of property. I worked fast. The weeks of training had steadied my hand.

As I started on my second point, with eight minutes left on the clock, I surveyed the prep room. Micah, hunched over his notepad in the shape of a crab, seemed to be moving with momentum. In the corner farthest from me, Debra had laid down her pen and was now peering out the window at an empty parking lot. I whispered in her direction, "Don't you have arguments to write?" She slowly turned toward me and, frowning at the interruption, said in a distant voice, "It'll depend." Then she returned her attention to the object of her distraction.

In the second-floor debate room, four adults, including Bruce, greeted us with forced and nervous smiles. This room, once familiar in most respects, was strange at this late time of day. The orange light of the streetlamps, faint against the darkness of the winter evening, cast strange shadows on the walls. I knew better than to sit down. Shivering from the cold, I walked to the center of the room and tried to count my way to a calm breath.

I felt the attention of the room converge on me, but this time I did not avert my gaze. Instead, I hardened my expression, reviewed the first few lines of my notes, then began.

"In the face of environmental destruction caused by rapacious companies and compromised governments, citizens confront a hard decision: give in or fight back. We on the affirmative team are not saboteurs and we do not argue that such actions should be legalized.

What we ask for in this debate is proper moral accounting for these acts of desperate resistance."

As I raced through my two arguments, spitting long verses of reasons and evidence, I noticed the judges strain to take notes fast enough. Behind me, the opposition team took shallow, uneven breaths and hissed at one another, "What do we say to this?" The plan to shock and awe listeners with the range and complexity of my arguments seemed to be working. So I increased my pace. "The fifth reason why no feasible political alternatives exist is the influence of corporate donations on setting the agenda for environmental policy. The sixth reason . . ."

Then, after eight minutes that felt, at once, like a flash and an eternity, I reached the conclusion of my speech: "Between the destruction of hardware and the decimation of habitat, side with the planet." My voice had gone hoarse and knotty. As the judges broke into applause, I lurched back to my seat, quietly wheezing. Spent as I was, I felt coursing through me a shot of adrenaline induced by the dangerous thought that I had done enough.

The next speaker, a colorful extrovert named Shreya, adopted a similar tack. She stood in a pose of confrontation—chest out, arms crossed—and rushed through a speech that brimmed with righteous analysis. "The opposition have been incredibly blasé about the very real danger that ecotage poses to the lives of workers who carry out these projects. Set aside possible injuries for a second. What about the economic insecurity that comes with constant disruptions to work?"

Beside me, to my left, a flustered Micah was awash in a sea of ripped pages and sticky notes, each one bearing rebuttal ideas written in red and green ink. However, on my right, Debra seemed to be zoning out of the debate. She kept her cool blue eyes fixed on the judges and only occasionally lifted her pen to mark her notepad. I tried a couple of times to offer ideas for rebuttal, but Debra rebuffed each of these attempts and returned to her reverie. "I'm trying to watch," she said.

Then it was her turn to speak. Debra rose from her chair and took slow, deliberate strides to the center of the room. Once there, she almost crouched down to meet the eyes of the audience, then delivered her opening line in a quiet voice: "A great number of claims have been made in this debate so far. This debate raises tempers, and that's a good thing. But I want us to scrutinize some of these arguments in closer detail."

In her speech, Debra seemed to be guided by an awareness of which arguments had and had not landed with the judges. If Shreya and I had been too abstract, she dug into the details: "Forget these words like 'violence' and 'calamity' or, on our side, 'interference' or 'resistance'. This is about spiking trees and blowing up construction sites in the dead of night to prevent further destruction of this planet." Where we had offered dispassionate proofs of various claims, she went in hard on the sell: "Look, here's why this stuff matters. If our existing laws enable environmental vandalism on a vast scale, it is our responsibility to resist them."

Debra and I relied on many of the same tools of argumentation. However, whereas I used these techniques to gain an edge *over* listeners and thus compel their assent, Debra used the same methods to channel and satisfy the audience's natural curiosity. When she asked herself the four Ws, she spoke for the listener who might be wondering "Why?" or "Who cares?" She made the other person a coauthor of her ideas.

This made for an unflattering comparison with my own performance. I had not once paused to consider what listeners might need to hear from me and had sought, instead, to overwhelm them. In the manner of unscrupulous politicians and pundits, I had used speech to exhaust rather than answer skepticism; to awe rather than persuade; to win admiration rather than sympathy. I spoke *at* and not *to* people.

Listening to Debra, I recalled this one story from near the end of the Second World War. In 1944, the Danish physicist Niels Bohr—the man behind the first physical model of the atom—was convinced the world was on the precipice of great danger. He had concluded after multiple visits to Los Alamos, New Mexico—the desert home of the Manhattan Project—that the only way to prevent a catastrophic arms race was for the U.S. to apprise the USSR of its progress toward the nuclear bomb. Within the course of this one year, Bohr managed to lobby his way to audiences with Winston Churchill and Franklin D. Roosevelt.

The meetings went terribly. Churchill was so turned off by what an aide called Bohr's "mild, philosophical vagueness of expression" and "inarticulate whisper" that he ended the meeting early, before declaring, "I did not like the man when you showed him to me, with his hair all over his head." Roosevelt, who had expressed misgivings prior to the meeting about whether he would be able to understand the scientist, was more polite in his meeting. But an adviser later expressed "doubt that the president really understood him at all."

Bohr's quixotic mission had likely been doomed to failure from the beginning. The allies' distrust of the Soviet Union ran deep, and so did their suspicion toward foreign-born scientists.

However, when I read the philosopher Karl Popper's description of disputes with Bohr—"One couldn't talk to him. He was talking all the time, allowing practically only one or two words to you and then at once cutting in"—I could not help but wonder about a counterfactual: How might the world have changed if Bohr had made room for his listeners' doubts and incomprehension?

Back in the second-floor classroom, Debra closed out the last minute of her speech and returned to the seat next to mine. Her warmth and perfume, tinged now with the faint smell of sweat, overwhelmed me. The four judges in the back of the room seemed neither flattered nor impressed. Instead, they wore the relieved expressions of people who had, at last, been heard.

. . .

I was not selected to the state team but was named a reserve, a position that allowed me to attend the national championships in August 2010 and wear the team's much-coveted uniform: a navy blazer with a red waratah (the state flower) blooming on the chest pocket.

Things moved fast from there. One year later, in 2011, I represented New South Wales at the national championships in Perth, where our team won the tournament, and I was selected as one of five members of the Australian national team. This allowed me to travel during the following year to Dundee, Scotland, and Cape Town, South Africa, to compete at the World Schools Debating Championships, where we bowed out in the final rounds.

Through these vertiginous years, spanning the ages of sixteen and seventeen, I found comfort in the knowledge that debate, regardless of the level of competition, came down to the arguments. Whereas I had once understood the ideal point as a magnum opus— the product of one person's genius—I saw it now as a nexus of many influences: the contributions of teammates, the expectations of listeners, and the values of loved ones.

Such arguments made audacious claims to truth. However, their quilt-like composition seemed to embody a view of truth as less a monolith than a shared reality, one that arose not from one person's speech but in the exchange of conversation.

On the last Friday in August 2012, a few weeks before my eighteenth birthday, I was selected at the national championships on the island of Tasmania to captain the Australian national debating team. Bruce had signed on to coach. Mum and Dad, who were in the audience for the announcement, committed to travel to Antalya, Turkey, in January to spectate at my last World Schools Debating Championships. Lying in bed that night, I counted nine years since my arrival in Australia and wondered where arguments might take me next.

3

REBUTTAL

How to push back

Bullshit, bullshit, bullshit," thundered the voice from the back of the room.

Over the three years I had known Bruce, starting from my first state team audition in the autumn of 2010, I had become expert at reading his expressions. The man's natural frame—six feet, with a rugby player's build—tilted at an angle of confrontation, and his manner of speaking leaned on jokes and denunciations. He was a country boy with a thick hide. However, I had learned to see in the movements of his more candid features—the folds at the corners of his eyes, the edges of his lips—intimations of approval, concern, and sympathy.

This Saturday evening on January 26, 2013, at a moody winter's dusk in Istanbul, Turkey, I learned something else about Bruce: genuine anger surfaced first on his face, in splotches of purple-red that eddied around his cheeks and crashed against his thinning hairline.

"Well, that was just—"

Whiiiing!

The sound outside began as a distant alarm, then within seconds swelled into an immense music. Soon it was coming through the thin walls of our second-floor rental apartment, filling the cramped space like a rich liquid. 6:36 p.m. marked the time for Maghreb, the sunset prayer for Muslims. Bruce sighed and sank back in his chair, resembling in sound and appearance a volcano asked to delay its eruption.

The eight of us—five members of the Australian team, Bruce, and the two assistant coaches—had been in Turkey for one week. From the apartment rooftop on the night of our arrival, the city skyline had seemed a mirage, shimmering and preposterous. Now only several hours remained until our flight to the nearby city of Antalya for the start of the World Schools Debating Championships, and the overcast sky set conditions for a dark and congested night.

For the past week, we had lived by a strict regimen: several three-hour debate sessions per day (one-hour prep, one-hour debate, one-hour debrief), interspersed with drills, lectures, and research. Aside from day trips to see the twenty thousand painted tiles of the Blue Mosque and the graves at Gallipoli, the site of a catastrophic defeat for Australian and Allied troops in World War I, we put our heads down and held out for delayed gratification.

Despite all that, we were making slow progress. Prior to this week, we had only spent time together as a group five months earlier at the national championships in Hobart. In many respects, the five of us—Nick, Tyrone, Zoe, James, and I—remained strangers to one another.

Our performances in training, though competent, had not been winning. As captain, I struggled to pull the group together and was beginning to fear that our team would be less than the sum of its parts. The pressure never relented. For the three of us due shortly to enroll at university—Nick, Tyrone, and me—this year's World Schools tournament would be our last. The same went for Bruce, who had tendered his resignation as national coach, effective at the end of this competition.

Back in the apartment, as the call to prayer downed, Bruce spoke into its echoes. Now a pensiveness weighed on his voice and lent his words a different kind of urgency: "You are giving away the debate. Seriously, you are barely contesting these rounds. Where is the rebuttal?"

He gestured to the two assistant coaches—Chris, a tall, soft-spoken man from Melbourne, and Kristen, a caustic, bookish woman from Brisbane—whose job was to demolish us in these practice rounds. "You are letting them get away with murder." The pair shot sympathetic glances in our direction.

The criticism was well aimed. In this most recent round, about the merits of public funding for the arts sector, my teammates and I had been so intimidated by the opposition that we had deferred to them. Instead of directly refuting their points, we took them as a given and looked for countervailing arguments. We said "Yes, but . . ." The coach had pointed out this tendency several times throughout the week, and now he appeared determined to settle the issue.

"This is what we're going to do: Whenever the opposition makes a new point, think 'Bullshit.' Then force yourself to come up with the reasons why it is so."

The coach spent the next few minutes demonstrating:

"They say the policy will increase the likelihood of nuclear war, you say . . ."

"They say this legislation violates the freedom of assembly, you say . . ."

"They say the opposition is being unreasonable, you say . . ."

There was a musicality to this refrain, like a profane call-and-response.

"In fact, let's try something different in the next round. Instead of repeating the word in your mind, say it out loud."

We went around the circle. The word sounded different coming from each person, but my delivery was conspicuously bad. I started too soft, overcorrected, and settled at an unhappy medium: "bULLshit." The coach didn't look up from his laptop, but I felt the weight of his attention all the same. I knew this activity was aimed straight at me.

*   *   *

For most of my life I had been terrified of conflict.

Behind the brutalist main building of my elementary school in Seoul had been an unpaved patch of dark-orange dirt. There, away from adult eyes, the older kids learned with their fists the uneven weight of bodies. The scuffles lasted a few minutes. Two kids circled each other, mustering the courage, then broke orbit to the animal noise of a cheering crowd. In the pivotal moments that ensued, strength never failed the losers. What broke first was the will.

I watched this unfold in the first grade and learned that proximity to violence elicited in me a gastric response. The acid soured my guts, then rose to the back of my throat. Though one could safely watch these fights as a member of the crowd, I felt in my bones the thinness of the line between spectator and participant. So I stayed at the other end of the school—the side with the gardens and parking spots—and kept my uniform bleach white.

But my parents had other ideas. Worried about their son's lack of preparedness for a cutthroat world, they opted for what was in Korea a national solution to shyness in children: enrollment in Tae Kwon Do. The dojang was in a steamy basement beneath a swimming pool. I never got used to the smell of chlorine and the vinyl stickiness of the mats. But I became fond of the sport, which in the beginning was ballet-like in its emphasis on stretching and rehearsing forms.

Within three years, I wound up at the Kukkiwon in Seoul, the global headquarters of the sport, competing for a black belt. The facility had been described to me as a kind of mecca but turned out to be a large gym built in the 1970s. In the shallow well of the amphitheater, one hundred of us demonstrated our forms for a dozen officials who sat on a dais and picked off from our number anyone who made a mistake.

The last part of the examination was the spar. I had prepared for weeks. But in this moment, the gap between practice and the real thing seemed impossibly vast. I locked eyes with the doe-like boy in front of me. We inched closer together and bowed. He threw the first punch—a jab that landed on my chest with a thud. I stepped back, shifted my weight, then kicked the side of his torso, a few centimeters below the ribs.

Beneath the starched white dobok, in the viscera between the bones, I felt again the part of me that hated all this. Soon after that, with my black belt in hand, I resigned from the sport.

Over the next decade I developed this gut instinct into a full-fledged ethic—a theory of how one should move in the world. In my everyday life I tried to dodge, ignore, and hide from altercations. I made an art form of nonanswers and deflective jokes. The reward of assiduous avoidance was likability. Whereas friends lost days of their lives to petty fights, I relished the comforts of getting along.

This view of conflict aversion as a life hack had a long history. Under the guises of propriety, complaisance, agreeableness, and good manners, it appeared everywhere from ancient Egyptian papyrus scrolls ("Silence is how you establish your superiority over him, / while he is bad mouthing, / greatly to the disgust of the assessors, / and your name is the good one in the mind of the officials") to *How to Win Friends and Influence People*, the seminal work of corporate trainer and former competitive debater Dale Carnegie ("There is only one way under high heaven to get the best of an argument—and that is to avoid it").

The wisdom of such advice seemed to me self-evident in the twenty-first century. If one feature of our public life was the absence of reasoned argument, another was growing rancor and enmity between political opponents (both phenomena dovetailed in the word *unreasonableness*).

Back home the very bad election of 2010, described by one journalist as a "new trough in Australian politics," had given way to a period of hostile and unrelenting partisanship. In one sign of the times, in 2012 Prime Minister Julia Gillard delivered a scorching fifteen-minute speech in Parliament denouncing the opposition leader as a misogynist for, among other things, standing at a rally in front of a sign that read DITCH THE WITCH.

The speech had gone viral around the world, but in Australia, the reaction was more mixed and polarized along party lines. For his part the opposition leader called on the government to "stop playing the gender card," a line also used in several major newspapers. At the lowest ebb of the discussion, people called one another misogynists and misandrists based on their reactions to the speech.

In this era of furious politics and culture wars, conflict seemed to me not only a prudent life choice but also a virtue. My aversion to political disagreements was not grounded in apathy or ignorance or fear. Instead, it resembled what the Italian philosopher Norberto Bobbio had once termed "mitezza," or meekness, that "repudiate[d] the destructive life out of a sense of annoyance for the futility of its intended aims." I even found for this moral position a theological justification. Turning the other cheek, scripture said, was neither stupidity nor weakness. It was wisdom.

So I lived this life of contradiction. Even as I climbed up the ranks of competitive debate, I remained staunchly agreeable in my everyday life. Friends who came to see me debate gaped at the transformation. My parents made jokes about Dr. Jekyll and Mr. Hyde. But I thought I had it all worked out.

Arguments had become the pastime of idiots and zealots. I was happy to stand with the silent, abstaining middle who rose above the fray.

. . .

The mood around the table was tense. In most training sessions, Bruce gave instructions and we wrote them down. As in an elite kitchen, we asked for clarification, not justification. But this time was different. Calling bullshit seemed to be at odds with everything we had been taught about treating our opponents with respect. It smacked of the dark side of the force.

Bruce looked around the table. He adjusted his glasses, scratched at his beard. He put down a half-eaten piece of simit—a chewy, sesame-coated bread—and continued: "I'm not asking you to do this just to get ahead. Right now, you're defaulting to agreement without really listening to the other side's arguments. You're deferring to the opposition without giving them the more basic courtesy of hearing them out."

I glanced down at my notepad. The column for our opponents' arguments was sparse: a handful of words and short phrases scattered its length in a random constellation. I had understood that the default to agreement was not an ideal strategy. However, I was learning that it could also amount to a kind of self-deception—the pretense that the other person's argument was too strong when, in fact, their rank and stature had overwhelmed us.

"Besides, you don't actually agree with the opposition on any of these points, do you?" Bruce said, his voice slowly rising. "No, you're just holding your tongue. That's cowardice—the same as saying, 'Mm-hmm, interesting,' and hiding what you actually think.

"Direct rebuttal isn't just something we do for ourselves. It's one of your basic obligations as debaters. You owe your opponents a proper response to their arguments and, with it, a chance to improve. You owe it to the audience to present the other side of the story."

The more Bruce spoke, the more I recognized in his advice a strain of optimism. Rebuttal was a vote of confidence not only in ourselves but in our opponents, one that contained the judgment that the other person was deserving of our candor and that they would receive it with grace. Calling bullshit entailed faith in our ability to make something positive out of disagreement.

By contrast, conflict aversion seemed to be premised on a much darker set of assumptions. It held that disagreements were bound to be ineffectual, if not divisive and outright destructive. It was a view that could have arisen only from an even dimmer judgment about people: that we could not be trusted to do right by one another.

I was not sure which of the two perspectives was correct, but as Bruce brought our last training session to an end, I felt I had arrived at the right question: Could rebuttal be more than a destructive force in a disagreement?

· · ·

In winter, the necklace of oversize resorts that hung around the coast of Antalya shone a little less brightly. The lights around the facilities dimmed shortly after the last dinner service, and the poolside bars were closed behind one-word signs that read OFF-SEASON. By the time we arrived at the tournament hotel, a flashy, sprawling resort named the Delphin Imperial, on Sunday evening, most of the other teams had already settled in.

The World Schools Debating Championships is the Olympics of high school debate. It began in 1998 as a six-way invitational among Canada, England, Hong Kong, New Zealand, Australia, and the United States and has since become an annual two-week competition with teams from as many as sixty countries, including Mongolia and Barbados. At the opening ceremony of my first World Schools in Dundee, Scotland, two years earlier in 2011, I had marveled at the array of national dresses and accents in the room. Sydney was diverse but not Romanians-and-Malays-learning-ceilidh-dancing diverse.

Such global representation seemed to offer a glimpse into how people around the world argued. For a group of sixteen- to eighteen-year-olds, many of them on their first overseas trip, the apparent stylistic differences among national teams was bewildering: the Singaporeans were technocratic speakers with flawless, intricate arguments; the Eastern Europeans recited Marx and critical theorists; the Canadians smiled and stabbed you in the front.

However, the shock of the new soon gave way to an appreciation of the similarities that lay beneath superficial distinctions. Almost everyone at the tournament spoke in terms of reasons and evidence and burdens. They drew from a common well of rhetorical references. This bookish and privileged group of teenagers seemed to be feeling their way to a global language of persuasion, one rooted in the vocabulary and syntax of good argument.

For much of its history, World Schools had been dominated by a handful of wealthy Anglophone countries. Among this group Australia had risen to the top with eight championships (next on the tally board were Scotland and New Zealand with four tournaments each). But now the competition was fiercer, with countries such as South Korea, Slovenia, and the United Arab Emirates regularly advancing to the final rounds. The last time Australia had won the competition had been some seven years earlier, in 2006.

Simple was the competition structure: every team competed in eight preliminary rounds, then sixteen of them entered a series of knockout rounds starting with the octofinals (an ideal run at World Schools comprised twelve rounds). In any given debate, the only thing that could make a team lose was an opposing argument that managed to convince the audience, and teams made an average of four such points per round. To win the tournament, all one had to do was defeat forty-eight arguments.

After check-in, my teammates and I turned our hotel suite, a two-story loft with strong heating and baroque furnishings, into a war room. Bruce pushed aside sofas and other niceties to make room for a large table and hard-backed chairs. The rest of us covered the surface of a bed with pages of news summaries and topic briefs, negotiated over electric outlets for laptop chargers, and set the television to the BBC. Then we got to work.

These last-minute sessions tended to reveal people's true anxieties. If you had a couple of hours left to prepare for the world championships, what would you do with the time? Some of my teammates practiced writing arguments, while others gamed out potential motions. For me, the only thing to do was to practice rebuttal.

Rebuttal, or the art of taking down an opposing argument, is straightforward in theory. As Bruce had explained to me years earlier, an argument has two burdens of proof: to show that its main point is true and that it supports the conclusion.

We should criminalize marijuana
CONCLUSION

because it is bad for people's health.
MAIN CLAIM

Truth: Marijuana is, in fact, bad for people's health.

Importance: If marijuana is bad for people's health, we should criminalize it.

No argument can succeed without meeting both of its burdens.

So it follows that one can take down an argument by showing that it is untrue or unimportant or both.

Un-truth: Marijuana is not, in fact, bad for people's health.

Un-importance: Even if marijuana is bad for people's health, we should not criminalize it.

This insight forms the basis of all rebuttal, on issues great and small:

We should buy a new car	because the old one is out of fashion.
CONCLUSION	MAIN CLAIM

Un-truth: The old car is not, in fact, out of fashion.

Un-importance: Even if the old car is out of fashion, we should not buy a new car.

There are several ways to show that an argument has failed to meet its burdens.

Truth rebuttal says the target argument contains inadequate information. Its content may be **factually incorrect** ("No, people are not buying fewer hatchbacks these days") or **lack evidence** ("You haven't given any reasons for me to believe that people's tastes are changing"). There can be conflicting information that makes the point **inconclusive** ("Yes, that's what Cars Daily says, but Motor Enthusiasts reckons something else").

Importance rebuttal takes two forms. One says the target argument is **unimportant**—that it does not provide a reason to support its conclusion. An opponent may be making a **logical leap** or misjudging the **relevance** of their argument ("Who says we have to drive a fashionable car?").

The second says the target argument is **outweighed** by other considerations—that it *does* support its conclusion but that there are good reasons to reject the conclusion nonetheless. There may be **better alternatives** ("Yes, we should drive a fashionable car, but we could do that by modifying the old one") or **competing considerations** ("Yes, we should drive a fashionable car, but we should also live within our means").

Of course, this was hard to do in practice.

In the Buddhist suttas, Saccaka, an argumentative man who quarreled with the Buddha, finds himself in an unenviable situation. The Buddha warns Saccaka that if he cannot answer a question after it has been posed thrice, "his head [will split] into seven pieces." This seemed to me to describe well the feeling of preparing rebuttal. One searched, under immense pressure, for an answer that might or might not take shape.

. . .

Later that night, after my teammates had gone to bed, I walked around the hotel grounds and settled in a plastic chair by the deserted swimming pool. From open windows in nearby buildings, the sound of other teams practicing streamed down toward me. One female voice, rich and full, cut through the rest. Her arguments came fast and at volume: just as I began to comprehend one idea, she moved on to another, so that I was left with nothing. I felt my chest constrict. For this was my fear: that opportunity would pass and leave me in the dust.

• • •

The first day of competition, a Monday, began at seven o'clock with breakfast. There was nothing remarkable in sight at the chandeliered function room on the first floor: a few hundred teens in ill-fitting suits moving through the stations of a hotel buffet. But then, as I entered the room, my ears adjusted to the sound. Everywhere around me—around the long tables, next to the lukewarm bains-marie—people shouted and explained and groaned in argument.

This aspect of debate tournaments had always puzzled me: How did people find the energy—before, during, and after a day of intense competition—to argue more? I gathered that some people wanted to size up the competition and that others enjoyed the free practice. For another group of people, the question barely arose. This was who they were. In any case, entering a room full of debaters unaccompanied carried the risk of being accosted.

Halfway through my breakfast at a table of Peruvians and Chileans arguing in Spanish, I saw a figure approach me. His tall and angular shape, clothed in a black suit, appeared as a narrow triangle in my peripheral vision. I looked at the empty seat to my right, then down at my plate of congealed scrambled eggs. "Anyone sitting here?" As he sat down, I caught a glimpse of his hair, which parted at the angle of a crow's wings in descent. "Gabriel, from the Philippines," he said, then fixed his dark, almond eyes on mine.

"You know that altruism is a myth, right?" I sensed that early capitulation could halt this interaction, but something about Gabriel's voice, reedy and smart, scratched at my pride. "There's a perfectly simple explanation. Those of our ancestors who were more favorably disposed toward cooperation were more likely to survive than those who weren't. So all this wanting-to-do-good-for-the-world stuff? It's nonsense." I began to twitch from the urge to interrupt.

One distinctive feature of the debate format at World Schools is the point of information (POI). Outside the first and last minute of a speaker's eight-minute speech, which are "protected," opponents are allowed to stand and offer a POI that the speaker can choose to accept or reject. If the speaker accepts, as he or she must at least once during a speech, the opponent then offers the point—by convention, a piece of rebuttal disguised as a question ("If altruism is a product of evolution, why don't we override the instinct as we do other impulses?"). The practice emerged from the tradition of oral questions in English parliamentary procedure. Some debaters abide by a gesture for offering POIs—raising one's right hand in the air while placing the left hand on one's head—as a hat tip to the past when parliamentarians had to hold their wigs in place as they stood.

People gave various justifications for allowing POIs, from making speakers more accountable to training competitors to think on their feet. However, I had always thought the main function of these permissible interruptions was to add to the spectacle of debate. A strong POI could throw a speaker off course and make its offerer seem dominant and otherwise formidable. On the other hand, a cutting response to a good point made the speaker seem invincible and elicited from the crowd howls of approval.

In societies that coded speech as strength and listening as weakness, interruptions held great power. Who cut off whom—in extended families, social groups, and workplaces—revealed even the best-disguised hierarchies. It also reflected ugly biases, such as the sexism that made women more likely to be spoken over and penalized for doing the same. In settings quotidian and elevated, a well-timed interruption could turn the tide of a conversation.

In the second U.S. presidential debate on October 16, 2012, Barack Obama and Mitt Romney, two of the more courteous candidates in living memory, spoke over each other an average of 1.4 times per minute (126 times across the ninety minutes). Obama deadpanned at one point, "I'm used to being interrupted." Both men had something to prove. As the challenger, Romney had to show that he could rival the president of the United States in gravitas. Obama was on the back foot after a disastrous first-round debate performance that had been widely panned as lackluster. They seemed to have settled on the same solution to their problems: interrupt.

The media headlines seemed to reward the decision: "Obama Hits Back in Fiery Second Debate with Romney" and "Rivals Bring Bare Fists to Rematch." But one political scientist, whose group counted the number of interruptions in the debate, saw the flickers of another danger: "President Obama may have benefited in the short run by adopting a much more aggressive style. But so many interruptions push the boundaries of civility in political debate."

Back at the breakfast table, as I drafted in my mind an acid rejoinder to Gabriel's argument, I paused over my instinct to interrupt. Our exchange, followed by a maximum of one other person, a bored Peruvian debater across the table, was not a public spectacle. So why was I treating it as one? The consequences of interrupting in everyday conversation seemed to me strictly undesirable:

At the outset, the response could miss. How an argument began often said precious little about how it might end. Some people buried the lede; others used red herrings to distract from the substance of their point.

Moreover, an interrupting speaker committed to attacking the conclusion rather than the argument. Most conclusions on most issues had at least one plausible point in their favor, but there was no guarantee that the other side had perfectly grasped one of those arguments.

An interruption also gave an opponent a chance to change direction. They could pivot to a new argument in favor of their conclusion ("Set aside evolution, then. We help other people because we will need their help in the future.") or move the goalposts of the original discussion ("Or at least we cannot ever say whether an act was motivated by altruism").

Lastly, interruptions could lead an opponent to conclude that they had not received a fair hearing. This allowed them to either disregard the rest of the conversation or use it to protest ("I can't get a word in edgewise. Why are you being so defensive?"). Too many interruptions foreclosed the possibility of changing an opponent's mind.

So then, why interrupt? One answer was to exercise some measure of power over the other person. Yet I wondered how strong I really felt at this moment. For there lay a certain fragility beneath the instinct to dominate. I feared the effects of Gabriel's speech, including its potential to persuade a listener or leave me tongue-tied. In such defensiveness, I saw the nature of the interrupter's bargain: they give up their chance to win so that, at least, they might not lose.

When I first started debating ten years earlier, in 2003, what I had appreciated most about the activity was its promise of freedom from interruption—and, in its absence, the room in which to find my words. However, the ban on cutting off a speaker had another crucial effect: it forced us to get even through listening. Unable to give immediate voice to our objections, we had to do the next best thing: listen closely and prepare the best possible rebuttal. So we learned to "flow" every round, a term that means writing down, in summary form, everything the opposition said.

Then, in the seventh grade, our coach, Simon, taught us to not only record but also *strengthen* the other side's arguments before responding to them. If the opponent had left out an example or a crucial line of reasoning, we had to supply it and say, "Now, the opposition could have said . . ." This sounded to us like an own goal. However, Simon insisted that responding to the strongest possible opposing case maximized our chance of persuading the audience and, maybe, even our opponents. It forced us to lift our game and take the other side seriously. Whereas good speakers gloated about opponents' mistakes, great debaters rushed to repair them.

Points of information detracted from a debate ethos grounded in listening. They turned "calling bullshit," once the final step of a long, thoughtful process, into a knee-jerk reaction. The advantages of such a move—engagement, accountability—were secured at the heavy cost of genuine persuasion.

. . .

In the breakfast room, Gabriel was nearing the end of his lecture on the evolutionary basis of altruism. This last stretch, on a study involving ant colonies, had been especially painful. Some of the others at the table had feigned interest in the beginning but were now pale with boredom. "So that about proves my point. Altruism comes down to selfishness in the end. QED."

What I wanted to say was that he had done nothing of the sort, that his argument was full of holes and pseudoscientific hand-waving. But instead I asked him a question: "Set aside evolution for the moment. What do you think about huge philanthropic organizations that do extraordinary work to save billions of lives?"

Gabriel adjusted his tie and swallowed a mouthful of juice. I saw his mind race from the anthills into the present day. "Well . . ." He paused. "Well, I would say that billionaires who donate to charity while running companies that exploit workers are hypocrites." The proceeding argument was hyperbolic and crude. Yet I could not help but to find aspects of it persuasive. When Gabriel asked, "Any objections?" I found myself briefly at a loss for words.

In both competitive and everyday debates, listening to the other side did not guarantee competitive success. Instead, it exposed us to the risk of being outshone by a better argument or being persuaded ourselves. However, we accepted the bargain so that we might be able to convince the other side and to take from the exchange an education richer than mere victory.

The thought brought to mind a long-buried memory from the fifth grade. In the winter of 2005, my class had taken an excursion to Canberra, the nation's capital city. There we spoke to an older woman in a neat woolen jacket whose job was to transcribe and edit the *Hansard*, a word-by-word transcript of the proceedings in Parliament.

Even at that young age, we had seen videos of politicians arguing on the news. Our reactions to these twenty-second clips tended toward the extremes. The better speakers seemed quite invincible, as if they possessed a wisdom beyond our reach. The others were boring and obvious.

But here was this public servant who had spent a career transcribing these arguments in their entirety—a woman who could credibly claim to be the best listener in the country. Someone in our class asked her what she had learned over her long career. She raised two fingers:

Most arguments are better than you think.

No argument is flawless.

• • •

After breakfast, my teammates and I boarded an unmarked bus to a picturesque school on the top of a steep hill. The view of the Mediterranean coast from this elevated spot would have taken my breath away. But by the time I set foot on the school campus, nervous anticipation had already left me winded.

In the first round of competition, between 10:00 a.m. and midday, we recorded an easy win against Germany. The German side was well researched but inexperienced. My teammates and I let down our guards and gave passable speeches filled with lazy rebuttal. Afterward, Bruce fumed at us. "You were too soft on them," he said. "This is not practice. You can't afford to leave a single one of their arguments on the table. That's not going to fly in this next round, so get fired up."

I knew what he meant: our next opponent, Mexico, had a reputation as one of the most aggressive and formidable sides in the league. "Give them one inch and, sheesh," one of the Danish boys whispered in the line for lunch. I tried to focus on the thick slab of mince-filled borek. Yet I could not stop looking to the back of the cafeteria, where the Mexican team stood in dark suits and bloodred ties, drinking only water and reserving their appetites.

Before the start of the second round, I paced up and down the corridors, blasting "Lose Yourself" by Eminem. I had never before chosen to listen to Eminem nor, for that matter, performatively paced around a common space. My usual preround routine was to sit in a quiet corner and take deep breaths. However, this afternoon, I wanted to access what I assumed was an innate human capacity for aggression. Hence, lose yourself.

Round two began at three o'clock in the auditorium, a cavernous, wood-paneled hall that seated two hundred people. Entering the venue, I noticed the sealed windows. The warm air inside smelled of recycled breath. As the two teams walked into the room, the crowd of students, sensing an opportunity to make some noise, burst into deafening applause.

The chair of the three-person adjudication panel, a bright Dutch woman in her early twenties, brought the house to order. She read the topic—"That the media should be prevented from intruding into the lives of public figures"—and invited our first speaker, Nick, to open the debate for the affirmative team. The audience, flustered from their earlier outburst, loosened the top buttons on their uniforms and settled in for the brawl.

Nick began in a ringing, boyish voice. "The right to privacy helps people lead lives of meaning. We should recognize in law this right because politicians and their families deserve protection from the remorseless tactics of unscrupulous media companies." Halfway through his introduction, our opponents began to loudly converse. They bickered and made gestures of exasperation. During the window for points of information, the three of them stood and offered one every ten seconds. I saw Nick struggle to keep his voice steady. At the desk, whatever anger I had tried to manufacture gave way to the real thing.

The first negative speaker, Paula, a short woman with a wild charisma, took to the podium before her name was announced. For a while she stood there, arranging her papers with a studied calm. Twenty seconds passed, then thirty. Just as the audience began to shift in their chairs, Paula raised her gaze and began to speak.

"Democracy lives and dies on the ability of citizens to choose good representatives. Politicians make decisions based on their personal beliefs, experiences, and relationships." Paula's voice, resonant and grave at first, began to climb in pitch. "Access to information is not a luxury. It is our right. The personal is political and information is power." Like an open flame, her voice swelled over the vowels and crackled on the consonants.

I gripped my felt-tip pen, then reached for Paula's argument: "The media should intrude because personal information helps citizens choose good representatives."

The argument had two burdens of proof:

> **Truth:** Personal information, in fact, helps citizens choose good representatives.

> **Importance:** If personal information helps citizens choose good representatives, then the media should intrude.

This gave me three openings for attack. I could say the argument was untrue, unimportant, or outweighed by other considerations:

> **Untrue:** No, personal information does not help citizens choose good representatives. The majority of this information is gossip and hearsay.

Unimportant: The fact that personal information may help citizens choose good representatives does not mean the media should intrude. Installing CCTVs in candidates' homes would also produce revealing information, but we'd never allow that.

Outweighed: Even if the media has good reason to intrude into politicians' lives, doing so would inflict collateral damage on their families and loved ones.

Paula wore her hair in thick braids that thumped against her neck as she spoke. Carried by this rhythm, she crescendoed to a conclusion: "Democracy cannot survive without a free and assertive press. I urge you to affirm this motion." The audience roared its assent.

Onstage, in front of the chattering crowd, I surprised myself with the steely and imperious sound of my own voice: "Everything the opposition told you about the media is a lie. For every one hard-hitting investigation there are hundreds of others about alleged affairs, weight loss, and misbehaving children. Such information dumbs down the public discourse. You should vote against Team Mexico because they are selling a fantasy."

My goal was to call bullshit on everything Paula had said. As I rushed through my rebuttal, I marveled at the trail of destruction—broken premises, dismantled connections, severed analogies—that I left in my wake. Soon, I reached the dangerous point when words began to outpace thoughts, yet I could not slow myself down. As I gained more confidence, I veered into personal attacks that, in number and kind, crossed the boundary of the acceptable: "less an argument than a string of nonsense ideas," "the product of a cruel imagination," "an irredeemably stupid point." The opposition made noises of outrage, but I kept pressing my advantage.

By the time I sat down, the air in the auditorium had noticeably chilled. Paula and her teammates fumed. Their coach—an intrepid and hot-tempered man known for setting up a debate circuit in remote parts of the world—looked ready to rush the stage. The audience sat upright, titillated by the hint of blood. I held my arms to disguise the adrenaline-induced shakes.

When the debate ended, we filed out of the room. Paula hesitated before shaking my hand. The resulting contact was brief and cold. For a panel of three adjudicators to reach a decision took, on average, between thirty and forty minutes. This sickening purgatory contained one moment of relief: we could ask the coach for his prediction.

Outside on the balcony, a grated platform overrun with wind, Bruce looked inscrutable. He gazed into the distance through dark sunglasses and ran his right hand through his hair. I blurted out a noise that resembled "Well . . . ?" He turned toward us but never quite met our eyes. "That was pretty good, guys. But I think you probably lost."

The coach said he appreciated our passion but that, in our rush to tear down the other team, we had missed a crucial point: disproving opposing arguments was not the same as proving one's own case.

"Your job in this debate was not to show that the other side had crap arguments or that they were bad people. It was to convince the audience to pass this sweeping restriction on media freedom. I don't think you did that. No amount of *no* is going to get you to *yes*."

Bruce explained that the best debaters ended their rebuttal with a positive claim. They switched from attacking what they opposed to advocating for what they supported, and thus answered the question: If not this, then what?

"If media companies are not driven to advance the public interest, then what drives them? If a right to information is the wrong principle to prioritize, then what is the right one?" He described this final step of rebuttal as providing the **counterclaim**. "After the destruction, you have to supply a better answer."

· · ·

In *Rhetoric*, Aristotle argued that anger contained a lick of pleasure. It began with the recognition that one (or an object of one's concern) had been wronged. This realization resulted in pain but also gave rise to a desire for "conspicuous revenge" against the wrongdoer. The thought of such vengeance—pleasurable merely as a prospect—was integral to anger: "Hence it has been well said about wrath, 'Sweeter it is by far than the honeycomb, dripping with sweetness, and spreads through the hearts of men.'"

Looking across the balcony at our opponents, I realized how easily this pleasure could hijack a disagreement. I had come into the debate with decent intentions, then had shifted my aim to wounding and humiliating the other side. Anger had become its own motivation. In a curious way, the resulting speech evinced the hallmarks of conflict aversion. When we chose to mock an opponent's missteps or attack their character, we exempted ourselves from the much harder task of wrestling with the actual disagreement at hand. The result was that, if and when the two sides returned to the original point, they had to start again at square one.

For Aristotle, the opposite of rage was calm, and the way out of anger was through those things that made us calm, among them laughter, the feeling of prosperity or success, and satisfaction. The philosopher included on this list "justifiable hope." The counterclaim seemed to me an embodiment of such hope. In the wreckage of old, flawed answers, one began to raise something new.

• • •

The adjudication, delivered by the judge from the Netherlands, went in our favor, 2–1. My teammates and I knew better than to look surprised, and the other side knew better than to protest on the spot. So we all wore the same blank expressions. Meanwhile, the audience began to whisper among themselves about the unexpected result. The dissenting judge from India, with her arms folded tight, looked inconsolable.

Over the next week I ran into Paula twice. Once was at the "cultural expo" on Thursday night, an event where each team set up a booth introducing their country to the other participants. Like almost every team, we overdid the snacks and undersold the culture. Once the chocolate-covered macadamia nuts were gone, we started teaching people how to swear in Australian.

The evening marked a happy milestone. Three quarters of the way through the preliminary rounds, we were on straight wins, which all but guaranteed a spot in the finals. Near the Indonesian stand I saw Paula standing next to me. She was holding an armful of mini sombreros but otherwise looked as she had in the debate. I managed a nod and a "mm-hmm" in her direction, then veered toward the wall.

Later that night I thought some more about the counterclaim. That pivot—when a speaker shifts from arguing *against* to arguing *for,* from your errors to my proposal—might be helpful in debate, but it was critical in everyday life. Naysaying could lay the groundwork for better answers to questions of fact, judgment, and prescription. However, the messy work of actually realizing the answer required people to sit up from the critic's repose and, at risk of error and rejection, commit to a position.

I next saw Paula on Friday night at the break party—the part of the competition when we found out which sixteen teams "made the break" and progressed to the finals. At the venue, an early Rihanna song was thumping and the lights were the color of Heineken bottles. Some teams came to the party in their uniforms only to hear the announcement at 9:00 p.m. Others arrived in black clubwear and cocktail dress, ready to dance into the wee hours. The strangest part was how natural everyone's presence seemed.

We qualified for the final rounds—in debating parlance, "broke into the outrounds"—with the fifth-highest number of points, owing to a loss to Canada in the last preliminary round. This was a respectable showing but one that placed us outside the top tier of teams. "Don't pay it any mind," the coach said. "Tomorrow is a new day."

I ran into Paula on the way out of the party. By the orange light of the craning lampposts she seemed to be standing at the center of things. I thought to pass by undetected, but the sound of my shoes on the pavement gave me away. Her eyes met mine and never hardened.

"Hi," we said, then, haltingly, found a way to talk.

. . .

In the fishbowl of debate competitions, where every triumph and misstep is on public view, news spreads at the speed of wildfire and reputations evolve in increments of hours. At this year's World Schools, one subject dominated the gossip among attendees: the team from

Eswatini, a kingdom in southern Africa with a population of one million people. The Swazi national debate team, in their second year of competing at World Schools, broke as the second-highest-scoring team in the preliminary rounds, then proceeded to slay giants—Scotland, Israel, Greece—on their march through the knockouts.

Early reports of the Swazi's success had been couched in faux-complimentary words such as *plucky*, *go-getters*, and *champs*. However, as the team progressed further in the competition, the chatter around them began to grow hysterical and the machinery of mythmaking went into overdrive. "They are geniuses reinventing the format before our very eyes," one Estonian woman told me in the elevator. "It's their coach: that anthropologist who hangs out near the hotel bar. He's devising all the strategies," a Greek adjudicator told me at the hotel pool.

The Swazi's own insistence that they had simply trained hard using videos of debate online induced suspicion and incredulity. When they defeated Singapore in the semifinals, on Monday, February 4, in a debate about paying homemakers a public salary for their work, the gasps in the room were said to have sucked the air out of the whole building.

By contrast, our team's run through the knockout rounds raised few eyebrows. Though Australia had not won the competition in several years, we were still considered the incumbents. News of our victories inspired occasional groans. When we secured our spot in the grand final on that same Monday, with a unanimous win over Ireland, we found ourselves cast as the Goliath to Eswatini's David. After the semifinal, on the bus back to the hotel, Bruce told us to buckle up: "Tomorrow, you will debate against the most inspiring story this competition has ever produced."

The evening of the grand final was crisp and moonless. So when the Swazi team and our own crossed the parking lot to the main ballroom of the Delphin Imperial Hotel, each side walked under the imperfect cover of night. The Swazis, three boys dressed lightly in shirts with rolled-up sleeves, moved with an ease that we, in blazers that pinched our sides, could not sustain. However, when we walked into the room and confronted the sound and heat of almost four hundred people, every one of us seemed to freeze at the legs.

As we took our seats onstage at seven o'clock, one of the nine adjudicators for the debate brought the house to order. The panel of judges comprised some of the most experienced debate teachers and coaches, as well as former world champions. Dressed in their various national garments, they resembled a United Nations Security Council of passing judgment. I scoured the audience to find Bruce and, next to him, my parents, whose eyes appeared blurry with jet lag and heightened emotions. Then I looked across the stage at the Swazis. Under the glare of the overhead lights, their foreheads glistened with sweat, but their eyes revealed no gaps in self-possession. I uncapped my pen and steadied my breath.

The chairperson for the debate, a mellifluous-voiced older woman on the tournament organizing team, announced the topic to the room: "The grand final motion is that Turkey would be better off outside of the European Union. Affirmative: Australia. Negative: Swaziland."

Beside me, our first speaker, Nick, subvocalized the opening to his speech on a loop. Under the desk in front of us, I forced my thighs together to prevent them from shaking, afraid that any such motion would send a tremor down our whole bench. Nick stood and approached the podium. Once there, he began his speech with a line that brought the house down: "There comes a time in every fairy tale when one side realizes they're the villain. And team Australia have come to terms with that. But as Voldemort said to Harry Potter: Turkish membership in the EU is a bad idea for Turkey."

Nick proceeded to make dense, intricate arguments about the harms of EU membership to Turkey's political dependence, then to its economic development. By convention, the grand final of the World Schools Debating Championships is a "prepared" round, which means that teams can research and write their cases ahead of time. In theory, this should reduce the pressure, but in fact, it has the opposite effect because expectations ratchet up to somewhere near perfection.

The Swazi first speaker, a poised baritone named Wabantu, unleashed a barrage of rebuttal on Nick's arguments. He presented two, three, four objections to every significant point in our case, all without breaking a sweat. The audience members whispered to one another in exhilaration as they toggled their gaze between the speaker and our bench. I disagreed with almost everything Wabantu said and kept my arms in constant motion, writing down four, five, six flaws in his reasoning. Then I saw Bruce in the audience, nodding with his arms folded, and I changed direction.

Soon my turn came. Standing at the podium, as the attention of the room pooled around me, I saw the audience as silhouettes in a fog of light. How familiar this feeling was: standing before others, exposed, on the cusp of an introduction. Peering into the crowd from a height, I could no longer distinguish friends from foes.

My role as a second speaker was to do maximum damage to the opposition's fledgling case. In a normal debate, I would have begun with a strident attack designed to divert all consideration away from the previous speaker. However, I opted in this round for a different approach. "So far, the two teams have focused on the disastrous consequences of either joining or spurning the EU. Each side has offered its prophecy of doom." I paused and cleared my throat. "What I want to do in this speech is paint a positive vision of how Turkey might look outside the EU: a nation that is more free, prosperous, and united."

Then, in rebuttal, I tried to pair each of my objections with a counterclaim: "So we don't believe Turkey will wield genuine influence within the EU. Instead, we argue that the best way to grow its global standing is to maintain a strong and autonomous foreign policy." The transition from criticism to positive argument reduced the thrill of rebuttal. It made our team a bigger target. What I got in exchange was the satisfaction of pushing the conversation forward. "So don't vote against the EU, against change, against team Swaziland," I concluded. "Vote for a better vision for this country." Then I sat down.

The Swazi captain, dressed all in black save a pair of white suspenders, stormed onto the stage while muttering under his breath. Fanele seemed an average, skinny kid, but the way he held the microphone—so close to its head, with a performer's dexterity—was for me the first sign that we might be in trouble. "Let's embrace the opposition's challenge. What is our positive vision of Turkey inside the EU? A bigger country that serves more of its people." Fanele spoke at great volume and speed, but every now and then, he slowed down and brought the mic within millimeters of his mouth to whisper some critical insight, a move that I had last seen at a Puff Daddy concert in the late 2000s.

Listening to Fanele's rebuttal, I noticed something remarkable. In response to my counterclaims, he offered not only objections but *another* counterclaim: "So let's talk about an autonomous foreign policy. Autonomy is as much about the range of options you have available to you as it is about the freedom to choose from a narrow set of options. Membership in the EU expands that range of options." The chain of counterclaims took us away from our original arguments and into unfamiliar terrain. Instead of simple offense and defense, we had evolution—the birth of new ideas and, with them, shifts in the borders of our disagreement. The debate concluded at a quarter past eight. As the nine adjudicators filed out of the ballroom, followed by the audience, my teammates and I held one another in a long embrace. Bruce came up to the stage and told us that he was proud of us. In the front row, Mum and Dad basked in the attention of well-wishers.

As the judges deliberated in another room, I sensed at the buffet dinner that opinion among the audience was divided. Friends told us the round had been close and strangers volunteered that, regrettably, they thought we had lost. So we had not embarrassed our opponents. Yet I felt at this moment a different kind of satisfaction.

• • •

For much of the history of parliamentary democracy, to be a member of an opposition (or minority) party meant spending a great deal of time on vacation. In eighteenth-century England there was not even a requirement that opposition members attend Parliament, so many of them decamped to their summer estates to lick their wounds and plot a return to power. The parties themselves existed as loose affiliations, beset by infighting and discipline.

The person who began to change this decadent norm was Edmund Burke. This Irish politician and scholar organized for his faction of the conservative Whig Party a "consistent program to be advocated in opposition." In doing so, Burke was motivated by a vision of what a party should be, "a body of men united for promoting by their joint endeavors the national interest upon some particular principle in which they are all agreed."

This view of political opposition was a tough sell in the 1700s. As one political rival wrote to a member of Burke's faction, "You can but serve the country by continuing a fruitless Opposition. I think it impossible to serve it at all except by coming into office."

However, over the course of the following century, norms shifted in Burke's favor. Terms such as *alternative government* and *his majesty's loyal opposition* began to enter the lexicon, and opposition parties were granted official privileges such as the ability to form a shadow cabinet and to influence the formal agenda of the Parliament.

Loyal opposition was to politics what the counterclaim was to competitive and everyday debates. Both grounded conflict and disagreement in the desire for shared progress. Whereas anger tended toward destruction (of the opponent or our relationship with them), opposition sought a form of competition that could be better or worse managed but never transcended.

Back at the Delphin Imperial Hotel, a pair of handbells called for our return. As the audience filed back into the ballroom and the two teams huddled at opposite ends of the stage, a hush descended on the room. In the front row, I saw Bruce and my parents contort with anticipation.

The individual results came first: I was named the best speaker at the tournament, and Fanele was named the second-best speaker. I nodded across the stage and he did the same, but both of us were too nervous to enjoy the moment. Too nervous, perhaps, even to see each other.

Then an older Scottish woman in a large tartan skirt came onstage with the trophy. The presence of the thin silver cup seemed to change the mood in the room. Audience members edged to the fronts of their seats. Our team huddle grew so tight that it began to implode. The head adjudicator, a wiry civil servant from Singapore, raised the microphone toward his mouth.

"The winner of the World Schools Debating Championships in 2013 is . . . Australia."

. . .

On the morning of departures, in the hotel lobby after breakfast, I ran into the captain of the Swazi debate team. In a worn athletic shirt and track pants, Fanele seemed more relaxed. He asked me where I was heading for university and I answered that I would enroll at Harvard in August. At this, Fanele burst into laughter so loud that people at opposite ends of the hotel lobby turned their heads. He told me that he had also applied to Harvard and was waiting to hear back. "You never know," he said with a grin. "Maybe in America we'll be teammates."

4

RHETORIC

How to move people

The afternoon got off to a bad start. A thunderstorm derailed the ceremony on campus, which was set to start at three thirty, and stranded a VIP party that included a former president and first lady of the United States. By the time the event got underway, it was five o'clock. The university president, a mathematician and clergyman, opened the ceremony with a prayer; speeches were delivered in Latin.

Then came the moment for which the small group had gathered. A reserved man—five foot seven, on the cusp of his forties, and recognizable as the son of the former U.S. president—took to the lectern and began his speech in English. The story he told was sad, but it arced toward hope.

At the revival of the letters in modern Europe, he recounted, the muse named Eloquence awoke from a thousand-year slumber to discover that her world had changed. She tried to get her bearings, still exhausted. But she discovered that her favorite languages were now extinct and people could not understand her.

Hers had been a long sleep. The muse had started noticing signs of physical decay—tremors, fatigue, paralysis—during the fall of the Roman republic, when speech was repurposed from persuading citizens to venerating dictators. She had persisted for centuries before passing out in the Dark Ages.

Wandering through this new world, Eloquence visited the three sites where she had once been most active.

The public fora—town squares and theaters—were empty. Or worse, they were filled with sophists and charlatans. But it was an even uglier sight that forced the muse to leave: the head of Cicero, one of her favorite orators, turned into stone and placed on the rostrum as an ornament.

What she saw at the courts was more disturbing. After climbing the steps to the courthouse, she saw her child, Persuasion, chained and shackled by the letter of the law. The muse also saw a version of herself, stammering in Latin and crushed by the weight of a thousand books.

The muse had better luck in the deliberative assemblies. She gained access to some of the fledgling parliaments around Europe and, with great effort, learned their languages and helped the politicians. But she was never again quite herself.

Thus began the story told by John Quincy Adams on June 12, 1806, at his inauguration as the first Boylston Professor of Rhetoric and Oratory at Harvard University.

Since the founding of Harvard in 1636, rhetoric, or the art of persuasive speaking, had been a feature on its curriculum. The subject was taught in lectures, and students were required, monthly, to deliver set speeches—an arrangement that reflected the school's initial mission to train Puritan ministers. But the endowment of the Boylston Professorship was a momentous occasion, one that ensured the teaching of rhetoric would endure through the generations.

Adams was not an obvious candidate for the job. Besides the fact that he was a politician as opposed to an academic, he was racked by doubts about his own speaking skills. He castigated himself in his diaries for a manner that was "slow, hesitating, and often much confused" and a tendency to end a sentence with the wrong word.

What Adams did bring to his role was a sense of political purpose. His father had once expressed hope that "eloquence" would be a feature of American political life—an ideal that traced back through David Hume to the ancient Greeks. But John Quincy Adams took it upon himself to teach rhetorical prowess to the next generation of American leaders.

Here, Adams believed, was the glimmer of hope for Eloquence. She had been oppressed by Europe's despots and had languished in its parliaments. But there might be a suitable new home for the muse: the United States. "Under governments purely republican, where every citizen has a deep interest in the affairs of the nation . . . the voice of eloquence will not be held in vain," Adams declared.

The first Boylston Professor began teaching on his fortieth birthday and left the job after three years to return to government service. His final lecture filled the chapel and, according to the writer Ralph Waldo Emerson, who arrived at the university many years later, "long resounded in Cambridge." In the year after his departure, Adams's lectures were published as a book, marking an American contribution to a genre dominated by classical and continental writers.

In 1825, John Quincy Adams was inaugurated as president of the

United States. He served one term, then lived out the rest of his life in the U.S. Congress. There, he developed a reputation for his impassioned advocacy against slavery, which culminated in an eight-hour argument before the Supreme Court on behalf of enslaved Africans aboard the *Amistad*. The reputation came with a nickname—a moniker for the ancient Greek orator Isocrates—"Old Man Eloquent."

I read about the old man's life on the twenty-four-hour journey from Sydney to Boston in August 2013. Everything about the flight was deadening: its length, density, air quality, food. But when I came across these pages in a book about U.S. history, I felt as though someone had cracked the window.

Part of the appeal was what the story said about my destination. To an eighteen-year-old prone to grandiosity, Adams's idea of America held layers of promise. Here was a young republic destined to revitalize the democratic tradition that was nonetheless open enough to allow one person to make a mark on its future.

For this vision, Adams seemed to me less a spokesman than an embodiment. His biography traced the arc of an underdog who learned through work and education to roar like a lion. I could see its mythic elements (the son of the U.S. president did not fit any fair definition of an upstart). But this, too, was part of America's romance: the country insisted on its place at the center of the world yet understood itself to be an outside challenger.

Oh, and the fact that Adams's story was about eloquence? Pure gravy.

. . .

My first encounter with the concept of rhetoric was in the winter of my sixth-grade year. In our redbrick classroom at the edge of the

Bush School, my classmates and I sat cross-legged on the floor as Mrs. Gilchrist, a purple-haired dynamo and the first teacher whom I loved, broke down the idea. "Rhetoric is about all the elements that go into the practice of persuasive speaking: words, speech, gesture, structure. If argumentation is *what* we say, rhetoric is *how* we say it.

"Look at me. How am I standing?" Mrs. Gilchrist moved through a series of poses, some expansive and others hunched, with uncanny ease. "Now, how does my voice sound?" Before our eyes, the middle-aged teacher grew into a stateswoman in the midst of a thundering oration. Then she turned into a shrinking violet whose voice could scarcely find its way out. So transfixed was our class that many of us forgot to blink.

However, as Mrs. Gilchrist turned from impressions to an introduction to the ancient origins of rhetoric, most of my classmates began to lose focus. I understood their lack of enthusiasm: When in our lives could we use the word *logos* without being branded a weirdo or a show-off?

Yet every word of Mrs. Gilchrist's lesson carried for me an urgent interest. No one had to tell me the manner of one's speech changed how one was understood. By this time, in 2006, I had learned English, but the subtle vagaries of accent, pronunciation, and idiom marked me as an outsider. I never believed that my ideas were less interesting or worthy than those of my peers, but I knew the distribution of credit was a fickler matter.

I also had no trouble accepting that one came to rhetorical prowess not through inborn talent but through an education. Since arriving in Australia I had acquired the language through a laborious process that involved stashing words and phrases in notebooks, sub-vocalizing sentences, listening to speeches on tape, rehearsing poses and gestures. To consider rhetorical skill a product of genius seemed to me a luxury I could not afford.

In the rest of that lesson with Mrs. Gilchrist, one detail stood out above the rest. The teachers of rhetoric in ancient Greece, known as sophists, were not Athenians. They were scholars and orators from distant lands. Immigrants.

Then, in middle school, I found in debate an activity that also approached rhetoric as a craft.

The coaches at Barker had neither the expectation of sublime delivery nor any tolerance for sloppy performance. They drilled us on a series of exercises to root out "tics," or distracting habits of speech (saying "um") and gesture (fidgeting, crossing arms):

> **Count:** Give a one-minute speech on any subject in front of another person. Ask them to count the number of times you engage in a "target tic." Repeat until you get to zero.

> **Restart:** Give a one-minute speech on any subject. Every time you engage in a "target tic," start the sentence again. Repeat until you go straight through.

> **Penalty:** Give a one-minute speech on any subject in front of another person. Every time you commit a "target tic," allow the other person to enact a penalty (e.g., throw some paper at you). Repeat until you get to zero penalties.

Whereas classroom discussions of rhetoric tended toward hyperbole and abstraction, debate took a no-nonsense approach. We cared about language and speech because they helped us win.

In other words, the tedium of speaking drills came with the promise of a reward: eloquence, or the kind of manner that made people stop and listen. What I could not have known then was that the pursuit of good rhetoric would not only take me around the world but also grant me admission to Harvard College—an important milestone in a brief lifetime of talking my way into places to which I had only a dubious claim of belonging.

I thought about the arc from Mrs. Gilchrist's classroom to the present as I wheeled two oversize bags into Harvard Yard on the morning of August 26, 2013. Such was the beauty of the late summer day that not even the university marching band could blemish its splendor. Several feet ahead, Mum, dressed in denim, dodged boxes and furniture while declaring that she should be the one moving in. "I would get more out of the place," she said, furrowing her eyebrows in mock protest.

My assigned dorm, Straus Hall, a four-story building in the colonial revival style, stood in the corner of the main yard. Lugging my bags up the steep main staircase, I greeted a dozen new neighbors, all of them baby-faced and sleek with sweat. In room C-31, a snug, wood-paneled suite with a filled-in fireplace, my three roommates and their families were busy at work, brooms and Allen wrenches in hand. My instinct in ice-breaker situations was to retreat but, resigned to the fact of cohabitation, I managed a smile and a sunny hello. Soon I was elbow to elbow with my roommates, assembling our shared furniture.

Of my three roommates, I gravitated toward Jonah. He had strong features—sharp blue eyes, red hair—and a taut, athletic build, but he exuded in gesture and movement a natural gentleness. The first book he produced from his bag was an exposé on the influence of big-money donations in politics. His parents, an outgoing and likable couple from Northampton, Massachusetts, found an easy rapport with Mum.

Over lunch with the families at Border Cafe, a raucous Tex-Mex restaurant with pink walls and relentless, cheerful music, I became tired of the polite conversation and decided to needle Jonah on his politics. "I think American liberals get too crazy about campaign donations. People advocate for their political causes in all sorts of ways. What's wrong with money?" I hardly believed the assertion, which I had picked up from a debate round, but I thought I could make a case for the position. Jonah set down his quesadilla as our two roommates rushed into a conversation of their own. "Are you being serious?"

In the next five minutes, Jonah's voice never rose in pitch or volume, but it nonetheless changed. He spoke with a graveness that thrummed with an urgent undertone. The argument he made tended toward exposition rather than polemic. Gesturing with outstretched hands, he told stories and used words such as *justice* and *fairness* without a hint of irony. "So yeah, that's why we get crazy about this stuff." By the time he finished, his hair seemed to have turned a darker shade of red.

I asked Jonah whether he had ever debated. "You'd be good, you know?" He paused, then said in a tone suggestive of a joke, "Not my cup of tea." I wondered if he thought I was British.

Outside the restaurant, I hailed a cab back to the airport for Mum. As I looked at her teary face, I felt a terrible realization descend: I would not see her for the rest of this year, and our next meeting, squeezed into the summer holidays, would measure in weeks rather than months or years. I wondered how I had failed to appreciate this fact and whether my parents had missed it, too. Then I wondered if the necessary cost of my choosing a college halfway around the world had been self-deception. Before she got into the cab, Mum produced from her bag a stone sculpture she had purchased from a local artist in Antalya, Turkey. "To keep you safe," she said.

For the rest of the day I shuttled from one orientation session to another and learned that the university was a hyperverbal place. None of my cohort of 1,600-odd freshmen seemed particularly wise, but almost all of them had cleverness and wit that expressed itself in the form of words. Everyone felt the need to explain themselves.

In such an environment, arguments played an important role. They served as a natural way for people to perform before an audience, to prove a point, and to size up one another. People disagreed on pop culture over dinner and on politics at the last debrief session in the evening. I stayed away from the fray but could not help feeling an affinity for these debaters.

By eleven o'clock I was exhausted. The roommates had gone to bed and I was horizontal on the couch sending texts back home. Then, as I began switching off the living room lights, I heard a knock at the door. "Who is it?" I wondered if it was the neighbor from downstairs, who had earlier professed his love of long conversations—a terrifying prospect at this late hour.

Another knock. "It's Fanele."

Fanele had been a scrawny kid when we had first met nine months earlier, but now he seemed more solid, relaxed. "Bo Seo. Bo Seo, man." His mercurial voice boomed on the verge of laughter as he walked past me into my living room.

I did not ask how he had found me. Neither this nor the small talk we exchanged on our experiences of move-in day seemed relevant to anything. Instead I told him that I'd had a question on my mind for months: "How did the Swazi team do that at World Schools?"

He laughed. "How did the Africans get to the final?" I made some sheepish noises in protest. Fanele explained that the team had watched hours and hours of debate videos, then filmed themselves delivering speeches to analyze every decision, move, tic, and gesture. "It was just work, man. No magic bullets." I told him I agreed.

Then Fanele said he had something to ask me: "Bo, I think we should try to win the world championships."

Before I could respond, he launched into a series of arguments, half rehearsed, half improvised. His voice grew louder and his expression more intense. I was baffled by the brazenness of his ambition, which made as much of a claim to my time as to his own. What I could not deny was his knack for summoning the right words. "This is who you are," he said.

Listening to Fanele, I started to believe that what had gotten me to this place might also get me through it.

. . .

Then classes began in earnest, and the campus changed.

At Harvard, undergraduates need not choose a major until the second semester of their sophomore year—an element of flexibility designed to allow for experimentation. I had arrived on campus expecting to study philosophy, a subject to which I, as a debater, considered myself well suited. So on the second Tuesday of the term, I rushed to the department's open-house event.

I walked in late to the grand, dusty library on the second floor of the philosophy building, Emerson Hall. At the front of the room, members of the faculty were describing their subject in increasing levels of abstraction: "Our aim is not to arrive at the right answer but to scrutinize the reasons for any given answer." "Even better is to pose better questions." "Or indeed to ask, 'What is a question?'" Thoughtful murmurs went around the room.

Afterward I stumbled into a conversation with a logician. The older man in a wool vest squealed that the cookies he had laid out were Leibniz biscuits. "Like the philosopher," he said expectantly. I took a sip of water before explaining that I had done a bit of debate in high school and asking whether he thought this might be useful training for philosophy. He adjusted his glasses. "Probably not," he replied. "We really side with Socrates over Gorgias on this one."

Later in the afternoon I searched for the reference that he had made.

Gorgias, born in 483 BC, was an itinerant rhetorician, or a sophist, who delivered public lectures—"Helen was not to blame for the Trojan War"—and tutored young people in the art of oratory. He had come to Athens in his sixties to seek military protection for his hometown of Leontini, on the island of Sicily, then made a life for himself in the big city. Some critics turned up their noses, but the man's effect on the people was undeniable. He drew them by the masses and put them in a trance.

One night, Gorgias was holding forth at a dinner party when he was cornered by another guest: a disheveled man named Socrates. The philosopher put the question to him directly: "What are we to call you, and what is the art which you profess?" Gorgias responded, "Rhetoric, Socrates, is my art."

In the beginning the sophist brimmed with confidence. He said rhetoric held the power to persuade the multitude that "if you have the power of uttering this word, you will have the physician your slave, and the trainer your slave." Then Socrates's questioning began.

The philosopher wrested from Gorgias an early admission: "Rhetoric . . . creates belief about the just and unjust, but gives no instruction about them." In other words, the art of persuasion was unallied to truth and used any means to win over the listener. Gorgias accepted the charge: "Socrates, rhetoric should be used like any other competitive art, not against everybody—the rhetorician ought not to abuse his strength any more than a pugilist."

Gorgias tried at this stage to pause the discussion supposedly on account of the company's boredom, but the crowd cheered for them to continue. So the philosopher went back on the attack:

SOCRATES: You were saying, in fact, that the rhetorician will have greater powers of persuasion than the physician even in a matter of health?

GORGIAS: Yes, with the multitude,—that is.

SOCRATES: You mean to say, with the ignorant; for with those who know he cannot be supposed to have greater powers of persuasion.

GORGIAS: Very true.

SOCRATES: But if he is to have more power of persuasion than the physician, he will have greater power than he who knows?

GORGIAS: Certainly.

SOCRATES: Although he is not a physician:—is he?

GORGIAS: No.

This gave Socrates the concession he needed, and soon the philosopher arrived at his conclusion: rhetoric was less an art than a form of flattery that produced delight and gratification.

"An art I do not call it," he said, "but only an experience, because it is unable to explain or to give a reason of the nature of its own applications. And I do not call any irrational thing an art." Rhetoric, said Socrates, was more like cookery than philosophy. In the rest of the exchange Gorgias barely spoke again.

Despite the result of this particular debate, rhetoric continued to flourish for hundreds of years. Ancient Romans such as Cicero and Quintilian greatly enriched the Greek tradition, while the Chinese and Indians elaborated their own theories and canons. In the universities of medieval Europe, rhetoric was among the original seven liberal arts, with arithmetic, geometry, astronomy, music, grammar, and logic.

However, some two thousand years on, I could not escape the conclusion that Socrates had prevailed. Nowadays the word *sophist* was an insult and *rhetoric* meant "mere rhetoric"—a term of dismissal for hollow, obtuse, and pretentious speech. Inasmuch as people ever thought about the art of rhetoric, they considered it an artifact of antiquity or an indulgence afforded to political and cultural elites. This exposed the term to further derision from demagogues and television hosts who spoke over chyrons that read STRAIGHT TALK and NO SPIN.

Even at this university, some two hundred years after John Quincy

Adams delivered his speech, rhetoric seemed to be in full-blown re-treat. As students settled into introductory courses in economics, com-puter science, statistics, and life sciences—the most popular classes at the college—meandering conversations in dining halls gave way to problem-set sessions. Even in the humanities, one detected a shyness about the spoken word. Instruction in public speaking, once a re-quirement for every student, had been reduced to an optional practi-cum with a cap of some eighty students. The two most recent Boylston Professors had been poets.

In this centuries-long decline of rhetoric, I saw the influence of overlapping trends. To start, the rise of modern science helped promote the view that rhetoric was imprecise and irrational. In seventeenth-century England, the philosopher Francis Bacon called for forms of rhetoric suited to communicating discoveries made through the scien-tific method. Though he made room for an "imaginative style," he also advocated for a plain one stripped of "ornaments of speech similitudes, treasury of eloquence, and such like emptiness." The idea had staying power.

Then the advent of printing and mass publication shifted com-munication from oral to written forms. In the 1870s, the new presi-dent of Harvard University, Charles Eliot, sought to move from a common curriculum to an elective model that allowed each stu-dent to choose classes according to the "natural bent and pecu-liar quality" of their mind. When it came time to select a handful of required subjects, he made elocution noncompulsory for the first time in 230-odd years and mandated instead a first-year writ-ing class. By the turn of the century, most colleges in the United States had followed suit and replaced "rhetorical work spread over four years with a single yearlong required first-year [composition] course."

Moreover, as a wider cross-section of society became culturally enfranchised, traditional notions of good language fell out of style. In the 1920s, the newly founded British Broadcasting Company formed an advisory committee of gentlemen luminaries to advise on correct pronunciation (e.g., privacy = prive-acy; respite = respit). The committee was disbanded after World War II, and a greater range of regional accents began to feature on the BBC. In more recent years, efforts to reclaim disfavored vernaculars such as Singlish in Singapore also evinced and contributed to declining interest in universal notions of good rhetoric.

Finally, declining interest in rhetoric correlated with the rise of anti-elite sentiment. The present-day contempt for "political speak" was a fair response to our political leaders' flagrant abuses of language, including lies and weasel words. It also reflected a suspicion that powerful people were waxing lyrical while acting against our interests. In this context, hearing then mayor of London Boris Johnson go on about the "descending tricolon with anaphora" in Churchill's speeches was, well, annoying.

For me, in early September 2013, barely weeks into my first semester of college, all of these trends seemed to have conspired to create the present. Taken together, they posed a simple question: What kind of rhetoric was desirable (and possible) now?

• • •

Every Monday evening, Fanele knocked on my door in Straus and the two of us walked to Lamont, a twenty-four-hour library with minimal ventilation, in time for debate training at 7:00 p.m. The university's parliamentary debate team, the Harvard College Debating Union, was among the best in the world. However, unlike counterparts such as the Oxford and Cambridge unions, the HCDU had no building or room of its own. So its fifty-odd members roamed the campus in search of venues for their disagreements.

University and high school debate differed in subtle but important ways. In college, the size of each team was reduced from three to two people, upping the pressure on each speaker and the partnership between them. The players also changed. Whereas in many high schools debate was the sole refuge of precocious kids, colleges hosted hundreds of clubs and activities. So only the true believers remained, and like sugar left in the bottom of the pan, they tended to be intense, stuck on, and prone to bitterness.

Fanele and I came into the union with no small sense of entitlement. Some thirty freshmen joined the team each year, and over the course of the next several months, twenty of those resigned upon realizing they had no prospect of competitive success. We intended to be the last pair standing.

What enabled our arrogance was mutual regard. While the rest of the school spoke the dry, precise language of academia, Fanele and I indulged—in conversations that lasted whole afternoons and evenings—our hunger for big ideas and flashy one-liners. Though only nineteen years old, a year older than me, Fanele had a self-assurance that was foreign to me. In his booming voice, he pronounced on politics and social mores. When a joke made him laugh, he rolled on the ground. In our disagreements, I often found myself conflicted: a part of me wanted him to come around to my point of view, but another part of me wished he would remain just so.

In these early weeks, the two of us had only one complaint about the debate union: our Monday training sessions gave us no opportunities to actually speak. Instead, our coach, a cerebral and wiry college junior named Daniel, recited earnest lectures on financial crises and the law of war. Even the more practical sessions were a slog. At our fourth training session, on the third Monday of September, a chilly night that seemed to prefigure the coming winter, Daniel told us to take out our notebooks. "Tonight we will practice 'flowing,' or note-taking during an opponent's subject." He opened his casebook, an immense gray folder filled with past cases and miscellaneous arguments, then began to read a passage produced by the People for the Ethical Treatment of Animals (PETA) in favor of veganism:

> Every year, tens of billions of animals are killed for food, and most endure lives of constant fear and torment. Nearly all the animals raised for food in America today are separated from their families and crammed by the thousands into filthy warehouses, where they spend their entire lives in abysmally filthy conditions. They're mutilated without the use of painkillers and deprived of everything that is natural and important to them. On the killing floor, many animals are conscious and struggling to escape.

What would you write down? The trouble was that the passage was descriptive. Each of the claims broadly supported the author's conclusion, but not every one of them required a discrete response. Disputing that warehouses were filthy, for example, was to somehow miss the point.

I had learned in high school that a better way was to isolate the main claim. This involved taking the opponent's conclusion ("We should be vegans"), adding the word *because*, then asking how the speaker might complete the sentence. That revealed the two key arguments hidden in the passage:

We should be vegans because . . .   animals are raised in appalling conditions.

animals are killed in an unacceptable manner.

This advanced version of listening comprehension was hard to do in real time. As Daniel raced through a dozen arguments, we freshmen kept up as best we could. Some people wrote at an extreme speed, cutting into the page with their felt-tip pens. Others moved at a workmanlike pace, never losing their cool as they steadily fell behind. The hour passed in the manner of a secretarial exam that everyone failed. "Practice makes perfect," Daniel offered on his way out the door.

Crossing the dark and windy yard on our way home, Fanele and I vented our frustrations. The precise discipline that the union prized seemed to be at odds with our own vision of debate—expansive, passionate, sexy. As we parted ways for the night, we took some solace in the fact that the past month had been a mere rehearsal. "Drills are drills. Debates are debates," Fanele declared. The first tournament of the American Parliamentary season, a yearlong league with weekly competitions held across the country, was set to begin at Columbia University in Manhattan at the end of the week.

. . .

Around noon on the afternoon of Friday, September 20, Fanele and I took a right turn on Broadway and paused to take in the unfolding sight. In the space of a few steps, imposing blocks of redbrick buildings gave way to a vast plaza teeming with life. The five-hour bus ride had matted our hair and soured our clothes, but now, in these currents of breeze, we felt our spirits revive.

From a modest height on the stairs to the main library, Fanele took pictures of Ionic columns and turquoise rooftops. Then he put his arm around my shoulders and said the time had come.

The atmosphere in the general assembly, a glorified term for any large room where competitors awaited the start of the next round, was tense and smelled of stale coffee. Around a hundred university students from across the United States milled around the warm auditorium, exchanging gossip and whatever ideas came to mind. Fanele and I hung around the back entrance to the room, afraid to engage, afraid to walk away.

In the first round, we faced a couple of jittery freshmen from Swarthmore, a liberal arts college in Pennsylvania. The two of them—a diminutive boy in oversize glasses, a girl mumbling something ferocious under her breath—led the way to our assigned room in the next building. When we settled around the main table in this small seminar room, I felt a nervousness that I had not experienced in a debate room in several years. However, as the first speaker from Swarthmore fixed his specs and began reading a case about banning the use of military drones, I felt my body settle into a familiar rhythm.

We won the round against Swarthmore and, by the late afternoon, were sailing through the competition, claiming victories on subjects ranging from paid parental leave to the downsides of free trade. Standard wisdom said to take it easy in these early rounds, to hide one's strength and bide one's time, but Fanele and I raced in the opposite direction. We showed off every skill we had ever learned—from answering the four Ws to crafting deadly points of information—and spoke to audiences of three or fewer people as though they were a vast crowd.

Later that night, around eleven o'clock, over dollar pizza slices and warm sodas, we allowed ourselves a moment of smug satisfaction. Our win-loss record, 4–0, guaranteed us a spot in the final rounds. Dreaming grand fantasies and uttering cruelties, we pushed our way out of the restaurant and descended Amsterdam Avenue to the dorm where Fanele's friend from home had cleared a spot on the floor so that we could crash for the night.

The next morning, thick and overcast, passed to the drumbeat of steady escalation. Fanele and I won the last preliminary round, then our octofinal against an established team of seniors from Brown University. Each of these results sent a shock wave through the anxious organism that is a debate tournament. Between rounds, in the hallways outside the general assembly, Fanele and I paced to music, subtly performing for the people who studied us from afar.

Sometime around two o'clock in the afternoon, the announcement of the quarterfinal sounded through the walls. "Quarterfinals in room EG014. Affirmative: Harvard. Negative: Bates. Judges: Connelly, Hesse, Ghosh." As Fanele and I walked into the auditorium to collect our bags, the crowd parted to give us passage. Seniors from our college debate union, many of whom had been knocked out of the tournament, mobbed us with advice—"Take the fight to them,"

"Don't forget to look up," "Breathe!"—as we descended to the basement floor.

Room EG014 had the scent and temperature of a boiler room but none of its functionality. Over thirty people, most of them strangers, had crowded into the space. They craned their heads to see us enter the room. Our opponents from Bates College, a liberal arts college in Maine, were already seated and busy at work, charming the judges with a verbal potpourri of self-deprecating jokes, compliments, and winning remarks. The more assertive of the two, a tall woman named Dana who sported a mohawk, greeted us with a yawn and a "Finally."

Soon a hush came over the room, and I stood up to face the crowd. The topic read, "That social justice movements should pursue change through the courts rather than the legislature." Surveying the faces in the crowd, many of them red with excitement, I reminded myself that I had to awe them from the beginning. For when a much-hyped team failed to meet expectations, the crowd could turn on it with vicious speed. So I gave the room a steely look, then began.

"Justice delayed is justice denied. For as long as craven politicians, who kneel at the altar of donations and self-perpetuation, hold in their hands the lives of those who have been denied far too long, yet another generation will know the coldness of rejection and indifference."

I sensed a movement in the audience. I thought I had imagined the sound at first, but then it grew. "The courts remain, in this period of political deep freeze, a bastion of hope," I pronounced. "Great is our debt to this most essential safeguard of our democracy." What began as a half-suppressed snicker in one corner of the room swelled as large as a giggle, then disappeared again. The brief moment set me out to sea, and only once I had hobbled back to my seat, weary and moist with sweat, did I feel I had returned to land.

Then Dana stood to deliver her speech. I met her green eyes as she approached the lectern, and I could see that she had grasped some important point. Dana laid down her notes, then, with a smile, asked whether everyone was ready. Her voice was relaxed but none-theless forceful: "What even was that?" She held the pause until the crowd sat forward in their seats. "These guys are pretty talkers. They sound good, but there's not a whole lot of *there* there. It's just rhetoric.

"Think about their argument about the courts delivering so-cially progressive outcomes. Justice, equality, democracy. Yeah, yeah. Have they given you actual reasons why we can leave our future in the hands of politically appointed elites who are bound by precedent?"

Few experiences in debate felt worse than sitting in a round headed toward defeat. There was no tapping out—only participation, as player and witness, in the theater of your undoing. Afterward, rivals gloated while friends and allies dissolved into coos. Around 4:00 p.m., after our defeat had been made official, Fanele and I packed our bags and headed to the Megabus station to see if we could talk our way onto an earlier bus back to Boston. As we walked down the city streets, crowded and indifferent, I consoled a particularly caring sophomore from our team: "Don't worry, Fanele and I will have more chances."

For the rest of the weekend, I denounced the local debate circuit to anyone who would listen, which was no one beside Jonah and Fanele. "They have no regard for rhetoric in this league. What could it mean to 'talk pretty' in a debate?" I wailed on the sidelines of a bleak dorm room party. The two of them indulged my complaints, but I began to see in their plaintive nods a hint of forbearance.

On Monday night at debate training, the freshman class drilled flowing again. The exercise felt no easier than in previous weeks, and I winced at Daniel's insistence that we had to "grow our hand muscles." As I listened to the coach recite a case about the proper structure of disability benefits, I recalled a curious detail from Saturday's quarterfinal round: during my introduction not one person in the audience had picked up their pen to mark their flow.

At first the realization upset me, but then I found myself asking a different question: What would they have written? The introduction had signaled where I stood on the issue and how I felt about politicians. It also told the audience that I considered it very important that they agree with me. Aside from that, I could not think of much else that a listener could have flowed.

On some level this had been my intention. I had wanted to leave the audience speechless with the force of my ideas. Yet as a result, I had failed to invite them in—to make my meaning transparent and give the audience an opportunity to consider the argument for themselves. In a bid to be spectacular I had become a mere spectacle.

I already knew that speaking manner had to get out of the way before it could help. That had been the point of drills such as Count, Restart, and Penalty: we had to root out vocal tics and other performance issues because the audience could notice those things over the actual message.

However, I had never applied the same effort to ensuring that my words were as clear as my speech.

Later that night after training, back at my desk in the dorm, I started to scribble some notes on achieving such clarity.

I began with a rule about individual words.

WORD		
Rule #1 No abstract words	Don't replace a word with the category to which it belongs, or use an abstract word when a more concrete one will do. We may be tempted to use this move to make our arguments seem more widely applicable and important. But the actual effect is to make our point harder to follow.	**Bad:** "Our educational institutions are failing." **Better:** "Our schools and colleges are underfunded."

Then, I moved to sentences.

SENTENCE		
Rule #2 No confusing metaphors	Treat metaphors like an overwhelmingly powerful spice: account for each one that you use, and almost never mix them. Note that some common fragments of language are, in fact, metaphors—"separate the wheat from the chaff."	**Bad:** "Injustice reigns and pervades the air that we breathe." **Better:** "Injustice reigns and makes subjects of us all."
Rule #3 No excess qualification	Qualifications, exceptions, and counterarguments can wait until the main point has been established. In a bid to be faultless we fail the more basic task of getting the message out.	**Bad:** "The right to life, notwithstanding the complications of how we define that term, is one of the more important rights we have." **Better:** "The right to life is paramount."

Finally, I thought about paragraphs.

PARAGRAPH		
Rule #4 No buried ledes	Start with the conclusion of your argument, and say the minimum amount required to prove it. This way we know where the argument is heading and whether we are on track.	**Bad:** "On one hand, the proposal is cost-effective, but I worry about the PR risks . . . so I would lean against it." **Better:** "We should not adopt this proposal. This is how I see the trade-offs. . . ."
Rule #5 No thoughtless repetition	Don't repeat the message without considering what the repetition will help you achieve. In general, many versions of the same claim dilute the message and, if the listener is unprepared to hear the point in this form, feel overwhelming. One rule of thumb: when you're 80 percent satisfied with how you have delivered the message, move on.	**Bad:** "The kids are unhappy about their new school. Their discontent is palpable. The school is not working out for them at all. They say it is horrible." **Better:** "The kids are palpably unhappy with their new school. We need to do something."

The rules were unglamorous. They involved subtraction rather than addition and lacked the mystique of antique terms such as *caesura* and *synecdoche*. For me, however, the rules seemed to embody another view of rhetoric: one that aspired to truth over awe and sought to enhance rather than supplant the underlying ideas, so that they might live more fully as themselves.

• • •

Over the rest of our freshman year, Fanele and I gained a steady footing on the competitive circuit. The two of us never won a tournament together, but we established ourselves as solid players and inseparable partners. Though some people continued to rib me for "talking pretty," the criticism lost most of its sting. Meanwhile, at college, I learned to write and speak in the ponderous style of scholars. In the spring semester, I inched away from philosophy to the freer pastures of political theory and English literature, but before that, I managed to wrest from a philosopher of mind some soggy praise for my "dispassionate writing style." All this I understood as signs of progress. Yet close to home a friend was headed in the opposite direction.

Jonah's freshman year followed the trajectory of an antidebater. He took classes in religion and English literature and sociology. As a natural empath, he spoke as often about feelings and intuitions as about reasons and evidence. His trim mustache grew into a full-blown beard. In politics, Jonah's bias was in favor of picking a side, then organizing for its success. He seemed disturbed by the idea that debaters could argue for libertarianism in one round, then for democratic socialism in the next one. "How does that work, exactly?" he asked, before adding in response to my blank stare, "Like, in a deeper sense."

While I crisscrossed the U.S. every weekend for tournaments, Jonah put down roots and became involved in a movement calling for the university to divest from fossil fuel companies. Near the end of the spring semester, on the last Wednesday in April, 2014, the group planned a blockade of the university president's office until the administration agreed to an open meeting on the subject. Jonah invited me to the rally: "It might be interesting to you. We also give persuasive speeches, you know."

The sit-in began before dawn on a gray Wednesday morning. From the window of my dorm room, through the dreary haze of the passing rain, I could see the bright orange of the protesters' T-shirts and picket signs. After breakfast, I went down to see Jonah. The air outside was surprisingly cold, and some combination of rain and wind had swept the protesters' hair into dramatic shapes. Jonah stood near the front of the crowd of fifty-odd people and held a large sign with both hands. I was concerned that the protesters seemed to have organized only coffee and various kinds of seeds for sustenance, but when I raised this point Jonah shooed me away.

Then the crowd began to form a semicircle and speakers lined up near the microphone. I retreated to the back row. The first few speeches were hard going. People spoke too close to the microphone. They went from zero ("Can everybody hear me?") to a hundred ("A mass extinction event is upon us!") in the space of several seconds.

I saw the dilemma. On the one hand, the stakes really were that high, but on the other hand, few people other than the true believers could stomach so much truth so soon after breakfast. I wondered if one solution might be for the speakers to bring their speech more in proportion to the particular intervention they were advocating—not yet a solution to climate change but an open meeting with the university president. This recalled a couple of other rules I had been thinking about in debate:

PROPORTIONALITY		
Rule #6 No emoting	Make sure the tone of your words fits the thing you are trying to describe. Otherwise it becomes emoting—a performance in which emotions no longer correspond to the situation at hand. The most obvious forms are exaggeration and euphemism.	**Bad:** "This thing is a catastrophe!" **Better:** "This inconvenienced me." **Bad:** "This was a regrettable error." **Better:** "Our mistake cost people's jobs."
Rule #7 No insinuation	Don't imply a conclusion that you are unwilling to directly defend. One common technique is dog-whistling, or the use of coded language to hint at a position that one can later deny. Another is the use of a rhetorical question in place of an argument.	**Bad:** "I want to protect our way of life." **Better:** "I believe in reduced migration and a commitment to assimilation." **Bad:** "What is the government hiding about the moon landing?" **Better:** "The moon landing was a hoax."

However, a few of the people who spoke next were outstanding. One slightly goofy kid from the American Midwest explained how he had joined the movement after spending most of his life apathetic about the environment. A lifelong activist told stories of how fossil fuel pipelines displaced regional communities.

These people made no grand claims. They spoke about one thing rather than many. In place of theories and abstractions, they relied on anecdotes and descriptions. For this reason their speeches would not have been considered effective by the standards of debate. However, I could not deny their appeal. I found myself returning again and again to how they enlisted personalities to persuasive effect:

PERSONALITY		
Rule #8 Reveal the journey	Besides explaining *what* you believe and *why*, tell the story of *how* you came to believe it. Listeners often find the prospect of changing their mind to be terrifying. They want to know where the speaker is coming from, so that they may be able to trust and even identify with the person.	**Bad:** "Mandatory sentencing is a grave injustice." **Better:** "I came to believe that mandatory sentencing is a grave injustice through the experience of . . ."
Rule #9 Name the stakeholder	Benefits and harms are rarely ends unto themselves. They are beneficial and harmful for *someone*. Tell the audience who that person is and why their interests are worthy of consideration.	**Bad:** "The prohibition of alcohol will lead to the creation of a black market." **Better:** "The prohibition of alcohol will incentivise criminals to set up an illegal market that preys on addicts and children."

Each of the speeches ran for several minutes. The staying power of their average sentence was near zero. However, some lines and turns of phrase lingered in the mind. They seemed as much a product of fancy as of effort and design. The speaker simply found the right words. In debate we called it the applause line:

PANACHE		
Rule #10 Find the applause line	There are no hard-and-fast rules, but applause lines tend to be short, expressive of a complete thought, free of redundancies, original, and idealistic.	**Bad:** "The good citizen does not make endless demands. He or she seeks to contribute in what ways he or she can." **Better:** "Ask not what your country can do for you; ask what you can do for your country."

Later in the afternoon I caught up with Jonah. I told him about the lessons I had taken from the rally: that the audience seemed to demand rhetoric that evinced proportion, personality, and panache; that each of these seemed to arise from some impulse we had as humans; that a speaker who wielded all three could persuade people in a way they could not with rational arguments alone.

Jonah listened to me, then made a face that suggested he already knew this. "Ideas don't move people on their own," he shrugged. "People move people."

Socrates said to Gorgias that rhetoric was bad because it exploited human frailties—our gullibility, unreason, and caprice. However, the opposite also seemed true: we needed rhetoric precisely because of our frailties.

When we tried to persuade another person, we battled not only ignorance and illogic but also apathy, cynicism, inattention, selfishness, and vanity. The sum of those barriers created the Butt Off the Couch threshold: the ridiculously high amount of energy required to persuade anyone to do *anything* in this world. The threshold made us right and unconvincing. It allowed our opponents to understand (or even concede) a point and still refuse to change their mind or behavior.

In response to these currents of inertia, a speaker needed to access extraordinary forces of his or her own. I wondered if the best chance we had was to meet vices with rhetoric that summoned our virtues—including empathy, compassion, pity, and moral imagination.

The third Boylston Professor, after John Quincy Adams and a minister named Joseph McKean, was a twenty-eight-year-old magazine editor named Edward Tyrrel Channing. At his inauguration in 1819, Channing pronounced the death of classical rhetoric. He argued that whereas society had once been "unsettled and irregular," it was now better organized and educated. Oratory could whip ancient crowds into a frenzy, but modern audiences were more discerning.

Consequently, the power of the individual speaker was greatly reduced. "He is not the important personage that he once was," Channing said. "[Nowadays] the orator himself is but one of the multitude, deliberating with them on common interests."

This seemed to me no great loss. So what if the materials for a modern revival of rhetoric could not be found in the ashes of antiquity? That just meant we had to make something new: a mode of speaking that did not force people's hands but grasped them.

. . .

On campus, the end of May marked the end of the academic year. As the sun arced higher and the days grew humid, my three roommates and I moved out of our freshman dorm and into sophomore housing. Jonah and I had elected to live together for another year and, along with our friend and soon-to-be roommate John, an easygoing ultimate frisbee champion from Atlanta, Georgia, we spent the last days before summer break cramming the sum of our possessions into small boxes.

Outside our half-dismantled dorm room, the groundskeepers unfurled enormous banners of crimson across the yard and set out vast phalanxes of foldable chairs. For most the year the university operated as a set of siloes. However, that changed for a brief moment in graduation season, when some 32,000 people gathered from every corner of the world. And for what? Diplomas and a bunch of speeches.

To speak at graduation was considered a great honor, and there were two such opportunities for students. The first was to be elected by one's peers to address the cohort on Class Day; the other was to be chosen by faculty to be a graduation speaker. These tracks were carefully managed by the university administration. But I had heard this one story from the 1800s about a man named Clement Morgan, who threw the process into chaos.

For much of Harvard's early history the unwritten rule for the selection of Class Day speakers held: "No Westerner, Southerner, Jew, nor Irishman, much less a Negro." Instead, the spot was held for the sons of Boston Brahmins. But the graduating class of 1890 decided to revolt. They elected as their speaker, by the margin of a single vote, Clement Morgan, an impressive student orator who had been born into slavery.

Newspapers around the country carried the story, and some sneered that "black washerwomen" would replace Boston society at graduation. But Morgan was not quite done. In May 1890, one month before graduation, the university held its annual competition to choose the six graduation speakers. Forty-four students, or around one tenth of the graduating class, auditioned before a seven-member committee. The selectors included two present and future Boylston Professors of Rhetoric and Oratory. Clement Morgan once again won a spot with a speech on the Garrison abolitionists. But this time he was joined, and indeed bested, by another African American student whom five of the selectors ranked first. His name was W. E. B. Du Bois.

The selection of two black graduation speakers was deemed a problem by some of the faculty. Over a weekend of deliberation, in which the university president, Charles Eliot, weighed in (against the inclusion of both speakers), the committee decided to replace Morgan with a white student. Law professor James Thayer resigned over this "pitiable rejection of a great opportunity," saying that "such a moving, deeply impressive statement for the cause of his race by a full-blooded Negro, the son of slaves, worthy to speak for them, will not come again."

On the morning of June 20, a Friday, graduating seniors assembled in the yard, then marched to Sanders Theatre for the Class Day exercises. The sky was clear, and a fresh breeze cut through the summer heat. But inside, the theater was somber and humid. Chandeliers, including a 1,040-pound behemoth in the middle of the room, lit rows and rows of mahogany benches.

Clement Morgan had entitled his Class Day oration after a line from Emerson, "Help them who cannot help again." He began the speech with standard graduation fare. There was talk of bittersweetness and flattering references to the alma mater. But halfway through the speech, Morgan drew this poignant analogy:

> Public speakers say that they make it a point to hit in
> their audience the man farthest off, assured that if he
> hear[s], all others must. Do you then in your relation
> with the world, in your service to humanity, make it your

> business to reach the lowest man? ... I mean him who
> has not like advantages with you, the man struggling
> against odds, who in the depths of ignorance, rudeness
> and wretchedness, it may be, is longing and striving, in
> his imperfect human way, for something higher, better,
> nobler, truer,—reach him.

With these words, Morgan reached from the particulars of his experience to a more general principle. The speaker's ultimate entreaty to graduates was for them to do everything in their power to "make it impossible for democracy to be a failure."

Five days later, in the same theater, W. E. B. Du Bois stood to deliver the graduation address. He had chosen as the subject of his speech the former Confederate president Jefferson Davis, whom he described as "the peculiar champion of a people fighting to be free in order that another people should not be free." The way in which Du Bois described Davis was not merely as a man but as an embodiment of a national contradiction:

> To say that a nation is in the way of civilization is a
> contradiction in terms, and a system of human culture
> whose principle is the rise of one race on the ruins of
> another is a farce and a lie. Yet this is the type of
> civilization which Jefferson Davis represented.

In this respect, Du Bois moved in the opposite direction from Morgan. He embodied abstract notions in the biography of this leader of the Confederate States of America. The speech was well received by the audience. One professor wrote in a Washington-based periodical, "Du Bois, the colored orator of the commencement stage, made a ten-strike. It is agreed upon by all the people I have seen that he was the star of the occasion."

• • •

Wandering the yard for the last time before summer break on a radiant Friday morning, as groundskeepers set up the great stage by Memorial Church, I found myself returning to the particular achievement of those two men in 1890. There must not have been anything terribly striking about the speakers as they walked onto the stage. Morgan stood five feet, six inches tall, with broad shoulders; Du Bois was skinny and wore a neat mustache. From the back of the theater, each speaker must have seemed miniature, no larger than an outstretched thumb. Then, as the distant figures began to speak, they must have grown before the audience's eyes.

The two speakers would go on to have trailblazing careers. Clement Morgan would train at Harvard Law School, then would work as a civil rights attorney and local politician. W. E. B. Du Bois would become the first black man to earn a doctorate from Harvard and would help form the National Association for the Advancement of Colored People.

In their graduation week, they were young men on the cusp of beginning their careers, and they had just proved a point. Morgan and Du Bois had arrived on the Harvard campus at a moment when rhetoric's star was on the decline, with writing classes taking its place on curricula around the country. They had sought to leave a mark through the eloquence of their speeches, even though oratory had been often used as a tool of vilification and exclusion. In doing so, they carried on a tradition—rhetoric—that for millennia had been criticized and mocked but had never been defeated.

Several days earlier, I had learned that Fanele and I would represent Harvard as the university's top-ranked team at the World Universities Debating Championship in December in Kuala Lumpur, Malaysia. I was daunted by the prospect and was already dreading the seven months of grueling training that lay ahead. Yet I also felt relieved to belong to a community that took words and speech so seriously that it would reward such preparation.

Across the yard, perhaps a hundred meters away, this year's graduation orators were rehearsing. The undergraduate speaker, five feet six, with thick, flowing hair, stood under the elm trees by the towering columns of Memorial Church. As she began to speak in her vital, crystalline voice about her childhood in the Middle East, I felt the distance between us close.

Her speech, a tribute to the Arab Spring, invited listeners to view themselves as people shaped by their settings but unrestricted by them. She quoted from the author Randa Jarrar to compare the experience of living in a place to "running barefoot, the skin of our feet collecting sand and rocks and cactus and seeds and grass until we had shoes, shoes made of everything we'd picked up as we ran." Then she asked graduates to walk out the gates of the university and leave a good "footprint" on the rest of the world.

The metaphor was simple, elegant. For as long as it lingered, I saw the speaker in the world, and in her the world.

5

QUIET

How to know
when to disagree

To get to the world championship, one had to pay one's way. Few activities had fewer expenses than debate—paper, pen, and newspaper subscriptions—but the cost of travel and accommodations in far-flung places mounted fast, and so our union was always strapped for cash. Throughout 2014, ahead of the World Universities Debating Championship in December, members of the union worked as coaches, adjudicators, porters, and chaperones at local high school tournaments in Boston. For me, these competitions offered a glimpse into the curious world of American high school debate.

Early on a brisk Saturday morning in October, I pressed against the heavy doors at Cambridge Rindge and Latin School and slipped in through the gap. Inside the heated main building, an immense noise flooded my ears and made me feel as though I had been plunged underwater. The first thing one noticed about American high school debate tournaments was their extraordinary scale. In the abstract, I understood the statistics: the National Speech & Debate Association served more than 150,000 students and coaches every year; a single tournament could involve thousands of competitors from across the United States. However, the experience of standing among this throbbing, verbal mass was something unique: it induced cosmic realizations about the insignificance of one's place in the world.

After judging a couple of debates in the morning, with time to spare before lunch, I decided to spectate at the round in the room nearest to the cafeteria. By the time I walked into the narrow, airless classroom and joined the audience of six or seven people, one of the speakers, a handsome kid from California, was standing at the lectern. He flashed an easy smile and, leaning forward, asked, "Everyone ready?"

Before I had a chance to nod, the speaker pressed down on his stopwatch and, instantly accelerating, began to speak at an inhuman speed—a feat he seemed to achieve by moving no part of his body, now frozen in a crouch, but the mouth.

> ThewarinSyriaisoneoftheworsthumantragediesofthepast centuryanditisincumbentonallfreenationstouseeverymeans necessarytobringittoahaltandtoholdthoseresponsiblefor theircrimesagainsthumanityresolvedthishousewould assembleacoalitionofthewillingtomilitarilyinterveneinSyria.

The boy gasped for breath. When he inhaled, he inhaled twice— *hurhhh, hurhhh*—in ravenous gulps reminiscent of drowning. As the edges of his face began to shade blue, I turned my head to the other audience members, all of them placid and silent, wondering about our culpability as bystanders.

Later that afternoon, through a fit of internet searches, I discovered that I had witnessed "spreading," a common feature of the competitive debate format known as "policy debate." The term *spreading* refers to the practice of speaking at between 350 and 500 words per minute. Such speed is not the fastest in the world—that distinction belongs to the Toronto-born Sean Shannon (655 wpm, 1995), who took the record from electronics salesman Steve Woodmore (636 wpm, 1990). However, it is twice as fast as an auctioneer in full flight and three times as fast as regular people in a regular conversation.

Few people came to such speed through natural means. Instead, aspiring spreaders committed themselves to a range of demanding exercises: shouting tongue twisters ("Peter Piper picked a peck of pickled peppers"), inserting a random word between every word in an argument ("Lying banana is banana morally banana unacceptable banana" or "My apple favorite apple pie apple is apple apple apple"), or delivering speeches with a pen in the mouth (to encourage over-enunciation). Hard-core competitors honored advice from the fastest talker in the world: "Practice holding your breath. . . . Breathing definitely slows down your average words per minute."

The spread could be dangerous. So much so that the policy team at Princeton University advised its members against spending more than thirty minutes on speaking drills: "You will hurt your voice. Don't laugh. It's possible." There was apocrypha about debaters who could never slow down, even in their regular lives; debaters who developed vocal polyps; debaters who developed cocaine addictions trying to keep pace.

Some people traced the origins of the great acceleration to the

University of Houston in the late 1960s—to an enterprising team that cracked the simple arithmetic: more arguments, more points. Others placed the genesis further back and elsewhere. Still another group of people were more philosophical on the question of origins. One debater who had been active on the policy circuit in the 1960s told the *Chronicle of Higher Education* in 2011, "When I was involved in debate, people spoke significantly slower than they do now, but debaters from the 1940s and 1950s accused many of fast talking. . . . Memory plays tricks on us here."

Policy debate allowed competitors to research topics ahead of time. This feature of the format combined with the spread to potent effect. Since the best spreaders could deliver a letter-size page's worth of material every minute, the amount of information they could present over an eight-minute speech was immense. So competitors did enough research to fill enormous fifty-pound tubs, which they wheeled around on trolleys. "We often competed against four-boxers or even the dreaded six-boxers," wrote one debater from northern Texas, himself a two-boxer, in 1986.

The spread had been a dominant feature of policy debate in the United States for decades, but there had been two serious attempts at resistance. The first began in 1979 at the national final for policy debate in Cincinnati, Ohio, when the executive secretary of the National Forensic League, Dennis Winfield, realized that the acceleration had gone too far:

> A billion seconds ago, Pearl Harbor was attacked. A billion
> minutes ago, Christ walked the earth. A billion hours ago,
> man did not exist. A billion dollars ago was yesterday
> afternoon in the federal government. After listening to the

1979 final round . . . I felt that I had listened to a billion
words being spewed forth in little over an hour.

Winfield was not alone in his conclusion. An executive at Phillips
Petroleum, then the primary sponsor of the NFL (not the football
organization), found the debate impossible to follow and relayed this
impression to the league's leadership. A reporter for the *Cincinnati
Enquirer*, assigned to cover the same debate, wrote: "One thing about
speech—you can get too busy talking to listen."

In the months after the round, Winfield and the other eight
members of the league's governing council approved the creation of
a breakaway format: the Lincoln-Douglas debate. A distinguishing
feature of the new format was that competitors had to be persuasive
to a lay judge. They had to avoid "massive use of evidence and ab-
breviated debate jargon" and be "slow, persuasive, and (when possible) entertaining."

Yet the spread proved hard to contain. L-D competitors began to
speed up their delivery to squeeze in extra material, and the practice soon became so widespread that people began to question the
point of secession from policy debate.

Some twenty years later, in 2002, an intervention came from a
most unlikely source. The billionaire founder of CNN and former
vice president of the (less profitable) Brown Debating Union, Ted
Turner, became the benefactor of a new format of debate. Public
forum debate sought to be in relation to L-D what L-D had been to
policy debate: a format for speaking that was persuasive to a lay audience.

The other attempt to thwart the spread was an inside job that began, in 2006, with the disillusionment of two California state champions. Louis Blackwell and Richard Funches, African American students at a low-income public school in Long Beach, came to believe that the esoteric features of debate marginalized already-disadvantaged people. One key target of their criticism was the spread: "Debate needs to be like an actual debate. If it's policy debate, let's argue. Let's not have a competition on who can say what the fastest."

Under a quirk of the policy format, competitors could use their speeches to raise objections, or "kritiks," against the underlying moral assumptions embedded in a discussion—such as anthropomorphism—then ask to be adjudicated on the strength of this criticism. In rounds, Blackwell and Funches began to aim their kritiks not against individual arguments or cases but against debate itself. They wore loose, casual clothes and cursed between recitations of Paulo Freire's *Pedagogy of the Oppressed*.

In the 2006 debate season, Blackwell and Funches recorded several notable wins but ultimately failed to qualify for the Tournament of Champions, the U.S. national championships, which is held every year in Kentucky. The documentary film about the pair, entitled *Resolved,* featured a line from U.S. Supreme Court justice Samuel Alito—a former debater at Princeton—that summed up a common response to the team from Long Beach: "I think debating has certain qualities that should not be changed. If you change those qualities, the benefits of debating will disappear."

Some debate observers described the acceleration of speech and the resulting overload of information as distinctly modern phenomena. The rise of personal computing in the 1980s brought endless tubs of facts and figures within easy reach. Then the rise of mobile technology and faster internet enabled the near-constant upload and download of information. In a 2012 article for *Wired* magazine, the writer Jay Caspian Kang described policy debaters as "highly efficient, thoroughly optimized information processors."

Late on that Saturday night, as I braced for another day of adjudicating debates at Cambridge Rindge and Latin School, I recalled what I had seen earlier in the afternoon. The spread was nothing more than a lark—a peculiarity in an already-peculiar activity. However, I could not shake the feeling that I had heard, in its guttural gasps and relentless, throbbing rhythm, the undertones of some dark motivation: the desire to overwhelm rather than persuade.

• • •

I belonged to a rival tradition known as parliamentary debate, or "parli." Whereas policy debaters tended to view themselves as elite performers trained in an esoteric art, parliamentary debaters identified as men and women of the people. The parli format rewarded plain speaking and even a degree of grand standing. Its insistence on short, closed-book preps placed a premium on "winging it." The resulting rounds resembled less Socratic dialogues than real arguments.

Though parliamentary debate drew inspiration from the lower house of the English Parliament, formed in 1341, the activity itself grew out of rowdy London pubs and coffeehouses. What began in the 1600s as impromptu public gatherings to discuss the day's politics, splintered and organized over generations into more formal and class-conscious debate societies. This culture of rambunctious, competitive debate, characteristic of the Enlightenment of the seventeenth and eighteenth centuries, then found a natural second home in the universities. In Britain, students formed debate clubs at St. Andrews (1794), Cambridge (1815), and Oxford (1823), adding to a tally of parliamentary debate societies that had grown, by 1882, to 105. Across the pond, a group of undergraduate students including James Madison and Aaron Burr were ahead of the trend: they founded the debate society at Princeton University in 1765.

Nowadays, university debate had global reach, and nowhere was this more evident than at the World Universities Debating Championship. Since its founding in 1980, WUDC had grown into an annual tournament that attracted some five hundred teams from sixty-odd countries and boasted (or rued) an alumni base that included the novelist Sally Rooney, U.S. senator Ted Cruz, and former McKinsey head Kevin Sneader. The best speeches at the tournament, watched by hundreds of thousands of people online, tended to create fashions and trends that filtered down to middle school circuits in Malaysia and South Africa and Lithuania.

For the rest of October and November, as Boston plunged into a bleak winter, preparation for the world championships took over my life. Aside from my roommates, Jonah and John, I saw few people on a regular basis. Fledgling love interests fled at the sight of Fanele entering my dorm room with a stack of *The Economist* magazines in hand. I also resigned from the student newspaper, *The Crimson,* my one other extracurricular commitment, and thus shelved my dream of working as a journalist. Life narrowed, fast.

Throughout the long journey to the world championships in December, Fanele proved a marvelous companion. His coursework in philosophy and economics had sharpened his mind and given him an enviable range in conversation. In a residential college environment that prized cheerfulness, Fanele insisted on biblical notions of decency and accountability. He stalked the campus, a brilliant crank, meting out judgment. Mostly, we made each other laugh.

After spending Christmas Eve in Dubai with Fanele's family, the two of us traveled onward to one of the few places in the world even more indifferent to the holiday season: Kuala Lumpur, Malaysia. The sun rose early on the morning of our arrival on December 25 and never relented. It coated us in a second skin of sweat that came through in photographs as a sheen. On the dusty cab ride to the hotel, I peeled off my hoodie and abandoned any thought of winning the competition in style.

At the Pullman Hotel, a utilitarian block within a kilometer of the Petronas Twin Towers, the follies and affectations of near-adulthood were everywhere in sight. A group of black-clad Marxists scowled through cigarette smoke by the revolving door, while the self-styled Falstaffs, barrel-bellied and barefoot, paced the lobby in search of a quarrel. From the safety of the mezzanine, future consultants in functional vests watched all this unfold with smug detachment. What sense of camaraderie and lofty purpose hung around World Schools was nowhere to be found at World Universities. Here, only the logic of competition applied.

The next morning, hours before the first round of competition, Fanele and I awoke from nervous sleeps to the buzzing sound of the alarm clock. While brushing my teeth and ironing a few shirts, I recalled how, as a high school student, I would stay up late to watch the livestream of WUDC rounds. I would record these rounds and replay them so many times that I could recite entire rounds from memory—a party trick with a biochemical effect. What I had not known then was how jet-lagged and terrified those shiny figures on the other side of the camera must have been.

On the heavily air-conditioned bus to the local university, Fanele and I tried to tamp down expectations. "First-time competitors rarely go far, let alone twenty- and twenty-one-year-old sophomores," I said to his "Let's pay our dues and set ourselves for a good run next year." However, as I set foot on solid ground, I realized the sense of motion that I had been experiencing had not come from the bus' movements. It had been my insistent heartbeat.

To our surprise, we kept winning rounds. Fanele and I sailed through the nine preliminary rounds, persuading judges to disable internet access in Syria and incentivise urbanization in developing countries. Then we passed through the octo-, quarter-, and semifinals—rounds about the ethics of racial "passing," the decline of secular pan-Arab nationalism, and the formation of special economic zones for women. Throughout these seven days, Fanele and I barely reflected on our progress, afraid that any element of self-consciousness would break the spell.

What we could not ignore was the deterioration of our health. Whether due to stress, poor diet, improper ventilation, or lack of exercise, one always got sick at a debate tournament. The only question was when. For Fanele and me, each 7:00 a.m. start at the Pullman Hotel had felt more painful than the last. The scratches in our throats had taken longer and longer in the day to subside. As I crawled out of bed on Saturday, January 3, the congested, humid day of the grand final, I noticed streaks of sweat on my sheets. Five feet away, in his bed, Fanele groaned and rolled around to no particular effect.

At 5:00 p.m., we arrived in suits and ties to the backstage area of the hotel's banquet hall. The narrow space had all the furnishings of purgatory. In the drafty corridor that connected four identical, gray rooms, I straightened my back and eyed the other teams with apprehension.

The format at World Universities, known as British parliamentary debate, began the same way as its American counterpart: a two-member affirmative team faced off against a two-member negative team—also known as the government and opposition, respectively. Then the BP format added another two-member team to each side, creating four teams: opening government, opening opposition, closing government, closing opposition. The idea was that each team competed against the other three: one had to not only beat the other side but also provide better arguments for one's position than the other team arguing the same position. Prep was fifteen minutes and the speaking times were seven minutes per person.

For tonight's debate, we had drawn closing opposition. This put us, on the negative bench, behind two older UK debaters who had enrolled at BPP, a for-profit university in London, to gain eligibility for the competition. On the other side, the Oxford team, a shiny Rhodes scholar from Australia and a brilliant, acerbic undergraduate, would open and a team from the University of Sydney, former contemporaries of mine on the schools circuit, would close for the government.

We and the other three teams remained in our own segments of the corridor, averting our gazes from one another. For almost ten minutes, I could hear only the sound of shoes scraping against the linoleum floor. Then one of the judges, a stiff man with a Napoleonic air, came to read the topic. He made no time for niceties and instead repeated the motion twice:

> That humanitarian organizations should, and should be allowed to, give funding, resources, or services to illegal armed groups when this is made a condition for access to vulnerable civilians.

In the greenroom nearest to the stage door, Fanele and I descended into panic. Neither of us understood the context for the debate, and the few points that came to mind—on the morality of funding illegal armed groups and the risks of legitimizing these organizations—were so obvious that opening opposition seemed certain to swoop on them. After ten minutes of arguing and staring at our blank notepads, we settled on a direction: paying ransom to armed groups would deplete public support for charity organizations. The argument was narrow enough, we figured, that the other teams might miss it altogether.

From my seat on the stage, the audience of a thousand people seemed to form one backdrop. The dark, oceanic mass rippled in parts and sparkled in others but, for the most part, remained a mystery. What I could not glean from sight I understood through sound. The currents of sighs and murmurs passing through the crowd revealed various tones of anticipation. During the first two speeches, I found myself straining to hear my opponents, so distracted was I by the sound of the audience, which held my attention like a siren's call.

For me, the first sign of trouble came in the second affirmative speech. The Oxford speaker, one of the smartest debaters on the circuit, half swung her right arm overhead, as if cracking a whip, then, bypassing any greeting or introduction, launched into her arguments. In thirty seconds, she outlined her four arguments—which ranged from a redescription of armed groups to the reasons why poverty prolonged conflict—then proceeded to elaborate on them at breakneck speed. Flowing her speech, I felt the tendons in my writing hand fray and snap.

Then, as I raced to think of rebuttal, the second BPP speaker, an elegant baritone in a tuxedo, walked to the podium and leaned over its farthest edge. He announced that his argument was that supporters of these NGOs would be "far less likely to give this money" if the resolution passed—or, in two words, our case. At these words, my heart seemed to skip a full beat.

In a debate round, Fanele tended to resemble a nuclear reactor. The clash between opposing arguments and his own ideas resulted in such a profusion of thoughts that he could scarcely give words to each one. Tonight he was silent. Under the glare of the stage lights, I saw in his expression a terror that might as well have been my own.

"Do you have anything?"

"No. Do you?"

"No."

For the rest of this speech and the next, we just sat there, sick and waiting for our turn to come.

On the short walk to the lectern, as the room trained its gaze on my gait and posture, I started to dissociate, so that by the time I began to speak, I was already watching myself from a distance. The voice sounded higher and reedier, and the gestures set to its intonation felt foreign to me. Then, around ninety seconds into the speech, I began to accelerate:

> Yes, these armed groups are going to have to find other funding sources, but that's good. First, the transition is time-consuming, allowing the state to intervene. Second, many organizations simply don't have the resources to do things like take over diamond mines. Third . . .

I found a perverse comfort in moving so fast. Behind the cloak of speed and volume, I felt invulnerable. The audience would surely struggle to understand my arguments, but at least they would not suppose that I was lost or incompetent or scared. So I craned my neck forward and took gulping breaths to sustain my speech. In this defensive posture, I discovered the pleasures of spreading.

I finished the speech, and my senses came back one at a time. The stage lights were still glaring; drops of sweat quivered on my brow, then came down my cheeks like tears. I sent a pulse down to the legs and reached for the papers on the lectern in front of me. The audience would, in a moment, burst into loud applause. Yet in this brief silence, I heard everything I needed to know: we had lost.

. . .

On the morning after the grand final, Fanele and I slipped out of the hotel and boarded a flight to the Philippines. We spent the next week at our friend Akshar's house, eating our body weight in chicken— fried and soy-basted on alternating days—and staying in bed too long. After ten days of high-decibel arguments, the more subtle noises (and silences) of everyday conversation, including the sumptuous *mmm* of vague agreement, sounded like music.

The truth was that I was exhausted, not from the championships in Kuala Lumpur but from a decade of obsessive commitment. Every piece of clothing that I owned was somewhere stained with ink or contained in its pockets a loose index card or sticky note. My voice always took a few days to recover from a tournament but had begun taking longer to regain its fullness. "Why do you do this?" Akshar asked one night. I opened my mouth, but nothing came out.

When we returned to campus on the last Sunday of January 2015, a quiet evening of steady snow, I told Fanele that I needed a break. There were too many friendships neglected, parties missed; the one potted plant that my long-suffering roommates, John and Jonah, had placed in my charge was dead; we were approaching the pointy end of our studies; besides, I wasn't sure whether I could make the commitment that our partnership deserved. Our stilted conversation followed the script of a breakup. Fanele said he understood. His glum expression prompted me to add that of course he was free to debate with other people.

But if I was winding down my debate career, the rest of the campus was just getting started. The year had begun with the murder of twelve people in the Paris offices of the satirical weekly *Charlie Hebdo*, which had published cartoons of the prophet Muhammad. In the months that followed, a "migrant crisis" erupted in Europe; the U.S. witnessed the killing of more African Americans by police and went to the polls for the midterms.

Harvard was not the most political place. Whatever counterculture had once existed on campus had been gone for decades by this time. The worst-abused drug on campus was probably Ritalin. Some of the most sought-after extracurricular groups on campus were the consulting and banking groups, which involved cosplaying various forms of white-collar work. Most people said they were simply too busy for politics.

This had the perverse effect of making whatever political controversy erupted on campus seem more polarized than it was in fact. The only people we ever heard from were those with the strongest views. That would have been fine if those arguments had remained a sideshow. However, as the disputes took over email lists and social media, then filtered into dining hall conversations, people felt the need to engage, often at the fierier register of controversy.

For the most part I ignored the commotion. Throughout February and March, as the weather thawed and the residents of Cambridge shook off their seasonal gloom, I grew close to a group of eight or so friends that included Fanele, Akshar, John, and Jonah. Together we suffered through homework—sometimes alternating sleep through all-nighters—and went to parties in three-bedroom dorm suites. The best times were those when we sat at the largest table we could find, in the dining hall or on the lawn, and talked until day became night or night became day.

Among the eight of us, we mostly exchanged jokes and talked about our personal lives. When other friends or neighbors joined, the discussion became more serious. People raised news items—the Obamacare case before the Supreme Court, preparations for the Paris Climate Accords—and pronounced opinions. In these conversations, people expected Fanele and me to intervene. "Wait, isn't your whole thing arguing?" they asked.

Fanele gave one answer to the question: "Hell, yes." The man seemed incapable of pulling away from a disagreement—not when there were points to be corrected and arguments to be made. For the most part this was to everyone's benefit, but every now and then, Fanele kicked himself for getting caught in some unending quarrel.

I went in the opposite direction. One lesson I had learned from debate was that arguments were easy to start and hard to end. Even in an artificial game with a beginning, middle, and end, the emotional logic of competition could easily take over. This often led speakers to make mistakes and saddled us with tensions and resentments that long outlasted the round. Given this danger, one had to be judicious about the decision to enter into a disagreement.

Around this time, I developed a mental checklist to decide whether to engage in a given argument. The list comprised four conditions that I thought gave an argument the highest likelihood of going well: that was if the disagreement was **real**, **important**, and **specific**, and the goals of the two sides were **aligned** (RISA).

Real: To begin, we should identify whether there is an actual difference of opinion. Some disputes unfold in the absence of a genuine disagreement. They are quarrels in search of a topic. Someone misinterprets the actions of another person or objects to something that turns out to be a difference in language or emphasis. The trickiest situations are ones in which there is conflict but no disagreement. A claim like "I don't like your cousins" may be objectionable, but it's an inappropriate subject for debate because there is no other side.

Important: Next we should decide whether a difference of opinion is important enough to justify a disagreement. We may not see eye to eye with another person on any number of things. The vast majority of these differences are unthreatening and even desirable. However, a small fraction of these differences occasions a disagreement because we judge them important enough to justify the debate. I do not want to be prescriptive about how people should make that judgment, but I do want to encourage the reflection. For me, the arguments that feel most important either touch on my basic values or involve an opponent whom I love and respect. Without considering the importance of an argument, we jump into disagreements out of instinct—pride or defensiveness—and at the provocation of someone with a lower threshold for conflict.

Specific: Third, we should ensure that the subject of our disagreement is specific enough to allow the two sides to make some progress toward resolving the dispute within the allotted time. This is another reason why an infinitely vast subject like "the economy" or "family matters" is inappropriate for debate. Disagreements tend to expand rather than contract. Think about the epic, earth-shattering arguments in Noah Baumbach's *Marriage Story* or Richard Yates's *Revolutionary Road*. These disagreements escalate until they become all-encompassing, and when an argument is about everything, nothing—not the speakers' motivations or backgrounds—is out of bounds. A clearly defined topic pushes back against expansionary pressures.

Aligned: Lastly, we should check whether our reasons for engaging in the disagreement are aligned with those of our opponents. People argue for different reasons: to get information; to understand a different perspective; to change someone else's mind; to pass the time; or even to hurt the other person's feelings. We need not have the same reasons as our opponents for engaging in a disagreement, but their motivations should be acceptable to us, and vice versa. For example, if we are in a dispute to change the other person's mind, but they want simply to learn something from the exchange, that would probably be acceptable to us. But if the other person wants only to prolong the dispute to express their anger toward us, or to hurt our feelings, we should walk away.

Real	There is an actual difference of opinion between the two sides.
Important	The difference of opinion is important enough to justify a disagreement.
Specific	The subject of the disagreement is specific enough to allow the two sides to make some progress toward resolving or ameliorating within the allotted time.
Aligned	The two sides are aligned in their reasons for engaging in the disagreement.

However, even as I applied the RISA framework with great zest and commitment, I still found myself wandering into bad disagreements.

In contrast to the fall semester, a remorseless slide into winter, the spring semester gave us reasons to hope. Around the end of March, one felt the first sign of warmth in the air; by April, the trees and flowers were full of vital color. What's more, the spring semester led into the glorious summer, a three-month holiday and the only extended contact we had, as college students, with the real world. However, one obstacle stood between us and vacation, obscuring the sun in the manner of an eclipse: exams.

Exam season at Harvard stretched over two weeks and tended to bring the worst out in the students. The word *exam* became a trump card that excused any failure of social grace or personal obligation. Since one's grades, in fact, had a material effect on summer and postgraduate work opportunities, incentives skewed in favor of selfishness. Students ignored their friends for weeks, and members of study groups turned on one another. "Only their parents can help them," Fanele said, shaking his head at the desolate social landscape. "Or God."

On a sparkling Tuesday afternoon in early May, less than twenty-four hours before an economics exam, I arrived late to the dining hall where I had scheduled lunch with Jonah. In the sun, my roommate appeared to be steaming. He had told me in the morning that lunch had to be tight because he had a shift at the bike repair shop on campus, and I, consumed by exam prep, had forgotten. As I pulled out a chair, Jonah began to unload. "This is becoming a pattern: I don't think you care about my time," he seethed. "The last five times we scheduled something, you were late. And today I reminded you in the morning because the shop was going to be short-staffed. This is going to be really bad for me at work. When was the last time I did something like this?"

Jonah's claim that I did not care about his time landed hard. Yet I managed to take a deep breath and consult the RISA checklist. The argument was real (I did care!), important (this was a question of character), specific (we were arguing about a particular instance of carelessness), and aligned (neither of us questioned the other's motives). So I began to respond: "Of course I care about your time. You're one of my best friends."

However, as I continued, some of Jonah's other claims began to resurface in my mind and I strained to respond: "What pattern? Last Friday you kept me waiting at the Science Center for close to half an hour." I scanned his face for a reaction before continuing, "Besides, your boss at the bike shop is a hippie who seems incapable of hurting a fly. I think you're taking that part-time job a bit too seriously. And look, I know I was late, but these things don't have to devolve into a character assessment, do they?"

Each of these sentences added a frown line to Jonah's forehead and deepened the red of his face. By the time he collected his tray and walked out to make the remainder of his shift at the bike shop, my roommate was the color of a beet. "We'll talk about this at home," he huffed.

Alone in the dining hall with a soggy salad, I tried to understand what had just happened. Our disagreement started out on solid ground but then grew and grew until it became quite unmanageable. On some level, I knew that refuting the other side's every claim was a fool's errand: it sapped time from developing one's own case and marked one out as an unreasonable naysayer. However, Jonah's irresistible wrongness had proved a fatal distraction.

This seemed to me a limitation of the RISA checklist: even the most promising arguments could degenerate over time into a useless quagmire. Jonah had begun the conversation with a wide set of complaints, and I had added my own grievances. The resulting discussion was unwieldy and full of sharp edges.

I wondered if preventing such an expansion required us not only to ask whether the overall argument was worthwhile but also to choose which claims *within* a dispute to contest. There seemed to be two good reasons for making such a choice:

> **Necessity:** Do we need to contest the claim in order to resolve the overall dispute?

> **Progress:** Does contesting the claim, necessary or no, get us closer to resolving the overall dispute?

If the answer was "yes" to either of these, one had a good reason to respond.

In Jonah's original complaint, only two claims seemed to meet these tests. One was the observation that I had been late to our last five meetings, which, as the main piece of evidence for my carelessness, *needed* a response. The other was the point that I had been especially inconsiderate this afternoon, which might be unnecessary to the overall dispute but could help us make progress given its immediate role in instigating the dispute.

The rest of his complaint I could afford to let go. They were issues on which we could disagree and *still* make progress on the overarching dispute. To prevent our disagreements from becoming all-out wars, we had to make room for acceptable differences of opinion.

Later in the afternoon, on my way back to the dorm, I stopped by the twenty-four-hour pharmacy on Massachusetts Avenue and picked out a few snacks as a peace offering. I spent the walk rehearsing what I might say to Jonah. Then, as I neared our suite on the second floor, I thought of the wisdom needed to disagree well—to decide when to fight and when to let go—and wondered where I might learn such a quality of judgment. What I did not know then was that the year would bring new and unexpected challenges against my resolve to stay out of bad arguments.

. . .

On the morning of June 16, a few blocks away from the office where I was working for the summer, businessman Donald Trump descended the gold steps of Trump Tower and announced his candidacy for president. His speech veered from hyperbole ("I will be the greatest jobs president that God ever created") to absurdity ("Nobody builds walls better than me, believe me. And I'll build them very inexpensively"). It also contained traces of malice ("They're bringing drugs, they're bringing crime, they're rapists, and some, I assume, are good people").

That night, over drinks on an apartment rooftop, friends from New York assured me that this would pass. "He's been talking about this for years. No one takes him seriously." The other expats and I made platitudes about the strangeness of American politics. Then we let the evening pass as one more in a long summer.

However, when I returned to campus in September for the start of my junior year, I found that people had Trump on their minds. The most vocal opposition came from women and immigrants and marginalized people, many of whom felt targeted by the candidate. In our cramped, second-floor dorm room, Jonah, whose research focused on social ties in local communities, supplied a running commentary on causes for concern: political disenchantment and economic despair in communities devastated by the collapse of manufacturing, the unchecked spread of misinformation on the web, and the streaks of xenophobia and bigotry that ran beneath respectable surfaces.

I understood these concerns but took none of them to heart. The depth of my analysis reached the observation that he was the host of the *Celebrity Apprentice*. However, I could see the dangers posed by a malign actor, protected by freedom of speech, spewing a great effluence of hate into the atmosphere. In the debates about the appropriate response to such a person—whether to limit their speech or accept it as a necessary cost of democratic freedom—I saw resonances of a controversy close to campus.

For much of the past year, universities in the U.S. and UK had been embroiled in disputes over the invitation of divisive personalities to receive awards or deliver public lectures. In April, less than ten miles away from my dorm, Brandeis University in Waltham, Massachusetts, withdrew the promise of an honorary degree to Ayaan Hirsi Ali, an outspoken critic of Islam, on account of her past statements about the religion. "What was initially intended as an honor has now devolved into a moment of shaming. . . . They simply wanted me to be silenced," Ali wrote in a widely shared statement in *Time* magazine.

Historically, the political Right had been effective at denying people with troublesome views a platform from which to spread their message. For example, conservative university administrations had banned revolutionaries such as Malcolm X from entering campus. Nowadays, right-wing politicians and media personalities wielded progressive demands for campuses to remain "safe spaces" as a weapon of the culture wars. They said such a vision poisoned liberty, higher education, and even Western civilization—an impressive escalation that gave everyone a stake in the decisions of minor student groups.

In many respects, the knotty debate about deplatforming was an echo from the past. In 1968, the British Conservative politician Enoch Powell delivered an incendiary speech arguing against mass immigration into the UK: "As I look ahead, I am filled with foreboding. Like the Roman, I seem to see 'the River Tiber foaming with much blood.'" The "rivers of blood" speech helped unleash a poisonous element in British politics. At the 1969 local elections, the National Front, a far-right political party with fascist origins, fielded forty-five candidates and averaged a vote share of 8 percent. Powell's prediction about his own speech had come true: "I'm going to make a speech at the weekend and it's going to go up 'fizz' like a rocket; but whereas all rockets fall to the earth, this one is going to stay up."

As the historian Evan Smith recounts in his book *No Platform,* leftist groups who sought to quell the rise of the far-right tended to use a common tactic: deny their leaders a chance to speak in public. The front page of *Red Mole,* the newspaper of the International Marxist Group, in September 1972 demanded NO PLATFORM FOR RACISTS and called on members to forcibly prevent the National Front and other such organizations from gathering or spreading their message to the public. The International Socialists added a crucial prohibition: a ban on engaging fascists in public debates. "Every liberal who debates with them gives them aid—much against their will."

The success of guerrilla actions to disrupt speaker events was necessarily ad-hoc but, in April 1974, student representatives of these leftists groups secured a more lasting achievement. At the National Union of Students (NUS) Conference, the activists helped swing a vote—by a margin of 204,619 to 182,760 votes—for the confederation of college and university student unions to adopt a "no platform" policy. The resolution urged members to prevent openly racist or fascist groups "or individuals known to espouse similar views from speaking in colleges by whatever means necessary (including disrupting of the meeting)." In response, *The Guardian* published a stinging critique: "Students should perhaps remember that frustration which leads to a denial of the right of one section of society is not something new. It is a classic pattern of fascism."

The NUS policy and public opinion toward the concept of "no platform" continued to evolve over the next forty years. For example, in the 1980s, Margaret Thatcher's government took a hammer to the policy by mandating that universities ensure "the use of any premises of the establishment is not denied" on the grounds of a person's beliefs or policy objectives. (Nowadays, the NUS maintains a more narrow version of the policy that applies to six "fascist and racist organizations.")

Many of the characteristic arguments of the UK's "no platform" debate recurred in conversations on American campuses about deplatforming. In January 2015, the University of Chicago issued a statement on freedom of expression that concluded, "Debate or deliberation may not be suppressed because the ideas put forth are thought by some or even by most . . . to be offensive, unwise, immoral, or wrong-headed." By September, the U.S. president, Barack Obama, had made his own contribution: "Anybody who comes to speak to you and you disagree with, you should have an argument with them. But you shouldn't silence them by saying you can't come because I'm too sensitive to hear what you have to say."

Nothing could persuade me to enter into a heated debate about deplatforming. In discussions about the subject, I gravely nodded my head and acknowledged the complexity of the issue. I deflected with a joke or an association. Then, on a tranquil evening in the last week of September, the controversy sought me out and demanded a response.

Every fall semester, our debate union hosted a competition for other university teams in exchange for a significant chunk of our operating budget. Though I had distanced myself from the day-to-day operations of the team, the union board had asked me to help with one of the most contentious tasks in tournament organization: choosing the topics. So around dinnertime, I pushed open the door to Quincy House and began climbing up the stairs to the dining hall. I realized halfway up that I had been holding my breath.

In the intimate back dining room of Quincy, the meeting place of the union board, we, the ten most senior debaters on the team, gathered around a narrow oval table. Our elbows bumped against one another as we tried to make progress on the chicken and salad. The first argument broke out within fifteen minutes. "If we don't push the boundaries with our topics, how will the activity advance?" charged Tim, an earnest slam poet from Hawaii. "Yes, but maybe a debate set on Mars is a bit much for a Saturday morning," responded Julia, a premed who volunteered in ambulances. Then the rest of the room, emboldened by this early clash, leaned forward into the posture of confrontation.

Our worst arguments centered on topics that were, for one reason or another, contentious:

> That Europe should legalize Holocaust denial
>
> That the government should not pay for gender-reassignment surgery
>
> That there is no God

This seemed to me a tricky case for the RISA checklist. Many of our most controversial arguments were real, important, specific, and aligned on intentions, but was that a good enough reason to engage in them? Or were some arguments simply better avoided?

In the mid-1600s, the English philosopher Thomas Hobbes provided one clear answer. He believed that debates were bound to result in terrible conflicts because the "mere act of disagreement is offensive . . . tantamount to calling [someone] a fool." The point went double for controversial issues such as religion. On such matters people had an obligation to refrain from open debate and, instead, maintain what the scholar Teresa Bejan has termed "civil silence."

Though I was not sold on civil silence, I believed the adversarial format of debate was inappropriate for some sensitive topics. The worst bullies on the debate circuit were self-identified contrarians who mistook the right to free speech for a license for cruel speech. Their notion that we ought to be completely unsentimental in our pursuit of truth—that anything else would be "coddling"—seemed certain to drive most people away from the marketplace of ideas.

While such thoughts swirled around my mind in the topic meeting,

I managed to blurt out a question that conveyed none of the nuances: "Can we, er, not make unnecessary trouble?" The room went still. Near me, the libertarians readied to pounce, but the first voice to speak up came from the far end of the table.

Dale was a long-serving team member who specialized in "equity" issues—a catchall term for measures, ranging from pronoun introductions to harassment policies, used to promote safety and inclusion in the debate community. Though retiring and soft-spoken, Dale carried herself with a moral seriousness. Her answer to my question took the shape of a story.

Growing up in conservative town, Dale had found in debate a space in which to explore ideas—about gender, politics, morality—that were otherwise considered taboo. "I've seen some terrible rounds," she said. "But at least in debate, arguments ruled the day, and people had to stick to the topic instead of veering off into personal insults. If we can't talk about this stuff in debate, then where can we talk about it?"

What Dale was describing seemed to me a different kind of safe space—not one that was safe from disagreement but one that provided the safety to disagree. "Rather than avoiding sensitive subjects, we should discuss how we can have good debates about them," she said. "Some people count on us doing that."

So we got to work on figuring out how to host good public debates on controversial issues.

First, we set a strict rule: a debate must not question the equal moral standing of persons. This was a matter not of nicety but of self-preservation. Debate was built on the idea that people had a right to be heard and have their contributions be given due and equal consideration. If you took out that premise, the exchange became a charade. So we could not tolerate a debate on whether "northern Europeans are immoral" or "Muslims are a threat to society" because it would contradict the activity's basic ethos.

Next, our group considered the symbolism of hosting a public debate. The decision to host or engage in public debate had political as well as personal consequences. Whether on cable television, in a town hall, or on a university campus, a formal debate carried certain connotations, namely that a subject was worthy of our attention and that there were two reasonable sides to the issue. The legitimacy conferred by the debate platform seemed to say the disagreement was real, important, specific, and aligned! This made me think that my RISA checklist was less a handy invention than an articulation of the expectations we already had for good disagreements. To confer credibility on a topic that fell short of these standards was to reduce confidence in the activity of debate itself.

Last, we reminded ourselves that the burden of arguing a case was borne by people. The experience of voicing one's ideas and having them challenged could be disruptive for anyone, but the weight of that disruption landed more heavily on those for whom the debate was raw, personal. As debaters, we had to be attentive to these people—not because they were "snowflakes," a term of derision meaning an overly sensitive person, but because they were human, prone to hurt and exhaustion. We had to think less about the freedom to disagree than about the responsibility to disagree well.

These checklists—RISA for personal disagreements and political considerations for public disagreements—seemed a drag. In the heat of argument, at precisely the moments that demanded urgent responses, they asked us to slow down and consider the situation.

One of my most formative mentors at the university, the literary scholar Elaine Scarry, thought that situations requiring consent benefited from "clogging"—impediments and checkpoints that slowed things down and forced people to repeatedly affirm their agreement. For example, marriage ceremonies afforded ample opportunities for either side to tap out (including the long walk down the aisle), and nonessential medical procedures often carried cooling-off periods of several weeks or months.

Professor Scarry argued that clogging was especially important in conflict situations. If one of the purposes of collective life was to guard against injury and maintain peace, a state and its citizens could make few more serious decisions than the one to deliberately injure a person. Such need for caution accounted for the many layers of appeal that stood between a guilty verdict and the infliction of punishment. Historical procedures regulating one-on-one duels, such as the *codes duello* from the European Renaissance, prescribed elaborate choreographies full of "breaks" and other opportunities for participants to withdraw. For Professor Scarry, the need for consent in conflict weighed most urgently against nuclear weapons, which in their vast destructive power foreclosed the possibility of rational deliberation.

I saw the implications of Professor Scarry's theory on a much smaller scale. On the average day, the most serious altercation we were likely to encounter was a verbal argument. Such disputes drained and hurt us. However, our arguments lacked breaks—chances to ask whether we consented to participating in the dispute. Instead, synapses fired and cruel words followed. The question of whether the disagreement was worthwhile occurred only in retrospect.

For me, the two checklists—RISA and the topic-setting considerations—provided necessary clogging for our disagreements. The aim was not to foreclose every argument but, rather, to exclude bad arguments *so that* we could focus on the most worthwhile disagreements. In a world with too many opportunities to disagree, we had to choose our battles. Besides, as I would soon learn, some time away from relentless debate could do a world of good.

. . .

In the weeks after the topic meeting, as an autumn chill descended on campus, I found myself thinking about debate again. It began innocently enough with web searches for the latest league results and videos of the rounds, then progressed to long conversations with Fanele about the debates in our past. By Columbus Day weekend, the second week of October, I was subvocalizing ideas and rhetorical punch lines on my way to class and back.

Nine months away from debate had been kind to me. I had grown out my hair and had started to regularly exercise. In the knowledge that I could be counted on to stay and not leave every weekend for debate, friends began to share more of their lives with me. Even romantic interests took longer to depart. For the first time since I had begun debating ten years earlier, in 2005, I won nothing, and that was just fine.

However, my time away made me miss some aspects of debate. One criticism of the activity that I had uncritically accepted was that debate was glib: How could one reduce issues as complex as commercial surrogacy or tax policy to a two-hour exchange of words? For me, time in the world outside debate dispelled such notions. In everyday life, I tended to react instantly—to offensive ideas, inflammatory op-eds—in conversations that swerved across multiple overlapping topics. By contrast, debate forced me to prepare, listen to opposing perspectives, and stick to the subject at hand. Sure, the activity was less meticulous than academic research, but it was also less sad-making.

On the dusty bookshelf in my dorm room, I kept the debate trophies at the very top, out of regular view. These cheap trophies had a
common shape: on the stand or cup stood one or two figurines, each
behind a lectern, delivering an argument. In the past, I had seen in
these trophies only the color—faux gold or faux silver—and the number indicating rank. Now I saw the people, straining to be heard.

Some days later, I went to Fanele's room and asked him to debate
with me at the world championships in December. I had dreaded
making the proposal but had taken some solace in the fact that he had
mustered the courage to do the same two years earlier on one of our
first days on campus. All Fanele said, before pulling me in for a hug,
was that he knew I would come back. So we began to prepare with
less than two months until the start of the competition. We spent
long nights researching topical issues and analyzing videos of past
debates. I lost entire class lectures to daydreams about various arguments and turns of phrase, but in this exchange of losses and gains, I
was a willing participant.

At the end of December, after spending Christmas with Fanele's
extended family in Atlanta, the two of us boarded a flight to Thessaloníki, Greece. As the plane descended for the last time, Fanele
told me he didn't think he could handle another tournament after
this one. "I'm tired, man," he said. "So this is going to be the end, one
way or another."

For those who sought out omens, the promise of victory was all
around. The namesake of the city, the second largest in Greece and,
once, the entire Byzantine Empire, was the half sister of Alexander the
Great. She was named after the victory (nike) in Thessaly, the triumph
of the Macedonians in the bloodiest battle recorded in ancient Greece.
But there were warning signs, too. The city's patron saint, a heroic

soldier named Demetrius, had been impaled by a spear. In the icons of the saint as a young man, he glittered but wore a sad expression.

Fanele and I cruised through the first twelve rounds of the competition. The force of reputation and experience gave us an easy momentum, but we knew those two things alone could never get us across the line. Before a large enough crowd and a fair enough judge, an argument afforded both sides no place to hide. In debate one had to prove oneself, again and again.

By the eighth day of competition, most teams had gone the way of the soldier. There were now four teams remaining: an affable pair from Sydney University whom I had known at school; a team of older Oxbridge debaters who had enrolled at a Serbian institution, Visoka škola PEP, to compete at the tournament; a formidable side from the University of Toronto who had been our rivals on the North American circuit; and us. As we boarded the bus to the grand final venue, we exchanged monosyllabic greetings. The rain drizzled overhead and muffled every sound.

Traffic was light, and the destination was close. The adrenaline had not yet kicked in, so I was afraid to close my eyes. Outside, ancient Byzantine structures whizzed past, somewhere between fast-food shops and mobile-phone retailers. I kept shaking my legs to ward off the fatigue. "Two more blocks," shouted one of the organizers, a philosophy student at Aristotle University.

The bus came to a stop outside the Thessaloniki Concert Hall. The banners that lined the entrance were emblazoned with the official motto of this year's championships: DEBATE COMES HOME. As we entered the air-conditioned building, we were met by an enthusiastic guide who reminded us there would be no eating or drinking. The thought of either one made my stomach churn.

In the backstage area of the main hall, a cavernous space with black walls, floor, and ceiling, the four teams drew their positions from an unmarked box. The slip of paper in my hand read "opening government." The topic came soon after that: "This house believes that the world's poor would be justified in pursuing complete Marxist revolution."

As Fanele and I raced to our prep room, I heard one of our competitors say, "What does this even mean?" There was a danger that this round would degenerate into a fight over definitions, so the first decision we made in prep was to keep our stance simple: a Marxist revolution seeks to abolish private property. Next we asked what it would mean for such a thing to be justified. We decided to make this a round about the principles. Our case would briefly explain why we thought the revolution would work but would submit that private property was such an affront to human dignity that we would be justified in seeking to overthrow it regardless of the practical outcomes.

This was a risky strategy: if we could not persuade the audience to view the debate this same way, we would be blown clean out of the water. Since we were focusing on a few arguments rather than spreading through a great number of them, the closing team on our bench would have room to maneuver. However, I recalled at this moment a piece of advice that my Australian team coach, Bruce, had shared ahead of the World Schools grand final three years earlier:

> Every debate contains a hundred disagreements. You'll
> have to choose which of these to contest, and which to
> ignore. That's especially true of the grand final. Winners
> never sweat the small stuff. They know to find the real
> debate within the debate.

When I related the advice to Fanele, he broke out into laughter. "So this will be our debate within the debate," he boomed. "What do we have to lose?"

The lights in the concert hall dimmed at 6:30 p.m. The crowd, 1,400 strong, had been chattering in anticipation, but as we walked onto the stage, their nervous energy took a more silent, concentrated form. Two felt-tip pens, black and blue, lay uncapped on the table; flow pads were at the ready. I walked to the lectern and began:

> Madame Chair, the global poor, all around the world
> and no matter the country in which they live, currently
> live in a system of dictatorship. They live under a
> dictatorship known as no alternatives.

An audience this size was like an Arctic ice sheet: it seemed immovable, at first, but then something cracked, and its immense weight began to shift. The problem? That moment might never come in one's speech. I took a breath and pressed on:

> Shackled by capital that's been unjustly acquired,
> constrained by landed gentry who have no incentive
> but to pursue their own interests, and chained by the
> demands of mere subsistence, the global poor cannot
> reach for the right to liberty and self-determination that,
> we believe, inheres in the human condition.

Murmurs moved through the crowd. I knew the material—a full-blown Marxist screed—was radical, and the rhetoric zealous. The words passed through my throat charged with strange electricity.

Yet I felt confident in the strategy: if we were going to persuade the audience to view this as a grand, civilizational debate, we were going to have to set an example.

> Use your imagination. People once lived in sharing
> economies where they defined themselves as something
> more than their labor and their productive capacity.
> That's the kind of world that we support.

I spent most of my eight minutes on a single point: that private property was inimical to dignity. The argument located the origins of wealth in slavery and colonialism, outlined the policy failures that led to its entrenchment, then explained the flaws inherent in competition and ownership.

Midspeech, a speaker rarely experiences the physical strain of thinking so damn hard. The adrenaline induced a mental fogginess that numbed the hard edges of experience. That did not mean, of course, that the stresses were not present and active. As I crescendoed to a conclusion, straining to be heard above a now-boisterous crowd, I felt my legs shake and my voice fray:

> What we need from an opposition is a comprehensive
> account of property, why it's just, and why it doesn't, as
> it has done throughout history, assault human dignity.
> We're very proud to propose.

The next speech, delivered by a meticulous, methodical speaker from Sydney, passed me by in a haze. He warned that the revolution would result in terrible bloodshed; the movement would be crushed, and the nascent utopia would collapse. "Results matter," he pronounced. The speech sounded reasonable, perhaps even persuasive, but I felt detached from its effects. So fully did I dissociate from the round that I barely noticed Fanele leave my side and take to the lectern.

What snapped me out of the daze was a moment in Fanele's rebuttal. He had been trying for a few minutes to bring the debate back into the realm of principles, when he paused and slowed down his speech. The sweat on his hairline was glistening in the stage lights. I caught his eye and knew that he had something.

His argument centered on the example of the Warsaw ghetto uprising. Fanele explained that many people in the Jewish resistance against Nazi forces knew they would face certain death, but that these individuals chose to fight nonetheless. Raising a finger in emphasis, he pronounced each of the next several words carefully:

> Self-defense even when you're guaranteed to fail is
> justified . . . because the resistance of evil is a good in
> and of itself.

When Fanele sat down to rapturous applause, I put my hand on his shoulder. More than half of the debate remained ahead of us. The win was nowhere near guaranteed, but we had found the debate that we wanted to have.

Four hours later, Fanele and I sat in the adjoining dining hall, stewing in anticipation of a decision. The closing ceremonies were playing out on the stage at the front of the room. University and local government officials gave lengthy speeches and exchanged ceremonial keys. Someone sang.

I alternated between being unable to stand the sight of food and stress-eating a plate of dolmas. At some point, the four finalist teams were called to the front of the room in preparation for the announcement. There were nods and a few hugs. Everyone knew that the debate had been close. That the adjudication had taken around three hours meant that anyone could have taken it.

The voice of deliverance, when it came, had a distinctive lilt: "Opening government." We had won.

6

SELF-DEFENSE

How to defeat a bully

The wedding took place on Mount Pelion, near the cave of the wise centaur Chiron, and attracted a pantheon of gods. So bountiful was the feast of food and drink that the occasion became, in the minds of generations of humans, a symbol for divine riches. The muses sang, accompanied by Apollo on the lyre. Gifts for the married couple, the hero Peleus and the sea nymph Thetis, ranged from an ashen spear to a basket of divine salt.

Most of the revelers failed to notice the small golden apple that was tossed into the crowd, but the three who did were the goddesses Hera, Athena, and Aphrodite. They read the inscription on the apple, "To the most beautiful," and each laid claim to the fruit. The ensuing quarrel was adjudicated by a mortal named Paris, setting into motion events that would culminate in the Trojan War. The little-known figure behind the debacle was Eris, or Discordia to the Romans—the goddess of strife, discord, and disagreement.

The typical version of this story portrays Eris as a jealous goddess, enraged by the bride and groom's decision to not invite her to the wedding. It says her act of vengeance proved more devastating than even she might have imagined: the Trojan War resulted in the death of Peleus and Thetis's son, Achilles.

Other accounts suggest that Eris was acting in cahoots with Zeus and the wise counselor Themis to save the world from environmental destruction. A fragment of *The Cypria,* an epic poem that some scholars describe as a prequel to *The Iliad,* posits an idea with new resonance in the twenty-first century: "Countless tribes of men, though wide-dispersed, oppressed the surface of the deep-bosomed earth, and Zeus saw it and had pity and in his wise heart resolved to relive the all-nurturing earth of men by causing the great struggle of the Ilian war, and the load of death might empty the world."

Both versions of the myth make the same connection: strife and disagreement ultimately result in death. The gods needed neither fire nor brimstone to level a city and decimate its people. They needed only some discord.

The ancient Greeks took inspiration from the goddess to describe a style of argument aimed not at the discovery of truth but at victory over an opponent by any means. Whereas a dialectic was beholden to truth and logic, an eristic conformed only in appearance to these virtues. The eristic was the charlatan, the quibbler, and the wrangler who won debates at the cost of undermining the integrity of the exercise.

Socrates schooled the eristics on several occasions, but in *The Republic* he took a humbler approach. While arguing with Glaucon

(Plato's brother), the philosopher remarked that people seemed "to fall into [eristic] even against their wills." Glaucon asked whether the observation applied to their conversation. "Absolutely," said Socrates. "At any rate I am afraid that we are unawares slipping into contentiousness."

The message was clear: eristics were impossible to avoid because the eristic was us. Anyone could be a bad debater or fall victim to one, unaware that the resulting discord contained embers that, under the right conditions, would grow into a blaze.

. . .

On the Monday afternoon of September 26, 2016, some nine months after the grand final debate in Thessaloníki, I paused in the snack aisle of the local grocery store to reflect on how much my life had slowed down. My retirement from debate at the tender age of twenty-one had meant the return of weekends and entire regions of my brain. Now, at age twenty-two, I felt myself settling into a more languid rhythm. Previously, the autumn in Boston had always seemed to pass in a flash, but now I counted the ways it held out for our attention.

This semester, the fall of my senior year, would mainly comprise work on my senior thesis, an original research project of around thirty thousand words. I chose as my subject multiculturalism and its political demands for recognition, aiming to connect high theory to the conditions of life on the ground. However, as I got to work in dusty libraries and austere seminar rooms, the real world seemed to recede from my grasp, so that all I had left were abstractions. On weekends out of town—to my professor Jamaica Kincaid's garden in Vermont, to friends' apartments in New York—the sensory richness of the world felt overwhelming.

The aloofness of academic work triggered in me a deeper anxiety about my place in the world. As the beneficiary of an expensive education, I had been marinating for years in others' high expectations of my success. However, when I scrolled through job listings and career guides, I saw few roles in which I could make a real contribution. What I knew was that I did not want to stay around the university. "Cambridge is a garden," one professor at the law school told me. "You have to get out while you can." I needed to find channels of escape.

So when an editor at the American news site *Quartz* approached Fanele and me to write a column ahead of the first U.S. presidential debate between Hillary Clinton and Donald Trump, I seized on the opportunity to leave the campus confines—if only virtually—and address a broader audience. The article, featuring our "top tips" for debate success, received a positive response from readers, prompting the editor to commission a follow-up piece reviewing the candidates' performance in the first round.

I had invited friends, many of them debaters, to watch the debate in my room. Though the consensus among our group was that the round would be a dispiriting mess, I held on to a measure of hope. Salesmen thrived in settings of their own design, but debates were sobering spectacles in which speakers provided live answers to hard questions, while an opponent and moderator held them to account. True, Trump had dominated the primary debates, but those had been variety shows with a dozen wacky contestants vied for attention. They were not real debates, let alone presidential debates. Or so I reassured myself as I picked out the snacks and chose the wines.

People started arriving at our place around 8:00 p.m. In our spacious living room lined with couches and chairs, I poured drinks and set up the livestream. Some people said they were nervous, but gathered together, we fell into a cheerful and familiar dynamic. Fanele sat with his laptop in the corner of the room nearest to the screen, looking sober and focused. Though the debate was set to start in an hour, the commentators on the cable television networks were already ruddy-faced. On mute, their performance resembled a repetitive and impassioned mime.

There was no clock in our room, but people sensed when it was time to sit. The network, scraping for usable content, was playing a montage featuring the moderators. In the footage from primary season, CNN anchor Jake Tapper said, "Our goal for this evening is a debate. A true debate, with candidates addressing each other in areas where they differ. Where they disagree—on policy, on politics, on leadership." Then the video cut and went live to the campus of Hofstra University in Hempstead, New York.

The debate began with displays of congeniality. "How are you, Donald?" said the Democratic candidate, as the pair shook hands and smiled for the audience. From his desk, the moderator spoke in a dignified way about vision, values, and the American people. In the first segment, both candidates provided sharp and reasoned responses to a question about jobs and the economy. Fanele and I exchanged thoughts on the finer points of strategy—subtle dodges and rhetorical moves—until a friend dug her elbow into my side. "Shut up, debaters."

Then something changed. The smiles receded and everything became second person. *You*, a vowel, does not make a natural cuss word, but the candidates found a way. Donald Trump began to yell and interrupt, turning the transcript into a dark poem. At times, the scribe gave up on disentangling their voices.

TRUMP: For thirty years, you've been doing it, and now you're just starting to think of solutions.

CLINTON: Well, actually . . .

TRUMP: I will bring—excuse me. I will bring back jobs. You can't bring back jobs.

CLINTON: Well, actually, I have thought about this quite a bit.

TRUMP: Yeah, for thirty years.

CLINTON: And I have—well, not quite that long. I think my husband did a pretty good job in the 1990s. I think a lot about what worked and how we can make it work again. . . .

TRUMP: Well, he approved NAFTA. . . .

The atmosphere in our living room became tense. People had been vocal at the outset, offering on-the-spot rebuttal or a fact check, mouthing "Shame" and "Unbelievable" while shaking their heads, or simply laughing in disbelief. But now things were quiet. The only noise in the room was people shifting in their seats. This was a burlesque, for sure, but at its bottom was a certain humorless-ness:

CLINTON: I have a feeling that by the end of this evening, I'm going to be blamed for everything that's ever happened.

TRUMP: Why not?

CLINTON: Why not? Yeah, why not? [laughter] You know, just join the debate by saying more crazy things. Now, let me say this, it is absolutely the case . . .

TRUMP: There's nothing crazy about not letting our companies bring their money back into their country.

When the debate came to a close, my friends clamored to find the upsides. "This is the reckoning," Jonah said. "It's messy and ugly, but no sane person watching that can say he just won the debate." Another friend noted that Trump had, after some hand-wringing, agreed to accept the results of the election, regardless of its results: "I want to make America great again. I'm going to be able to do it. I don't believe Hillary will. The answer is, if she wins, I will absolutely support her."

However, I had found something profoundly unsettling about the debate. In my days on the debate circuit, I had been in those kinds of rounds, against bullies who lied, shouted, interrupted, slandered, then claimed the whole thing was rigged. Those people did things one could not imagine, but they were hard to beat. Those people could bring down great debaters. Those people could win.

The presidential debate also made me realize something else: bullies won debates not by evading the debate format but by hijacking it. Bullies used the adversarial format to bludgeon opponents and used rhetoric not to enhance but to elide reason. They took advantage of the debate's openness to ideas by introducing lies.

Bad debates seemed to point back to some weakness in the activity itself. They showed that a debate, so hijacked, could be a harmful force in the world.

As friends moved around the room and music replaced the sound of television, Fanele and I remained on the couch. The mountain of notes we had compiled at our feet in preparation for our piece seemed more and more beside the point. Treating the events of the last ninety minutes as a regular debate seemed dishonest, but explaining what they had revealed about this activity, our activity, was outside our immediate grasp. We never filed the article.

• • •

In 1831, the German philosopher Arthur Schopenhauer, at age forty-two, finished writing one of the stranger works in his corpus. The work, which was not published in his lifetime, was a debate manual.

Schopenhauer was a mercurial man, prone to quarreling with colleagues, publishers, neighbors, and even random people on the street. As a young academic at the University of Berlin, he had picked fights with the luminary G. W. F. Hegel, whom he later described as "a flat-headed, insipid, nauseating, illiterate charlatan." Schopenhauer brought this brass-knuckled sensibility to his treatise on debate, entitled *The Art of Always Being Right*, or in the original German, *Eristische Dialektik*.

The book starts with a definition: eristic dialectic is the art of winning an argument "whether one is in the right or the wrong—per fas et nefas" (through right or wrong). It then outlines thirty-eight unscrupulous techniques, from subtly changing the topic to goading the opponent into anger, for succeeding in debate. The best one? "Claim victory despite defeat. If your opponent is shy or stupid, and you yourself possess a great deal of impudence and a good voice, the trick may easily succeed."

Schopenhauer had a pretty dark view of the world, and this comes through in the book. At age seventeen, the young German likened himself to the Buddha encountering sickness, pain, and death for the first time. "This world cannot be the work of an all-good being but rather of a devil who had brought creatures into existence in order to gloat over the sight of their anguish," he concluded. This was the year, 1805, in which his father drowned in a canal by their family home in Hamburg.

This pessimism extended to Schopenhauer's view of other people. He wrote in *Eristic Dialectic* that bad debates emerged from the "natural baseness of human nature." If people were honorable, a debate would aim at nothing other than the truth. But, in fact, we are vain and, precisely in these moments of vice, prone to "loquacity and innate dishonesty." Even if a debate started out in good faith, it could not stay so for long.

The most common reading of *Eristic Dialectic* is that the text was a parody. Schopenhauer was skewering the depraved way in which most people debate by adopting the voice of a vile coach. "Put objective truth aside," he urged, before drawing an analogy between an eristic and fencing. What led to the duel is not all that important; "thrust and parry is the whole business."

But the perennial puzzle with parody is to what extent it is motivated by cynicism or idealism. Does Schopenhauer believe that a better debate is possible, and attempt to nudge us toward it through his satire? Or does he think people are eristics at heart?

There is some evidence that Schopenhauer held on to hope. He writes near the beginning of the book that understanding the ways of the eristician can help us defend the truth against his or her attacks: "Even when a man has the right on his side he needs [eristic] dialectic in order to defend and maintain it. He must know what the dishonest tricks are, in order to meet them; nay, he must often make use of them himself, so as to beat the enemy with his own weapons."

In fact, Schopenhauer suggests that a widespread understanding of bad arguments may prevent them by deterring eristics from misbehaving. After advising the reader to be rude against an opponent who is pulling ahead, Schopenhauer issues a warning. Debaters must ask "what counter-trick avails for the other party? For if he has recourse to the same rule, there will be blows, or a duel, or an action for slander." When both sides have mastered eristic debate, a mutual deterrence sets in, paving the path, perhaps, for a different kind of disagreement.

The trouble was that, in order to learn the ways of bad argument, one had to step into the ring with the eristic.

. . .

Four years earlier, when I was on the Australian debate team, Bruce would invite the bullies to practice. They were his friends, the best university debaters of their time—some of the people whom we admired most. The coach's rationale was rooted in his experience on the rugby field: "To get better, get hit by the biggest, baddest players in the league."

Through the window in our prep room, we could see the interlopers mucking around. The hour allocated to us for prep was barely enough to calm our nerves, let alone to devise a winning case. Our opponents spent most of the time watching funny videos. Their cackles echoed down the hall and rang in our minds.

By the time we entered the room, they were in position, like gunmen at the firing wall, cold and unblinking. The people themselves were normal college students: a pale guy in sensible slacks, an artistic type with no shoes, a woman who spoke with a husky voice. "How're we feeling?" "Hope you prepared." The trash talk was poorly done. But the debaters' stature imbued even those things that were disappointing about them with plausible deniability.

Their speeches were designed to shock. Every argument we made was feeble, idiotic, outrageous, and we had to be foolish or wicked for having thought otherwise. Their manner was expansive, triumphant; sometimes a voice cracked with glee, but it never slowed down. The debaters misstated our points and twisted our words. They called out "Lies!" and "Wrong!" in the middle of our speeches.

At the end of the round, we shook hands with our fallen idols. The small talk was awkward. This was a strange way to meet for the first time, we agreed. "Sorry guys, your coach told us to do that," one of them said.

The coach was unsympathetic to our complaints. "Do you know what one of the Queensland coaches used to say to her teams? 'Go for the throat.'" He stretched out that last word, so that every consonant and vowel became its own syllable. "Now, you guys are good, clean debaters. But there are teams out there who will play dirty and sling the mud. Sure, you can look down on them. But guess what? You will also lose to them, unless you know how to respond.

"Good debaters lose to bad debaters when they get outmaneuvered," he said.

Over the next few sessions, we analyzed our opponents' playbook. Bad debate, we learned, could manifest in a million different ways, but the basic physics was straightforward. The bullies tended to take on one of four personas.

The Dodger

Dodgers never respond directly to an argument but understand they must be subtle in evasion. Their signature move is the pivot. Instead of ignoring the point, which would be too obvious, dodgers comment on some aspect of the broader subject, but not the particular argument they need to address:

> "Coal-fired plants are bad for the environment. They exacerbate *climate change*."

> "*Climate change* means we need reliable energy sources like coal-fired plants."

Sometimes the pivot works as an offensive tactic. Ad hominem attacks, aimed not at the argument but its advocate, are one example. ("Bad for the environment? You drive an SUV.") Tu quoque, or the "you also" attack, is another example ("Bad for the environment? So are windmills.").

The best response is to stay the course and pursue the original argument. This can be hard when the attack is personal or incorrect. But dodgers escape scrutiny when we relent on the arguments they would prefer to ignore. Where this is untenable, we can engage without surrender, issuing a correction while insisting that the discussion return to the original subject.

The Twister

Twisters misrepresent opposing arguments. Unable or unwilling to respond to the original point, they create a distorted version of the argument (straw man) and make a show of tearing it down.

> "Individual citizens should have the right to own a firearm."

> "Are you saying that communal safety should be sacrificed for individual freedom? This is a typical libertarian argument."

Straw-man arguments often expand what the original speaker must defend. That is, they push additional burdens of proof (burden push). They do this by generalizing a broad principle from a specific claim ("right to own a firearm" to "communal safety should be sacrificed"), analogizing to a similar case ("If you're happy with guns, why not other weapons?"), or categorizing the argument ("typical libertarian argument").

The best move is to correct the record. This involves spelling out the A to B of the twister's distortion—the original argument and its distortion—and, where necessary, explaining the misrepresentation, before returning the discussion to the actual claim.

The Wrangler

Wranglers are excellent at rebuttal but never put forward a positive argument of their own. Nothing is good enough for them. Their basic strategy is all attack, all the time.

The concept of wrangling can be traced back as far as the *Nyaya Sutras*, a Sanskrit text from around the sixth century BC. The sutras distinguish among three types of disagreements: good debates (vada), which keep to clear, well-reasoned arguments; bad debates (jalpa), which involve a range of underhanded tactics; and wrangling debates (vitanda), which involve a critic who never establishes his or her own counterthesis.

Since wranglers never commit to a position, they can constantly move the goalposts for their opponents. This is what Toni Morrison meant when she wrote, "The very serious function of racism is distraction. . . . Somebody says you have no art, so you dredge that up. Somebody says you have no kingdoms, so you dredge that up. . . . There will always be one more thing."

Sometimes wranglers get away with this by implying a position that they can plausibly deny. For example, dog-whistling refers to the use of vague language that signals a more specific message to some people ("law and order" instead of "increased policing in low-income communities").

The best response is to pin the wrangler to a position. This might involve asking questions—"So what *do* you believe?" or "What would I have to prove to convince you?" or "What do you mean by that?"—then holding them to that argument.

The Liar

Liars lie. They make statements they believe to be false in order to mislead other people.

The mistake we make in response to liars is to assume that calling them out—"You're a liar!" or "That's a lie!"—is enough to defeat them. In fact, this is how liars get ahead. They make us emotional and provoke us to make personal attacks.

What we need to do instead is to prove the falsehood of the liar's remarks. In debate, we use a two-step method called "plug and replace":

1. Plug the lie into a broader view of the world, then explain what problems arise:

    "Let's imagine that immigrants *are* violent people. How do you explain the fact that they are less likely to be convicted of a violent crime than native-born citizens?"

2. Replace the lie with the truth, then explain why the latter is more likely the reality:

    "The truth is that immigrants *aren't* any more violent than other people. They live in tough, heavily policed neighborhoods and are still less likely to get caught up in crime."

This does not prove that the opponent lied but shows it would be unreasonable and dishonest to persist with the claim. That such obstinate disregard for the truth must be condemned in a well-ordered society is a point to which we will return.

Liars pose two other dangers.

First, they engage in bluster, which is dishonest speech that hides behind the excuse of being nonliteral. When a liar is challenged for saying, "Every media outlet is corrupt," they respond, "I don't mean it literally." The best response is one we have already used against the wrangler: to ask the liar *precisely* what they mean, until we have pinned them to a position.

Second, we should be wary of being overwhelmed by a spread of lies. Liars exploit the reality that fact-checking takes time, and that inundating an opponent with falsehoods distracts them from their arguments. As the British writer George Monbiot said of his refusal to debate a climate skeptic, "It takes 30 seconds to make a misleading scientific statement and 30 minutes to refute it."

The best thing we can do is to focus on a couple of representative lies, which exemplify the liar's distortion. Once we have proved the falsehood of these claims, we may be able to draw out a pattern.

DODGER	
Pivot	Stay the course
Ad hominem	
Tu quoque	
TWISTER	
Straw man	Correct the record
Burden push	
WRANGLER	
Moving goalposts	Pin them to a position
Dog whistle	
LIAR	
Lie	Plug and replace
Bluster	Refute representative lies
Liar's spread	

At the end of these training sessions, we felt better prepared for the intense debates that lay ahead of us. What's more, we harbored no ill feeling toward our tormentors because, in the back of our minds, we knew they were fake bullies—decent people playing a part. Their antics could only go so far in an activity that penalized evasion, misrepresentation, wrangling, and lies. Like most people in the world, they were constrained by a sense of shame.

. . .

On the day of the second presidential debate, Sunday, October 9, the temperature barely deviated from a perfect fifty-five degrees. The wind had been stirring all day but it, too, subsided in the early evening, lending these hours an eerie sense of stillness. However, inside the dining hall of Pforzheimer House, an echoey two-story space with long tables, people were abuzz with excitement. Some groups tried their hands at ESPN-style prematch analyses; others exchanged assurances that their side would prevail. Dinner was a fibrous meal of beef stir-fry on brown rice, a high risk for indigestion.

This time we had no party in our room. After a long day in the stacks of Widener Library, I packed a container of the quasi-Asian food at the canteen and carried it up to my room. Jonah and John, who had both recently entered into new relationships, were nowhere to be found in the suite. So I cracked open a bottle of beer and sank into the couch. Then I opened my computer to a livestream channel and a social media feed.

Before 9:00 p.m., the stream cut to Washington University in St. Louis, Missouri. The set had the same aesthetic as the one from two weeks earlier—bald eagle, Constitution(s), stars—but stools had replaced lecterns, and undecided voters sat in a broken circle around the candidates. This time, the candidates did not shake hands: they stood at a distance, nodded, and smiled. Somehow this felt to me a violation, for debate, like a duel, was a fight enmeshed in rules of respectability.

In the first ten minutes, as the candidates presented the equivalent of opening remarks, the discussion was civil. Hillary Clinton began the debate with an uplifting message—"If we set those goals and we go together to try to achieve them, there's nothing in my opinion that America can't do"—and Trump responded with a gesture of conciliation: "Well, I actually agree with that. I agree with everything she said."

Then a question about Trump's taped comments on groping and kissing women without consent sent the debate on a different trajectory. Once the descent began, there was no sense of a bottom:

> If you look at Bill Clinton, far worse. Mine are words,
> and his was action. His was what he's done to women.
> There's never been anybody in the history of politics in
> this nation that's been so abusive to women. . . . Hillary
> Clinton attacked those same women and attacked them
> viciously. Four of them [are] here tonight.

When Clinton tried to take the high road, the format of the discussion seemed to block her. The physical proximity between the two people onstage, and the rapid-fire exchange between them, left no room in which to breathe.

> CLINTON: It's just awfully good that someone with the
> temperament of Donald Trump is not in charge of
> the law in our country.

TRUMP: Because you'd be in jail.

CLINTON: Please allow her to respond. She didn't talk
while you talked.

TRUMP: Yes, that's true. I didn't.

CLINTON: Because you have nothing to say.

For at least an hour after the debate, I could not step away from
the screen. The ugly highlights looped across the cable channels and
multiplied on social media as gifs and memes. "You okay?" John
asked as he took off his shoes and hung his coat. The question
stumped me.

If there was a bright spot in the evening, a sign that things might
turn out okay, it was the fact that almost every postdebate survey
seemed to punish Trump for his behavior. The percentage of respondents who believed he had won the debate trailed the percentage of
those who believed the opposite by double digits. I ran through these
numbers while brushing my teeth. They were meaningful results, uniform and quantitative. So why did they leave me cold?

Back in my elementary school, children had different approaches
to bullies. Some fled the scene; others alerted the teacher. The most
terrified ones crossed over to the dark side. My own approach was to
bargain with the bullies and urge them to "talk things over." I often
thought myself ahead in these exchanges—"No, what I am wearing
is not, in fact, unreasonable" or "I'm not looking at anything, except
in the most general sense."

However, the bullies possessed dark tools: cuss words, personal
insults, non sequiturs. The effect of a "yo mama" joke, well deployed,
was transformative. It changed our interaction from a debate to a

brawl, so that reasoned arguments no longer applied. The game had changed. Friends and family consoled me, "You won the argument. They resort to insults and fists because they've nothing to say." True enough, but what use was moral victory against a bruised arm?

Though the genteel rules of competitive debate shielded against many bullying tactics, the protection was incomplete. Back on the middle school debate circuit in Sydney, my Barker teammates and I dreaded one particular team from a boys private school in the city's wealthy lower north shore. Our opponents had slight physiques, but they had somehow absorbed the movements and gestures of rugby jocks. Between rounds, the three boys swore in broad Australian accents, and in the debate room they scoffed and guffawed and leaned forward in threatening poses, glaring at the adjudicator and audience. Most of the time, their charm backfired and came to nothing, but, crucially, it sometimes worked. An inexperienced judge, stunned by the boys' certainty and dominance, would hand them the win.

The occasional tendency of debate to reward bullies stems from a feature of its adjudication. At first glance, the basis of victory in debate appears straightforward: one side *persuaded* the judge to vote for their position. But what does it mean, exactly, for us to claim that a team has persuaded an adjudicator, say, in a debate about supporting the invasion of Iraq? Clearly, we cannot mean the judge must now believe the invasion is a good idea—she may be a pacifist for all we know. Rather, we mean the winning team has convinced the judge that they were the more persuasive side.

Many bullies are expert at exploiting the gap between *persuasion* and the *perception of persuasiveness*. Whereas one pertains to a decision on the issues at hand, the other uses the present discussion as a proxy to glean a broader set of qualities, such as eloquence and intelligence. If persuasion refers to the result of one round, persuasiveness is a kind of social cachet that one carries across multiple settings. In a culture that encodes certainty and dominance as winningness, our perception of persuasiveness, in particular, tends to filter through twisted lenses.

In most debates, participants seek to persuade and demonstrate their persuasiveness. For this reason, debate has always been a dyad that combines *spectacle* and deliberation, *artifice* and truth seeking, *contest* and cooperation. The demonstrative aspects of debate are not bad per se. Spectacle gives people the motivation to engage in politics, metes out social judgment, and spreads ideas further than they might otherwise reach. However, we had to be honest when the elements of performance cut against the more sober, deliberative aspects of debate.

So, then, back to those opinion polls. Each of these surveys had relied on a version of the same simple prompt: "Who won the debate?" However, this was not the only question one could ask of the round.

Donald Trump might have lost the debate as a debate, but this might not have been the only way of viewing the exchange. What he had done was to brawl on the debate stage and try to convince us that it was a brawl we were there to see. I wasn't sure whether this would work. But the animal thrill that I felt during moments of his performance—the basic instinct to side with the bully—made me think that it just might.

The debate recalled a fifth kind of bully: the brawler. Unlike the four others I had encountered at debate practice, brawlers did not seek unfair advantage within the logic of debate. They sought to explode the logic altogether and turn the argument into a free-for-all in which the only measure of success was the perception of dominance. The brawler's aim was not to persuade but to silence, marginalize, and break the will of their opponents.

Formal debates could set up defenses against such bullies. Moderators could be empowered to mute the microphones of speakers when it was not their turn to speak and intervene to fact-check or call out bad behavior. In most of the bad disagreements we encounter on an ordinary day—at work, at home, or in the public square—these options are beyond our reach.

Faced with a brawler in our daily lives, we have only one hope: to restore the structure of debate. But as the presidential debates showed, this is hard work, even with dedicated moderators. What hope do we have when it is just us, alone, against the bully?

. . .

In the summer of 1959, near the height of the Cold War, a delegation of U.S. officials arrived at Sokolniki Park in Moscow to launch an exhibition. The display was designed to show Soviet citizens the enviable lives of Americans.

Among thousands of images and umpteen other displays, the pièce de résistance was a handsome model house, which at $14,000 was affordable to the average American steelworker. The replica of a property in Commack, Long Island, was divided into sections to maximize the number of visitors. For this quirk and the hope riding on its appeal, the house was named "Splitnik."

The exhibition was opened on June 24 by U.S. vice president Richard Nixon, who took it upon himself to tour the Soviet leader around the display. The bellicose Nikita Khrushchev did not much enjoy the exhibition and, for reasons personal and strategic, decided to pick a fight. He zeroed in on an automatic lemon squeezer in the model kitchen: "What are you showing us that for? Do you want to lead us astray with a display of unrealistic objects?"

Standing five feet three inches, with the proportions of a blueberry, Khrushchev was an unmissable physical presence. He gestured with his whole body. One signature move was to point a finger at an interlocutor's chest, then follow through with his weight. The premier had a resonant laugh that spilled through his gap teeth. But his good cheer could turn to fury in a split second, a turn that first showed on the impressions around his smile lines.

Behind this expressive face lay a genuine political cunning. Khrushchev was born in 1894 to a poor peasant couple in Kalinovka, a village near the Ukrainian border. The man possessed an innate intelligence that allowed him to climb the ranks of the Communist Party and, more important, stay there. He helped carry out Stalin's purges without himself being purged, outmaneuvered rivals to win the leadership upon Stalin's death, then proceeded to denounce his predecessor's legacy as a "cult of personality."

Richard Nixon, the son of Quakers, was not yet the Nixon of Watergate. At the time of his visit to Moscow, the forty-six-year-old had begun to display some of the political skills that would launch him to and from the presidency. But relative to Khrushchev, who was twenty years his senior, Nixon was a novice. The former senator from California had risen to the vice presidency in the same year that the Russian had become the leader of the USSR.

The physical asymmetry between the two men touring the exhibition was striking. Khrushchev, dressed in a gray suit and a white hat, was expansive. He moved on the offbeats, veering into one person, then backing into another. By contrast, Nixon cut a svelte figure.

Though he was the taller man, he carried far less heft and was in danger of being muscled out of the frame and into the shadow of his adversary.

Now, in this model kitchen, the latent tension between the two men was boiling over into an argument. Nixon was about to debate one of the most formidable brawlers in the world:

> NIXON: I want to show you this kitchen. It is like those of our houses in California.
>
> KHRUSHCHEV: We have such things.
>
> NIXON: This is our newest model. This is the kind which is built in thousands of units for direct installations in the houses. In America, we like to make life easier for women.
>
> KHRUSHCHEV: Your capitalistic attitude toward women does not occur under Communism.
>
> NIXON: I think that this attitude toward women is universal. What we want to do is make life more easy for our housewives.

The barbs came thick and fast. They were prickly things, made to break up the speaker's flow. On the sidelines, cameras snapped and scribes wrote in shorthand.

Nixon's opening tack was to pretend it was a debate. That is, he continued to act *as if* he was entitled to continue making his arguments and receive a fair hearing for them. It helped, of course, that Nixon had been a champion debater in high school. His speech coach used to tell him: "Speaking is a conversation. If you have an audience, you may raise the level of your voice, but don't shout at people. Talk to them."

When an opponent is being disruptive, the worst thing to do is cut short or rush through our argument—thus allowing the opponent to control the flow of time in the exchange. The second-worst thing to do is seize on the heckles (especially if they're good!) instead of finishing our own argument—thus letting the other side set the agenda.

We must also avoid the temptation to respond like for like against bullying tactics. The truth is that few of us have the energy and shamelessness to sustain an all-out brawl. Even if we were to score a point or two, we are unlikely to outdo the bully in his or her game.

The best thing to do is to press on with the argument, at pace. If the other side interrupts, we can pause, and count these minutes as ours to use later. It may feel as if the two sides are having different kinds of discussion. This is precisely the point: a brawl is not a debate, and we will not allow the opposition to unilaterally change the rules.

So the first step to preventing a debate from becoming a brawl? Pretend it's a debate.

This bought Nixon some time. Instead of swapping one-line zingers, the two men made competing points about the affordability and longevity of homes in their respective countries. But once the Soviet leader got on a roll, he was hard to stop.

> KHRUSHCHEV: The Americans have created their own
> image of the Soviet man. But he is not as you think. You
> think the Russian people will be dumbfounded to see
> these things, but the fact is that newly built Russian
> houses have all this equipment right now.
>
> NIXON: Yes, but . . .

KHRUSHCHEV: In Russia, all you have to do to get a
house is to be born in the Soviet Union. You are entitled
to housing. . . . In America, if you don't have a dollar
you have a right to choose between sleeping in a house
or on the pavement. Yet you say we are the slave to
Communism.

[. . .]

NIXON: If you were in the Senate, we would call you a
filibusterer! You—[Khrushchev interrupts]—do all the
talking and don't let anyone else talk. This exhibit was
not designed to astound but to interest. Diversity, the
right to choose, the fact that we have one thousand
builders building one thousand different houses is the
most important thing. We don't have one decision made
at the top by one government official. This is the
difference.

To stop Khrushchev from taking over the debate, Nixon used a
second tactic: stop and name. That is, he paused the conversation and
named the specific behavior ("filibustering") that was starting to break
down the debate.

Brawlers thrive in chaos. Their tactics work best when they seem
unrehearsed, and their corrosive effects on the debate are concealed
in theatrics. Naming the behavior, like revealing a magician's tricks,
can help us resist these tricks and reset the discussion.

There is a danger that this tactic verges on an ad hominem attack
and makes the disagreement even more intractable. Nixon came close
to this point. So we should stick to the behavior rather than the person behind it.

The two leaders took their conversation from the kitchen exhibit to an adjoining television studio. Before the media, Khrushchev was the more natural performer. The Soviet leader made declarative statements and big gestures. He used his white fedora as an occasional prop. The camera lights brought out the showman in him:

KHRUSHCHEV: [interrupting] No, in rockets we've passed you by, and in the technology—

NIXON: [continuing to talk] You see, you never concede anything.

KHRUSHCHEV: We always knew that Americans were smart people. Stupid people could not have risen to the economic level that they've reached. But as you know, "we don't beat flies with our nostrils!" In forty-two years we've made progress.

NIXON: You must not be afraid of ideas.

KHRUSHCHEV: We're saying it is you who must not be afraid of ideas. We're not afraid of anything. . . .

NIXON: Well, then, let's have more exchange of them. We all agree on that, right?

KHRUSHCHEV: Good. [Khrushchev turns to translator, asks] Now, what did I agree on?

Near the end of the exchange, Nixon decided to defer the round. Rather than persisting with a debate that, despite his best efforts, was becoming a brawl, he won a commitment to a rematch.

There is no more consequential decision that a debater can make than to end a debate. But when we make this call not to run from disagreement but to save our energy for the right kind of disagreement, we set ourselves up for a better conversation.

These three moves—pretend it's a debate, stop and name, defer the round—may seem like the countermeasures we developed to the bullies in debate practice. But their aim is far more ambitious. It is not only to beat back nasty arguments in the moment but to restore an environment that reduces their potency.

One year after the confrontation in Moscow, Richard Nixon faced an entirely different foe on the debate stage: a U.S. senator from Massachusetts named John F. Kennedy. The first round took place in Chicago on a Monday in late September and marked the first time that candidates for the president of the United States faced each other in a televised debate. Some 66.4 million people tuned in to watch.

What followed was a political disaster for Nixon. Under the glare of the stage lights, the man seemed pale, nervous, and sweaty (he was recovering from a knee infection at the time). Meanwhile, the young senator was tanned and winning in his demeanor. The polls flipped against Nixon after that night, and enshrined the debates as a feature of American democracy.

The narrative that has emerged from the 1960 presidential cycle says that Nixon's inaptitude for debate and television helped seal his fate. But one year earlier, he had managed to hold his own against the leader of the Soviet Union. He had ensured that what could have been known as a brawl would be remembered instead as "the kitchen debate."

For us debaters, the lesson of Nixon's rise and fall was painfully familiar: debate giveth, and debate taketh away.

On the day before the 2016 presidential election, Monday, November 7, I took an early morning flight from Boston to New York to interview for a postgraduate fellowship in Beijing, China. The Schwarzman Scholarship, founded by the American billionaire and cofounder of the private equity giant Blackstone, Steve Schwarzman, promised funding for a one-year master's degree at Tsinghua University. I had no particularly good reason for wanting to live in China but was drawn to the prospect of witnessing a nation, and indeed a region, in the midst of rapid transformation.

The interviews took place on the thirty-first floor of the storied Waldorf Astoria Hotel. Prestigious fellowships relied on a particular top-down theory of change: that a group of already expensively educated people, through access to postgraduate study and a community of peers, could enrich themselves to better serve the world. As a new program, Schwarzman Scholars could not yet prove this hypothesis, but it provided, in its selection of interviewers, a model. In the gilded hotel, a veritable who's who of former world leaders, captains of industry, and media personalities intermingled with twentysomethings. I perceived in the group a clubby calmness. At lunch, over a salad of shaved vegetables and ornamental fronds, the political discussion was contained. "Hillary will do great," said a distinguished-looking gent on my right.

For most of the next day, as I crisscrossed town to shop and see friends, I barely checked the news. In public spaces, canvassers and get-out-the-vote campaigners made all the right noises about participating in democracy, but I heard the weight of exhaustion pulling on the edges of their voices. Later in the evening, I arrived on time at LaGuardia Airport for my 7:59 p.m. flight back to Boston and read the first set of projections—Indiana and Kentucky for Trump and Vermont for Clinton—on the boarding line. Take-off was perfectly smooth and, once out of internet range, I felt as though I had fallen out of time.

After I disembarked from the plane, collected my bags, and readied to face the night, at around 10:00 p.m., I read on my phone that *The New York Times* was projecting a 95 percent likelihood of a Trump victory. On the Silver Line bus back to downtown Boston, a slow and uneven ride, nothing felt so stable anymore.

In the days after the election, the three presidential debates proved a rich source of media showing the polarization (and attendant ugliness) of contemporary politics:

"Bad hombres"

"You're the puppet"

"Such a nasty woman"

Throughout the campaign, political pundits had been critical of the debate format. "A mélange of showmanship and complaining, obstinacy and irrelevance" was one journalist's description of the spectacle. A political scientist even proposed that the format be scrapped altogether and replaced with televised "crisis simulations."

I never believed the debates would be canceled, but now, in the aftermath of a most divisive election, I sensed another danger: that people would give up on the possibility of what debate could be, not only at the level of national politics but in their own lives. Such a loss—caused by despair rather than outrage, exhaustion rather than anger—would be immeasurable, indeed.

In conversations with friends, I tried to make the case that debate, as a dyad, had another register and that debaters could speak in a voice that was as gracious and thoughtful as it was candid and passionate. I made the argument with great confidence. Yet in my heart I wondered whether we would find it in ourselves to raise and amplify that other voice. In these moments of doubt, I got solace from a most unlikely source.

Some twenty years after writing *Eristic Dialectic*, Arthur Schopenhauer seemed to cool on the prospects of good debate. In 1851, he wrote in his last major work, *Appendices and Omissions*, that he had once tried to make "a neat anatomical specimen" of the formal aspects of bad debate, or what he called the *Ultima ratio Stultorum* (the last resort of the stupid).

As an old man, Schopenhauer became even more convinced that men revealed in argument not only "their intellectual incapacity, but . . . moral depravity." He said he would not revisit the specimen but would more earnestly urge "avoiding an argument with the common ruck of people" for the "result is always detestable." We could attempt to debate, Schopenhauer said, "but as soon as we notice in his rejoinders any obstinacy we should stop at once."

Yet in the depth of his cynicism, the philosopher could not help but leave the door slightly ajar. "Whoever does not admit an opponent's sound arguments betrays an intellect that is either directly weak or is so indirectly through being suppressed by the mastery of his will," he wrote. "We should, therefore, go for such a person only when *duty and obligation require it.*"

This seemed to me exactly the point. As citizens, we *did* have the

duty to disagree well—to settle our disputes through the force of persuasion and not violence; to deliberate on matters of shared interest; to
tell those with whom we disagreed why and give them a chance to respond. These obligations applied double to those with whom we shared
a home, a workplace, a neighborhood, or a nation. To walk away from
debate was to shirk these responsibilities, too.

The ancient Greeks tended to conceive of their gods in opposing
pairs. Zeus was the god of the sky, and his brother Hades was god of
the underworld. Apollo was god of the sun; Artemis, his sister, was
goddess of the moon.

According to the myths, the goddess Eris also had a sister. She was
the goddess of harmony and concord and was thus named Harmonia
by the Greeks and Concordia by the Romans. There were only a handful of stories about her, and these accounts suggested that her powers
never rivaled those of Eris.

Hesiod, an ancient Greek poet whose name means "he who emits
the voice," saw things a different way. He said there were, in fact,
two goddesses named Eris. Whereas one brought wars and strife, the
other fostered disagreements and conflicts that were "far kinder to
men." This benevolent goddess was she who "stirs up even the shift-
less to toil" by placing them in competition with their neighbors.
"This strife is wholesome for man," he wrote.

The myths tell us that the opposite of bad disagreement is not
agreement but rather good disagreement. For now, the dark Eris
seemed to reign. However, the lesson of the past millennia was that
the contest between good and bad arguments—and the impulses
that pulled toward each—never resolved finally for either side. Like
any rich debate, the struggle went on and on.

7

EDUCATION

How to raise citizens

By the end of seventh grade, Malcolm Little had turned things around. The past few years had been tough. He lost his father and saw his mother endure a nervous breakdown. He earned a permanent suspension from the Pleasant Grove School in Lansing, Michigan, and got involved in minor crimes. But here at Mason Junior High School on the cusp of the 1940s, Little was starting to find his feet. He was a ward of the state and the only African American in his cohort. He was also the class president-elect, and his grades placed him near the top of his class.

Then, over the course of a year, things came undone. Little's best subjects were history and English. "Mathematics leaves no room for argument," he recalled. "If you made a mistake, that was all there was to it." Trouble began in those classrooms. Little had already cooled toward the history teacher, Mr. Williams, due to his habit of telling racist jokes in class, but he trusted Mr. Ostrowski, the English teacher. So when the older man began to offer some advice, the teenager listened:

> OSTROWSKI: Malcolm, you ought to be thinking about a career. Have you been giving it thought?
>
> MALCOLM: Well, yes, sir, I've been thinking I'd like to be a lawyer.
>
> OSTROWSKI: Malcolm, one of life's first needs is for us to be realistic. Don't misunderstand me, now. We all here like you, you know that. But you've got to be realistic about being a [n-word]. A lawyer—that's no realistic goal for a [n-word]. . . . Why don't you plan on carpentry?

Little could not forget. He played the moment over and over in his mind, reminding himself that the same Mr. Ostrowski had been extraordinarily supportive of the other children's aspirations. "I was smarter than nearly all of those white kids," Little said later. "But apparently I was still not intelligent enough, in their eyes, to become whatever I wanted to be." From then on, the teenager withdrew into himself. He refused to explain what had come over him.

The week he finished the eighth grade, Little boarded a Greyhound bus to Boston. He moved in with his half sister, Ella, and over the next several years worked a series of menial jobs while becoming enmeshed in crimes and hustles. He never again returned to school.

In February 1946, the twenty-year-old Little arrived at the state prison in Charlestown, Massachusetts, to start serving a ten-year sentence for burglary and related charges. He was assigned inmate number 22843 but soon earned the nickname "Satan" on account of his hostility toward religion.

Behind bars at Charlestown, Little fell under the influence of another inmate. John Elton Bembry, or "Bimbi," was the same height as Little (six feet two inches) and shared his light, reddish complexion, but in other respects the men were completely unalike. Whereas Little was given to vicious, swear-ridden exclamations, Bimbi spoke with eloquence on subjects ranging from commerce to the works of Henry David Thoreau. When Bimbi raised his voice, even the guards listened. "My approach sounded so weak alongside his, and he never used a foul word," Little observed.

Bimbi's example—his erudition, eloquence—stayed with Little as he transferred in 1948 to the Norfolk Prison Colony. The Norfolk had been designed by a reformist warden as a model prison community, and Little took to its education programs and well-stacked library with gusto. He copied words from the dictionary, starting with *aardvark*. He read everything from history (ancient Egypt, Ethiopia, China) to philosophy (Socrates, Schopenhauer, Kant, Nietzsche) to the political theology of Elijah Muhammad. "My reading had my mind like steam under pressure," Little recalled, and what he needed now was an escape valve—an outlet for his views. This he found in competitive debate.

The Norfolk debate society trained teams to compete against local universities and held a weekly competition between inmates. Topics ranged from politics ("Compulsory military training—or none?") to history ("What is the true identity of Shakespeare?") and even nutrition ("Should babies be fed milk?"). The rounds attracted upward of several hundred people. Little described his initiation in debate as a "baptism":

> But I will tell you that, right there, in the prison, debating, speaking to a crowd, was as exhilarating to me as the discovery of knowledge through reading had been. Standing up there, the faces looking up at me, things in my head coming out of my mouth, while my brain searched for the next best thing to follow what I was saying, and if I could sway them to my side by handling it right, then I had won the debate—once my feet got wet, I was gone on debating.

Little grew as a debater alongside his teammates. In December 1951, Norfolk hosted its first international debate, against a team from the University of Oxford. The prisoners had a decent record against college teams—thirty-four wins and fourteen losses. But the Brits, who had made Norfolk the last stop on a two-and-a-half-month undefeated tour of U.S. universities, were sure to be hard work. Little had been transferred back to Charlestown by this time, so the task of opposing the motion on creating a national health service fell on Murdo the Robber and Bill the Bad Check Passer. The judges awarded the debate, 3–0, to Norfolk. "They're extraordinarily good, you know," said one of the Oxford debaters, William Rees-Mogg (the future editor of *The Times* and father of the British conservative politician Jacob Rees-Mogg).

Some eight months after the Oxford debate, Little was released from prison on parole. By this time he had adopted a new name: Malcolm X.

In his career as a minister and activist—first for the Nation of Islam, then as a free agent—Malcolm X relied on few things more than his skills in debate. To make the case for racial separatism and against nonviolence, he brought the argument to his opponents. He challenged them on campuses, on radio, on television. "Malcolm nearly always won these encounters, or at least the crowds who attended them," observed one biographer. "He prosecuted [his case] with a bleak moral fury."

When people asked how he had learned to speak with such great force, Malcolm X credited his prison days and, in particular, the influence of one person: "It had really begun back in the Charlestown Prison, when Bimbi first made me feel envy of his stock of knowledge." But sometimes, while reflecting on the strange course of his life, he recalled an earlier moment with another mentor: "I've often thought that if Mr. Ostrowski had encouraged me to become a lawyer, I would today probably be among some city's professional black bourgeoisie, sipping cocktails and palming myself off as a community spokesman."

The Norfolk debate society prospered, too. Before it went dormant in 1966, the team achieved a record of 144 wins and only 8 losses against college teams, including a win against a Canadian side led by the musician Leonard Cohen. In 2016, a group of inmates revived the society and began, once again, to train teams for competition. One of the Norfolk debaters, James Keown, said of the society's first public debate in fifty years, "This is a humanizing event for me. . . . I mean, this is about, you know, we have a place in this world and we have a voice and we have something to share." So, the education resumed.

. . .

In the last week of May 2017, an uneven time of blazing sunshine and torrential rain, another chapter of my education came to an end. My parents had flown out from Sydney to attend the graduation ceremony—known at Harvard, as at many American colleges, as commencement. So had a beloved aunt from Seattle. Throughout the week, I suggested outings to see the sights around Boston: Fenway Park, the Isabella Stewart Gardner Museum, Chinatown. My parents seemed to prefer sitting around my room, speaking with my friends, divining some outline of the life I had led for the past four years.

I spent the evenings with friends at Grendel's Den, a moody underground pub, covering too many subjects over too few drinks. The largest segment of our graduating class was bound for major American cities such as New York and San Francisco, but my friends had resolved to disperse more widely. After graduation, I would move to Beijing in August on the Schwarzman Scholarship; Fanele would start work as a consultant in Atlanta; Jonah would finish one remaining semester, then move to Madrid, Spain. The directions of our life paths, forking apart, served as a reminder that apartness, not togetherness, was the natural state between any two people.

In these late-night conversations, my friends and I wondered what we had actually learned these past four years. Against the tedious obligations of the real world, the content of our liberal arts education seemed a series of non sequiturs: political theories of recognition, history of sexuality, the novels of Thomas Hardy.

The graduation ceremony on Thursday, May 25, sharpened some of these concerns. Despite the downpour, the spectacle of commencement—a show of regalia, Latin oration and song, before a crowd of 35,000—was dazzling. The sight of honorary degree recipients Dame Judi Dench and James Earl Jones, between university officials and chemists, sent shock waves of thrill through the audience. In the afternoon, Facebook founder Mark Zuckerberg spoke on the future of technology and democracy.

The ceremony made clear that our degrees had a market value—one that placed us in the company of celebrities and afforded us a platform to pronounce on the future of technology and democracy. In the faceless crowd, I wondered about the gap between this external value and the substance that our education had actually comprised: failures of understanding, spells of confusion, and long nights in the library that yielded no satisfaction.

I took solace in the fact that I had some runway left. Before the move to China, I had unfinished business on familiar territory: in a couple of months, I would coach the Australian national team at the World Schools Debating Championships in Bali, Indonesia. Fanele would also be at the tournament, coaching the U.S. national team, and this would be our last time together for a while.

Most debaters retire twice. They stop competing. Then, sometime after that, they withdraw altogether from the activity, including as adjudicator, volunteer, and coach. Since most tournaments require competitors to be students, most people first retire around the age of twenty-five. The timing of the second retirement widely varies. Some people delay until, well, the end.

The tournament in Bali would be my second and final retirement from debate. Though the council asked me to stay on for another term as the Australian team's coach, I stuck to my resolve. For the past twelve years I had not known a life completely outside the world of competitive debate. For five of those years I had been a coach to younger debaters—at my old high school, at Harvard, and at schools and summer camps around the world. I still enjoyed the work, but the potential costs of leaving too early seemed to me now minuscule compared with those of leaving too late. I figured it was time.

So, on the third Wednesday in July, after a quiet few weeks of vacation at home, I boarded a flight to Indonesia for my last-ever trip for debate. On the late-afternoon flight from Sydney to Bali, several rows of vacationers ordered drinks before the in-flight safety video. Their excitement was palpable—and so, too, the desire to make the most of a vacation that was already beginning to end. I had planned to review the training schedule for the upcoming week but decided instead to join the party.

Our plane descended through thick, viscous clouds and touched down around 10:00 p.m. local time. I declared to customs that the reason for my visit was "conference"—an old debater's trick for avoiding a painful conversation about "debate, kind of like arguing, but a sport"—then joined the tourists rehearsing "Selamat malam" at the taxi stand. The airport wi-fi held out long enough for me to message the team, who had been on an earlier flight, to gather for a meeting in one hour.

On the bumpy drive to the rental house, I thought about what I might say to the team. The tradition was to start these boot camps with a pep talk—an earnest, motivational speech laced with benign nationalism. But in a year marked by bad-faith debate and its political consequences, such a narrow focus on winning seemed inappropriate. The value of the activity I was there to teach no longer seemed so self-evident.

What I knew was that debate was a powerful tool of education. In my case, I felt the activity had not only taught me a bunch of things but also taught me how to learn, and instilled in me the actual desire to do so. This I sometimes tried to explain to others with a simple formula: Information < Skills < Motivation

Debate exposed children to an extraordinary range of information—in terms of subject matter (politics, history, science, culture) and source type (news, studies, data, theories)—and required of them a deep enough understanding to sustain a live argument.

But the real learning occurred at a level above the content. Debate was a synthetic activity. The skills involved—research, teamwork, logical reasoning, composition, and public speaking—formed a tool kit that students could apply across many settings. Perhaps most important, the activity gave children a reason to care about learning. Whereas much classroom work was top-down and passive, debate encouraged constant participation and made a sport of that most basic impulse: to be heard and to hold one's own in an argument.

The empirical evidence was that debate could be equalizing and scalable. Though the activity had long been a mainstay of elite education, recent efforts to expand access had produced great results. For example, a decade-long study of the Chicago Urban Debate League—one of twenty-odd such organizations in the U.S.—found that, controlling for self-selection, at-risk high school students who debated were 3.1 times more likely to graduate than nondebaters.

Debate was also (relatively) easy to organize. Since 2013, Broward County in Florida had managed to roll out a debate program in every one of its middle and high schools. Efforts were underway around the world to introduce the principles of debate into regular classes, and thus "debate-ify" the curriculum.

I stood by each of these claims. Yet I wondered if that was all debate was: a pedagogical tool that conferred some measure of personal advantage—knowledge, skills, motivation, relationships, and prestige—but produced no societal benefit. There was nothing wrong with that, per se, but the thought somehow left me cold.

The cab took a right turn onto an unpaved road. I had chosen the rental property for its secluded location, but I was nonetheless surprised by the absence of other houses. In their place were rice fields, acres of them, bubbling to some conclusion. James, one of the assistant coaches, greeted me at the gate. "The kids are already asleep," he said, with a hint of apology. "But they're excited to meet you."

Later that night, alone in my room, I reflected on the madness of what I had come to Bali to do. The experience of coaching a debate team mostly involved heartbreak. Coaches made plans; debaters broke them. When things went bad, there was no bottom. Yet we took the bargain—and surrendered our hopes to teenagers—because, on the good days, we got to see tradition change hands.

* * *

The job of debate coach came with no script, only examples one could emulate. Arguably the greatest coach of all time taught English at a historically black college named Wiley College in Marshall, Texas. This was one of many things that the fourteen-year-old James Farmer did not know in 1934 when he enrolled at the college as a freshman.

What Farmer knew at the time, as a teenager on a campus of young adults, was loneliness. His father was a professor of religion and philosophy at Wiley, so the campus—with ivy-covered walls and gardens filled with daffodils, zinnias, bluebonnets—was familiar enough. But his age foreclosed the prospect of romance, and most students treated him with the distant admiration with which the world greets prodigies.

There was, however, one person who showed interest in the wallflower. On an autumn day, the English professor, a man in his late thirties, spotted Farmer on campus and decided to make his approach. He shouted across hundreds of yards to ask what the boy was reading. Pleased by the response—"Tolstoy, *War and Peace!*"—the teacher boomed back, "I'm glad to know that at least you are drinking the broth of knowledge; why don't you eat the meat?"

Then came the invitation, along with a threat. After class one morning, the teacher chastised Farmer for not applying himself and ordered him to add more books to his reading list. "Then we'll get together and argue about them. I'll take a devil's advocate position, and you defend your views. That's the way you sharpen your tools— in the clash of opposing views." Or else? A failing grade. Farmer was speechless, so the older man seized the moment. He explained that the university's debate team trained at his house every Tuesday and Thursday evening. "You come over, too," he said, before adding, "all right, Farmer, I'll see you tonight." Thus the freshman fell into the orbit of Melvin Tolson, educator, poet, and coach of the Forensic Society of Wiley College.

The birth of the American university debate society dates to the time of the Founding Fathers. But competitive debate, which pitted these societies against one another, spread across the country in the Progressive Era—a period from the 1890s to the 1920s marked by intense demand for democratic reform, including women's suffrage, direct election of senators, and crackdowns on corruption and monopolies. This extended to historically black colleges and universities, where a generation of future African American leaders, including Martin Luther King Jr. (Morehouse), Supreme Court justice Thurgood Marshall (Lincoln University), and state senator Barbara Jordan (Texas Southern University), received an education in debate.

Another such graduate was Melvin Tolson. He competed for Lincoln University with his partner, Horace Mann Bond (the noted college administrator) before graduating in 1923. When he arrived at Wiley College the next year to teach English and speech, Tolson made one of his first acts the creation of a debate society. By the time James Farmer arrived on campus, the coach had honed for ten years the "mighty Tolson method."

Farmer soon discovered that the training sessions were grueling. Tolson was the center of the action, playing the adversary, drill sergeant, and professor. He cross-examined each debater for an hour and critiqued every gesture, every pause. Then he sent the group home with reams of reading. Sometimes Tolson tended toward cruelty, evincing a "deep-seated disgust for anyone who was incompetent, unknowledgeable, and unconcerned about bettering his lot." But the man inspired fierce loyalty. For Farmer, "the evenings at Tolson's were feasts at the end of days."

One reason for the tough training regime was that being a black debater in the Jim Crow South took serious fortitude. Farmer's teammate, Hobart Jarrett, recounts that a white supremacist once shot a rifle at the team outside a general store, and that they evaded a mob while driving through Beebe, Arkansas, by having the darker members crouch down. "Almost every debater during this period either observed or was threatened with lynching," wrote one historian.

The way Tolson saw debate was as preparation for the battles that awaited his students. "My boy, it is customary for a professor to tell his students that the world is waiting for them with open arms. Well, that's a lie. There are men waiting for you, all right—with a big stick. Learn how to duck, and counterpunch," he told Farmer. This was a fight not only for personal survival but also for political progress. As Tolson once told a debater named Henrietta Bell Wells, "You've got to put something in there to wake the people up."

In Farmer's first year at Wiley, the debate team was consumed by one goal. They planned in early 1935 to travel some five thousand miles across the Southwest to face various teams in California and New Mexico. But there was one round on this tour that dominated their attention: a debate against the University of Southern California, reigning national champions.

The debate took place on a Tuesday night at the Bovard Auditorium on the USC campus. Tolson was said to have confined the team to their rooms the previous night to ensure they would not be intimidated by the enormity of the rival university. Before a crowd of over two thousand people, the trio of Hobart Jarrett, James Farmer, and their teammate, Henry Heights, decked out to the nines in tuxedo suits, affirmed a motion on banning the "international shipment of arms and munitions."

Five years earlier, Tolson's 1930 Wiley side had become the first African Americans to compete against whites in debate. But this round, owing perhaps to USC's stature or to Wiley's growing reputation, came with its own sense of history. The audience was rapt with what Tolson described as the "thrill of seeing beyond the racial phenomena the identity of worthy qualities."

Wiley won the debate. News of their victory soon spread around the country. Hobart Jarrett's article from this time offers a glimpse of the chutzpah and seriousness that helped the team prevail:

> Many folk have asked me how I felt on the platform in an interracial debate. Many have inquired if I were afraid. This is rather amusing. After a debater has thoroughly prepared himself for several months in debate work, after he has weighed all the pros and cons and mastered the art of delivery and refutation, there is nothing to fear.

Coach Tolson built on the triumph over USC to achieve an extraordinary record: under his direction, the Wiley debaters won seventy-four out of seventy-five debates. James Farmer went on to captain the varsity debate team, then to become one of the most prominent civil rights leaders of his generation. In this latter capacity, he used his skills in debate to spectacular effect. There was only one person who could ever rival him in an argument: Malcolm X.

• • •

At the house by the rice fields, I worked the Australian team harder than might have been wise. The kids—Arth, Zoe, Jack, Isy, Daniel—woke up at eight o'clock and were in their first prep by nine. They debated in the afternoon, then again in the evening. In between, I ran strategy sessions and reviewed their research. The truth was that World Schools was becoming more competitive every year. Whereas the competition had once been a round-robin for a handful of wealthy, English-speaking nations, the field was now more open. I reminded the team that ascendant countries, such as India and China, worked their debaters into the morning.

But on the second-to-last day of boot camp, when I detected genuine anger creeping into my voice while chastising the team for the weakness of their substantive arguments, I called an early time-out. The kids elected that afternoon to visit the Mandala Suci Wenara Wana, a sanctuary for the Balinese long-tailed macaque. I mostly hung back as the team communed with their fellow primates, but when I spotted two of the kids at the foot of a moss-covered shrine, asking for good luck at the world championships, I nearly burst into tears.

The rhythms of a tournament were different for a coach than for a competitor. Whereas the debater structured his or her day around a series of sprints—one round in the morning, another in the afternoon—the coach endured the slow burn of thinking about the competition as a whole. There was not a lot we coaches could do, once the competition got going. So we obsessed over the few things that were within our control. We weighed up each piece of feedback, agonized over the lineup (who would speak, and in what order), rehearsed nodding for our side and glowering at the opposition. Even then, one sensed that, in the main, the die was already cast.

I shared a room at the tournament hotel with Fanele. For the first few days of the tournament, I felt an unspoken distance between us. Our teams had been scheduled to meet in the fifth preliminary round. It was only after this debate was over—and Australia had prevailed—that my relationship with Fanele thawed and our conversations regained their sparkling quality. I was somewhat ashamed by this glimpse into my capacity for pettiness, but mostly I was glad to have my best friend back.

Every debate tournament has a bellwether round, a matchup that intimates a team's chances of winning the competition. For us that was the eighth preliminary round, against South Africa. The South Africans were formidable. They debated clean and shared our antipodean sense of humor but also had the capacity to steal the stage with displays of flair and earnestness. "Treat this as the finals," I told the team on a balcony next to the venue. "Don't let them get close, not for a minute of the round. This is a chance to make your intentions known."

The motion was "This house believes that states should be able to prioritize asylum seekers on the basis of cultural similarity with the existing population," and we were on the negative side. I had arranged our lineup the previous night. Arth would lead the offense, stunning the opposition with his natural gravitas. Then Daniel, a more personable speaker, would consolidate our positive arguments. Jack would use his quick wits and salesmanship to showcase our best material while skewering the other side. The team enacted the plan to a tee. They spoke with such passion and immediacy that, for long periods, the audience of Indonesian schoolchildren were wide-eyed, their mouths agape. Australia won 3–0.

When the team went on to beat Greece, 4–1, in the next day's octofinals, I let myself dream. There was in my ambition for the team an aspect of vanity. To win the world championships three times—as a high school and university debater, then again as coach—was to achieve the EGOT (Emmy, Grammy, Oscar, Tony) of our world. I had coached the United Arab Emirates team to the quarterfinals and the previous year's Australian team to the semifinals. The progression seemed promising. When the tournament organizers announced that our opponents in the quarterfinals would be South Africa, I warned the team against complacency but made no real effort to conceal my glee. "We have their measure," I told them. "So look sharp and have fun."

The first warning sign came before the start of the quarterfinal debate. "Prep was crap!" exclaimed Isy. I was bewildered but, for the benefit of the judges who were within earshot, made a point of shouting back, "I'm sure it was just fine. You always say that." Zoe, the other alternate, came to my aid: "Yeah, it was actually *pretty good*!" Once this sad pantomime was done, I glanced at the front of the room. Our three speakers were ashen-faced, scrawling on their pads in unintelligible script.

"That we should impose additional taxes on employers who use automation to replace human workers" was the topic, and we were on the negative side, with the same lineup as last time. Everything that could have gone wrong did. The speakers spent far too much time on rebuttal and left the substantive case underdeveloped. As the debate spun out of control, their manner began to swerve between bombast and sheepishness. An off-color joke added a scandalous touch to the proceedings. Somehow, we managed to pick up a judge. But we lost four others and were eliminated from the competition on a 4–1 decision.

I managed to keep smiling on the bus back to the hotel, even as my stock of canned consolations—"There's always next year," "Getting to the quarters is no mean feat"—began to run low. In truth the kids seemed to be handling the loss far better than I, and this made things feel worse. At the hotel, I made another effort to reassure the team, then excused myself for a couple of hours. I opened the door to my room, crawled into bed, and lay there immobilized by a pain that was worse than anything I had experienced as a competitor.

Fanele did not return to the room in the afternoon because his team, the U.S. national team, had progressed to the semifinals. Yet even in his absence, I could hear his voice, conspiratorial and glistening with thought. Fanele used to say to me that debate was an education in losing. Every single debater lost more tournaments than they won. Most of them had the experience, weekly, of seeing their ideas demolished before a live audience. He used the word *stew*—as a noun ("Are you still in the stew?") and a verb ("I'm stewing")—to describe that sticky, self-pitying feeling that set in after a loss and lingered for hours, sometimes days.

Over the years, Fanele and I had come to see that the stew, for all its unpleasantness, had its uses. The stew made hard lessons stick, strengthened our resolve to improve, and brought us closer as teammates. What's more, repeated exposure to the feeling of being in error made us more humble. For debaters, the idea that we could be wrong, and that even our most cherished opinions could be flawed, was no abstract notion: it conformed to our experience.

I believed in the value of the stew but nonetheless felt relieved that Fanele was not in the room to remind me. For his team was still in the competition and mine was not.

By the time I woke up, the sun had gone down. I got dressed in the same shirt that I had worn to the quarterfinals, then discarded it on the floor of my room. The text message from the team read, "Gone swimming." At the hotel pool, I saw the team hanging out with a group that included some of the South Africans from the afternoon debate. I cornered one of our team members and asked, "No hard feelings? Really?" He responded, "The score is one-all."

One common criticism of debate is that it is too adversarial. The linguist Deborah Tannen famously decried what she described as an "argument culture," which prized debate over dialogue and thus blanketed society in an "atmosphere of unrelenting contention." Such a culture, she wrote, evinced agonism, or a tendency to "take a warlike stance in contexts that are not literally war." This last point seemed to me especially on the nose. As a debater and even as a coach, I had been guilty of appropriating the language of combat—"Crush them" or "Demolish their case"—to stir the passions before an important round. In these moments, I was not so far from those demagogue politicians and cable television hosts whom I regarded with disdain.

But watching these kids on the night of our defeat, I saw another aspect of debate. The activity taught us that our adversaries might be defeated but they would never be vanquished—not only would they return in days or weeks to hash out another disagreement, but they would be waiting for you at the damn swimming pool. As a competitor, one's goal was to get runs on the board. For this, a warlike mind-set of destroying an opponent by any available means was unsustainable. In the long run, one needed the goodwill of the other side and the protection of well-established rules to be able to keep playing the game. Debate taught us these truths, which in our daily contests of politics, commerce, and personality were too easily forgotten.

The word *agonism* derives from the ancient Greek word *agon*, which means struggle and conflict but refers most directly to an athletic contest (as in Olympiakoi agones, or the Olympic games). For me, this seemed a better way to understand debate—not as war but as a recurring contest or game, in which losing is inevitable, winning is impermanent, and wisdom lies in responding to both with a measure of grace.

. . .

James Farmer never said much about the first time he debated Malcolm X. The year was 1961, and the pair—Farmer, now forty-one, and Malcolm, thirty-six—met for a one-hour radio debate on Barry Gray's show. "I had underestimated him," Farmer wrote in his memoirs. "I was saved, perhaps, by a booming voice and speed of delivery as we fought for the microphone, but I must confess to being surprised by his quickness and sharpness of repartee." The round gave the old Wiley debater a new resolve: to never again misjudge his opponent.

When the pair met again the next year at Cornell University, Farmer thought he had his opponent's measure. He failed to persuade the organizers to let him speak after his opponent and thus have the last word on the discussion (Malcolm won this predebate jostle for position), so he devised another plan. Farmer figured that his opponent was stronger on diagnosing the problem than on proposing solutions. He opened the round with a searing indictment of racism, then turned to his rival: "Brother Malcolm, don't you tell us any more about the disease. That is clear in our minds. Now, tell us, physician, what is thy cure?"

His strategy had the intended effect. Malcolm X was slow to rise to the microphone and gave the impression of a man "searching for a speech." He regained his footing in rebuttal, arguing that despite the "support of the Senate, Congress, President, and the Supreme Court," integrationists had failed to desegregate the country. But it was too late. Farmer had focused the audience's attention on Malcolm's proposal. "Mr. X, you have not told us what the solution is except that it is separation, in your view. You have not spelled it out."

The two men debated several more times over the next four years. Perhaps the best of these rounds was in 1963 on a panel for PBS's *The Open Mind*. Seated across a narrow table from each other in a darkened studio, each of them cut a distinctive figure. Whereas Malcolm X shifted from one dramatic, angular pose to another, Farmer maintained his perfect posture.

For almost ninety minutes they debated. Each side had better and worse moments, but most of the exchanges were so even that it was hard to say who had won. What was clear was that both men understood each other enough to refute, revise, and adapt the other person's ideas and words:

MALCOLM X: The only time the black man in this country has made any progress in this country is wartime. When the white man has his back to the wall, then he lets the black man come forward a little bit....
It'll take another war for the black man to take any more steps in the right direction.

FARMER: Minister Malcolm.

MALCOLM X: I didn't cut you off when you spoke for fifteen minutes.

FARMER: You tried.

MALCOLM X: Moderator wouldn't let me.

[...]

FARMER: You say that progress is only achieved in wartime. We're in a war now. The war is being waged in the streets of Birmingham, the streets of Greensboro....

If you don't like this war, that's all right. But don't deny this is a war.

MALCOLM X: Is it a gain to go to a theater for a man who hasn't got a job?

FARMER: . . . It's a gain because it's not the theater so much; it's not the cup of coffee at the lunch counter. It's the dignity that a person achieves. . . . If we're not members of the public, then what are we?

MALCOLM X: Why do you have the race problem in this country if we're members of the public? . . . You will never wipe [racism] out with a desegregated theater.

Behind the public spectacle, the relationship between the two rivals was beginning to transform. Some weeks after the PBS debate, Farmer and Malcolm X made a pact to refrain from debating each other in public. They agreed instead to hash out their disagreements at one or the other of their homes. In these meetings the affection on display between the two opponents could give the impression of a "mutual admiration society." Each of them professed, for example, that his wife thought the other was the better debater. But the relationship never lost its competitive edge. Farmer once said that during these arguments he thought, "Come off it, Malcolm, you can't win. You didn't come up under Tolson."

These debates were not the only settings in which Farmer and Malcolm X encountered an opposing perspective. The clash between the mainstream Civil Rights Movement and black nationalism helped define the politics of that era. It is nonetheless striking to reflect on how the two opponents' positions evolved alongside their ongoing conversation.

Malcolm X left the Nation of Islam in March 1964. In the following month, he declared his continued belief in black nationalism and the principle of violence as self-defense. But he also urged African Americans to strategically engage with the electoral process: "It's time now for you and me to become more politically mature and realize what the ballot is for." Meanwhile, Farmer remained steadfast in his commitment to integration but tried to accommodate some aspects of nationalist thought. For example, he advocated in 1965 for a "both-and" approach that combined direct action with a greater focus on community organization.

Remarking on these changes, James Farmer and Malcolm X joked at one of their last meetings that they would soon have swapped political positions. "And we may well have been right," wrote Farmer.

However, the idea of a swap, or even that of movement along two poles, could take us only so far. In my experience, good debates rarely resulted in one side "winning over" the other side. The far more common outcome was a slight adjustment in the beliefs of both parties. These new ideas did not always map onto the binaries of the past—say, less integrationist and more nationalist. They were a synthesis. Both-and. Neither-nor.

In 2006, a professor of organizational behavior, Christina Ting Fong, proposed a link between emotional ambivalence (the simultaneous experience of positive and negative emotions) and creativity (the ability to recognize unusual relationships between concepts). Discussing the results of two experiments, she suggested that ambivalence may signal to people that "they are in an unusual environment, which in turn increases sensitivity to unusual associations." Her con-clusion? There was not sufficient evidence to believe that managers should actively promote emotional ambivalence in the workplace, but there was good reason to take a "more balanced view of potential consequences of mixed emotions."

Debates, and the experience of intellectual ambivalence, tend to work in a similar way. Faced with a genuine challenge to our views, the options are not only to double down or jump ship but to think again—and thus to find a third way. That is the other aspect of debate as a tool of education. The activity teaches people how to keep learning and to learn from one another, if only they could keep the conversation going.

• • •

Two weeks after the end of the tournament in Bali, on August 27, one of the last days of summer, I landed in Beijing and hailed a taxi to Tsinghua University. In the passenger seat of the old Hyundai Elantra, I felt the foreignness of my surroundings hit me from all sides: the smog, the scale and number of gray buildings, the cab driver's growling Beijing accent, and, through it all, the forbidding charisma of the unfamiliar. Then, as the car pulled in to the sprawling, green campus, I knew through its motion that I was near my new home.

The architects drew inspiration from traditional Chinese courtyard houses in their design for Schwarzman College, the residence and teaching facility for our program, but the building's imposing walls, accented with rich-red wood details, put me in mind of a fortress. Our program—comprising fifty Americans, twenty-five Chinese, and forty-five internationals—aimed to serve as a bridge between

China and the United States and, to a lesser extent, the rest of the world. The articulations of its aim ranged from the vague (promote cross-cultural understanding) to the epic (overcome the Thucydides Trap, the proposition that the clash between an emerging power and an incumbent hegemon tends toward war). As I wheeled my bag through the air-conditioned lobby to my room on the third floor, I wondered how this social experiment would turn out.

For the first few months of the program, we, the students, aged in our twenties, approached the task of cultural exchange with stiff professionalism. In class discussions, people spoke with ambassadorial reserve: "As a Chinese, I would say . . ." "Most people in America would say . . ." The more practical portions of the curriculum—a mix of classes in public policy and business administration—framed the ability to work across social and ideological divisions as a professional skill: one of our classes was named "Ambicultural Strategic Management." This put a damper on the quality of the conversation.

This was fine by me. For I had intended these ten months to serve as a break from those things that had possessed me in the rest of my education: competition, self-presentation, and the unsolicited seizure of public platforms. Most weekends I traveled with two friends—an artist from China and a poet from Pakistan—and tried to delay interpretation in favor of experience. The three of us packed light and covered a great distance, through the canals of Suzhou to the mountains of Xinjiang, all the while speaking our own language of affection.

Over the course of my year at Tsinghua, the world changed at a dizzying pace. Three months into the program, as my classmates and I prepared for Christmas dinner, the U.S. declared China a "revisionist power" that sought to challenge American influence, values, and wealth. Beijing called this "malicious slander." In February 2018, a short month of intense work on our master's theses, the Chinese president abolished the term limit for his position. Several weeks after that, in March, the United States imposed tariffs on Chinese steel and aluminum, producing a cascade of retaliatory actions that was named a trade war.

Meanwhile, the community within Schwarzman College was changing, too. In shared living rooms and bars around the city, people formed friendships and dove—with caution, then abandon—into romance. They reaped the complicated rewards of intimacy.

Then, as our inner and outer worlds transformed, my classmates and I began to speak to one another in an unfamiliar tone. Whereas before our classrooms and common spaces had been filled with passionate recitations—hard on the consonants and long on the vowels— or plodding diplomatese, now they echoed a quieter sound. People spoke for themselves instead of some collective. Their speech was speckled with doubts and open questions. Sometimes pauses took over entire sentences, then conversations.

In such moments, I felt I was listening to the sound of people engaged in genuine education. This was less the preening, defensive noise of assertion than the tender voice of receptiveness, one that proceeds on the confidence that one will receive a fair hearing and that disclosure will beget the rewards of a richer conversation. Debate—and its lessons in losing—could help people access that voice, but the activity could surely benefit from it, too.

From the time I had arrived in China, local debaters had been inviting me to come speak at tournaments and training sessions. I had sent my apologies with a note explaining that my debate days were behind me. Then, toward the end of the academic year, in April, I accepted a couple of these invitations—partly as a response to their persistence and partly out of curiosity.

On a gorgeous Saturday afternoon, while cycling to a local university to judge a small tournament for middle and high school students, I wondered about the rounds that awaited me.

In the debate world, China had been competing on the global stage for years without extraordinary success. The same was true of most Asian countries, with a handful of exceptions such as Singapore and Malaysia. This was owing in large part to language barriers and the incumbency enjoyed by Western, English-speaking countries. I also thought the more rigid, top-down education systems in Asia—which I had experienced as a child in Seoul and more recently in Beijing—shared a portion of the blame.

What I saw at the tournament exceeded my every expectation and made me believe that a great pipeline of talent was at work. The kids, aged between fifteen and eighteen, spoke fluently the language of debate. They defended their side of the motion with passion, creating the rare feeling: that something was at stake. What was more, the students seemed to possess a natural sense that theirs was not the only perspective on an argument or issue—and that they would have to overcome doubts and objections to win over the audience. This element of circumspection made me wonder if our single-mindedness in disputes was a bad lesson we adults had to unlearn.

I envied these kids. They stood exactly where I had been thirteen years earlier—on the cusp of a steep learning curve—and so much remained ahead of them. Cycling back to Tsinghua at dusk, through narrow channels between the Beijing traffic, I wondered what would happen to these students, such interesting minds. Some of the kids aspired to international careers, but most of them said they wanted to stay at home.

As I parked my bike near the gates of Schwarzman College, I wished for these kids every opportunity to use their debate training—to use their knowledge, skills, and motivation to persuade others; to win and lose with grace; to embrace ambivalence. I also hoped that, for our sake, democratic societies would commit to this education, so that when the time comes to defend our values in a debate on the global stage, we may have a chance.

8

RELATIONSHIPS

How to fight and stay together

The handsome redbrick duplex on Kissing Point Road had come on the market in April 2009 as a result of the previous owners' messy divorce. When my parents and I arrived to tour the property on a clear autumn morning, the real estate agent told us we had stumbled on an "opportunity." Inside, the air was stale and acrid. An older woman sat in the dark, purple-walled living room, watching television. Looking around the bedroom, still made for two, I wondered what misery had flowered in this home. Later that night, Mum called the agent and bid the asking price. Then, in less than a month, the three of us got to work making the place our own.

In August 2018, after one year in China and a sum of five years abroad, I returned to Kissing Point Road to a home that looked a little the worse for wear and moved back in with my parents. The garden around the house was overgrown, and the lights in several rooms shone less bright than they should have. After years of living in dormitories maintained by custodial staff, I recoiled at the responsibilities—and tolerance of imperfection—that come with living in a real home.

Mum and Dad had gotten on in years, too. Now on the cusp of their sixties, they spoke openly at dinner about the prospect of retirement. Dad had stopped using hair dye, and his silver mane brought my grandfather to mind. My parents told me they had wept for months after I first left to attend college in 2013. Sitting around the table as a whole family, I could see that some measure of mirth had returned to my parents' faces, but I wondered what had been lost in those months and years.

Against the growing sense of obligation to home and family, I felt mostly impotent. I had envisioned my stay at home as a pit stop en route to life as a young professional—a too-brief period on which the family would look back with fondness. However, no job was forthcoming, and the city's inflated rental prices made moving out unrealistic. In my childhood bedroom, a cozy room that smelled of disuse, I woke up to dusty displays of school prizes and debate trophies. These and more recent preoccupations of distended adolescence—internships, fellowships—were supposed to provide clues about the life ahead. Now their promise seemed to sallow by the day.

Toward the end of my time in Beijing, I had resolved to become a journalist. The decision was based less on calculation than on infatuation with the foreign correspondents I met in China. To one raised to respect authority and seek its approval—first as a migrant, then as a meritocrat—these scribes embodied a spirit of dissent. They dressed badly and hunted for stories. As a career choice this was inconvenient. I had no experience in a newsroom; an industry in decline was not known for its generous hiring drives. Yet the intention, once formed, proved hard to shake.

Mum and Dad never asked me to reconsider my decision. They were steadfast as the chorus of meddlesome friends and relatives grew loud and accusatory. "So what is Bo doing these days?" Without my parents I would have come undone, but even with them I lived in a welter of private doubts. I had turned my nose up at wealthy peers who set aside their life's ambitions for lucrative jobs in consulting and finance. Nowadays I wondered how long such idealism could last and whether it had been misguided from the beginning.

In these months I found myself yearning for some drama—anything to distract from the rhythms of a job search. My wish came true in November, in the form not of an event but of an aftershock.

One year earlier, in August 2017, the Australian government had asked every registered voter a question: "Should the law be changed to allow same-sex couples to marry?" Though the survey was voluntary and nonbinding, the government pledged to respect the people's choice. All we had to do was mark and return our ballot in the postage-paid envelope between September and November.

The postal survey had not been especially well received. LGBT advocates argued that a public campaign would unleash latent hatred in the community. They favored direct legislation for marriage equality. Religious conservatives worried that the process would stoke antireligious sentiment and divide faith-based communities.

However, the conservative prime minister Malcolm Turnbull, a supporter of same-sex marriage, had remained steadfast in his commitment to defer to the people—and their ability to disagree:

Do we think so little of our fellow Australians and our
ability to debate important matters of public interest that
we say, "You're not able to have a respectful discussion
about the definition of marriage, which is a very
significant, important, fundamental element in our law
and culture?" Australians are able and have demonstrated
that they can have a respectful discussion.

In the end, the result had come back in favor of same-sex marriage—
with 63.6 percent of the vote. The campaign had brought out the
best and worst in the nation. In private, many families and communities found constructive ways to disagree, but the public conversation was marred by general antagonism and instances of abuse. Once
the legislation passed in December, and the issue slid from the headlines, most people were glad to consign this period to history.

Now, one year on, new fights loomed on the horizon. Under the
law, religious organizations were not required to perform marriage
ceremonies for same-sex couples. But in some faith-based communities there was growing support for the notion that they should volunteer to do so. In July, the Uniting Church in Australia—Methodists
and Presbyterians—had recognized two separate definitions of marriage, giving ministers the option to endorse same-sex unions. This was
vigorously opposed in some segments of the church, including the
congregation to which my parents belonged.

An effort was now underway to repeal the decision, and congregations were openly discussing the prospect of defection from the
Uniting Church. To gauge community opinion, the minister at my
family church called for a meeting to be held on the second Sunday
in November.

In my experience, outside perceptions of the church tended to swing between two extremes. One held that there were too many disputes within religious organizations, and that these tensions were always on the verge of breaking out into conflict. The other said there were too few disagreements within the church, and that the force of dogma and indoctrination quashed internal dissent.

But neither described the churches where I grew up. It was in Sunday school that I first learned to pose ethical questions and argue about them—"Is lying always wrong?" "Wait, why is God drowning everyone?" Every now and then, the passage itself described an argument. Abraham urged his maker to consider the innocents in Sodom and Gomorrah; Job quarreled with his friends about the problem of suffering. We children understood these stories in different ways and argued over our conclusions. In these moments, church felt like an elaborate book club.

There was also something distinctive about congregations of Korean migrants in Australia. The community rented space from an English-language church and held services during their off-hours. To describe the group only in religious terms would be misleading. The church was a one-stop shop for various forms of care—fresh food, free childcare, emotional support, financial advice—and to one another the congregants were also friends, coworkers, and neighbors.

Being so tightly knit carried risks. People got close enough to hurt and betray one another, and the gossip could be relentless. But for the most part the community flourished. Though I had strayed away from religion in high school and college, the congregation had remained for me a paragon of community.

So there were good reasons to be optimistic about the upcoming forum on same-sex marriage. The congregants knew how to disagree with one another. They had a great deal in common. There were no bullies or villains. Plus, as a result of similar debates in other churches, a certain theology of good disagreement had entered the mainstream. The archbishop of Canterbury, Justin Welby, told his church in 2015: "The plumb line doesn't judge disagreement. But it does hold me and each of us to account for how we disagree.... Untidiness in relationships is normal, not fearful: it expresses the richness of who we are." If ever good disagreement was within our reach, it was now.

What, then, could explain this sinking feeling in my stomach?

• • •

In the week leading up to the discussion at church, my parents and I did not talk much. At home we were quarreling more and more. Some of the fights centered on important topics. For example, I had been urging my parents to downsize their home and move into an apartment closer to town—two prospects that made them recoil. However, the worst and most consuming disagreements seemed to concern trivial matters: chores, loose words, failures of situation. Such disputes began small, then grew in proportion to what we fed them.

To their credit, my parents never gave one inch. Dad was a former officer in the Korean military whose many qualities—pride, generosity, discipline—seemed to have a common root: an abiding belief in something he called "dignity." Mum had been raised by a feminist father who read her *The Second Sex* in translation and urged her to put career before marriage. Neither was the type to take any nonsense from their only son.

There was a similar dynamic among my friends. Most of them

were already a year or two into their careers, and had long-term partners waiting for them in swell rental properties. I felt like an overgrown child around them. I had spent the past five years overseas, mostly reading, and to what end? For this and other reasons, I took to heart loose barbs and careless comments—by-products of banter among friends—and instigated arguments about anything I could get my hands on, from politics to petty personal grievances. My friends gave me no false consolation or indulgence. Each of us had the others' measures, and we always gave as good as we got.

The manufacturers of the laundry detergent Finish once commissioned a study of the state of dishwashing in the United States. The survey found that six out of ten respondents experienced stress while doing the dishes, and that three quarters of them prerinsed their dishes. But the most interesting set of findings concerned household disputes. The average household reported having 217 arguments related to dishwashing in a year, or 18 arguments per month. They mostly argued about who should empty the dishwasher but also fought over dishes that had been left to soak in the sink.

These results seemed to underline two things people implicitly understood about disputes:

1. Some of our most persistent disagreements are with those with whom we are closest.

2. They are waged over trivial matters.

Both phenomena were strange. In the literature on negotiations, few pieces of advice recurred more frequently than *find common ground*. Even if the shared attribute was trivial—"Hey, we're both human" or "Both our cultures eat hummus"—its recognition could reorient people's approach to disagreements, or so the experts said. Another tip was to break down a large disagreement into smaller parts. This way one could reduce the stakes of the discussion and ensure that each dispute was a manageable size.

But disagreements in our private lives seemed impervious to such hacks. One did not need to find commonality or connect on a personal level with friends or families or lovers—that was the premise of the relationship. Nor did it seem especially useful to break down an argument over chores—could there be a simpler issue? In fact, the combination of intimacy and low stakes often made disputes harder to resolve.

When I argued with my parents over trivia, I could afford to be careless. And so I was. Home gave me the self-assurance to set aside a decade of training in debate—and to think less hard about what I said and how I said it. This was generally good for everyone's sanity. But it also led to mistakes, misunderstandings, and mistreatment. In such disputes, I also had a high degree of confidence that I would be able to resolve the disagreement quickly and in my favor. So I became inconsiderate and quick to anger when the other side refused to yield. How could such conditions *not* result in a shouting match?

Herein lay the tragedy of the Dirty Dish Dispute: if one loved the other person less, or had disagreed on a more pressing matter, the argument might not have been so painful.

Another way to understand the unique challenges of personal disagreements was through the RISA checklist. The background conditions for good disagreement are hard to secure, but especially (and perversely) so in the relationships that matter most:

Unreal: Misunderstandings are rife in personal relationships. It is hard to listen and easier to presume. This is partly due to the certainty that comes with greater knowledge of the other person, but also to the romantic notion that we should understand our intimates implicitly—perhaps better than they understand themselves. The result? We fight over a misunderstanding until we stumble into a genuine disagreement.

Unimportant: Minor disagreements take on an exaggerated importance in intimate relationships. We expect our loved ones to agree with us, even to be like us, and we get upset when those hopes are dashed. We also read into trivial disputes all kinds of signs—about mutual compatibility, relationship strength, and our status in the mind of the other person. So molehills start to look like mountains.

Unspecific: Personal disagreements tend to have few natural limits. We are so entangled with the other person that any single dispute unfolds against the background of a thousand others—say, that other time your partner did a similar thing. As soon as we start expanding the scope of the disagreement, we risk making it irresolvable.

Unaligned: People quarrel with their loved ones for complicated reasons. Some of these are unrelated to the issue at hand. We argue to cause pain, signal our unhappiness, and test whether the other person still cares about us. This makes it harder to ensure that the two sides' motivations are aligned.

What seemed clear was that argumentative skills would not save me. In fact, whenever I gained an advantage in these personal disputes,

I found myself on the losing end of this devastating barb: "Don't debate me." Instead, the problem was that I had gotten as far as I could arguing passionately for my interests—and fallen short.

This seemed to me an urgent problem. The poisonous dynamics of Dirty Dish Disputes did not just apply to relationships with family and friends. They drove spats with lovers, rows with neighbors, conflicts within like-minded groups such as sports clubs, school boards, and religious congregations. In these settings, disagreements reached extremes of ugliness and consequence.

When I was a child, Mum would read me Aesop's fables. One story began with two goats meeting on either side of a narrow bridge over a valley. Each trod carefully across the panels, knowing that a fall would be fatal. But when the goats met in the middle, they were both too proud to step aside. So they locked horns and eventually fell to their deaths. In some versions of the story, the two goats were friends; in others, they were kin.

· · ·

That Sunday at church, lunch was miyuk guk, a seaweed soup with garlic and slices of beef. It was served with rice and massive plates of kimchi that were placed at regular intervals along the communal tables. The family responsible for this week's meal had made everything in excess, as was customary, and had packed the leftovers for young families and students to take home. Conversation was breezy and the hot soup made people moan "Ahh!"

People started filing into the main hall around 2:00 p.m. They carried over facial expressions from whatever they had been doing before; some were smiling, others were working things out. Parents told the children to go play for a while. The pastor, a quiet man with the work ethic of a farmer, was already seated. He opened the meeting with a prayer for wisdom.

In the beginning the conversation was stilted. Senior members of the community outlined the facts of this "difficult situation." The mood in the room was not unpleasant but was draining, in the manner of treading water. That the hour would pass without a single interesting development, rendering this a failed but harmless experiment, seemed entirely possible.

Then an older woman near the front of the room raised her hand. She was a quiet and conscientious member of the community—one whose faith had been cultivated through periods of undisclosed suffering. By this time most people had let their minds wander far enough to miss this subtle gesture, and its intimation of purpose.

"Scripture is clear on this point," she said. "Why are we even discussing this question?"

Her voice wavered. The words themselves were audible, but the meaning of the sentence was ambiguous—suspended between a joke, an indictment, and a plea. Yet as she continued, she seemed to discover a new resolve. The intention, once formed, ran through the rest of her speech like an iron rod. It steadied each syllable and imparted to them a trace of metal.

"The purpose of a church is to uphold the faith. That means saying yes to what is right and no to what is wrong. If we bend to fashions, we lose our integrity."

For a while the room was quiet. The speaker slumped back in her chair and seemed suddenly fragile. Those who had been waiting for their turn hesitated; a young parent slipped out of the room to check on a child. Then something broke. The next few speeches were flecked with unreasonable anger and an earnestness that teetered on the verge of tears. Time between contributions shrank. Time between words shrank. Soon the room was abuzz on every register of sound.

The arguments raised were various, and they did not always intersect. Dad spoke in favor of recognizing same-sex marriage. His argument was framed in bureaucratic terms. He talked less about scripture and ethics than about strategy and process—how to maintain good relations with the synod. But from a country boy raised in a conservative postwar family, this was a radical intervention. The person who spoke after him made an entirely separate point; and so did the person after. So the unresolved disagreements began to pile up and fester.

Even moments of genuine contact released their own kinds of poison. In response to one person's argument that opposition to same-sex marriage would confirm public perceptions about the church as an outdated institution, another said: "That's ridiculous nonsense." But what was ridiculous? The conclusion or the reasoning or the area of concern or the person raising the point? All of the above or none of them? Such ambiguity, left to linger, could spoil the air.

· · ·

In 2010, cognitive scientists Hugo Mercier and Dan Sperber caused a ruckus with an unusual answer to the question "Why do humans reason?" They argued that reasoning had evolved not to help people discern truth and make better judgments but rather to win arguments. "[Reasoning] was a purely social phenomenon. It evolved to help us convince others and to be careful when others try to convince us," Mercier told *The New York Times*. Under this view, supposed flaws in our reasoning, such as confirmation bias, were not bugs but features. They might not get us closer to the truth, but they helped us make arguments. The name of Mercier and Sperber's thesis? The Argumentative Theory of Reasoning.

I had no idea whether this was correct as a theory of evolutionary psychology. But I saw at church how the desire to win an argument could *become* all-consuming—how it overtook the impulse to seek truth and show mercy to others. Such a competitive drive was dangerous, and nowhere more so than in personal disagreements. It made us forget the most important objective in an argument with our loved ones: to fight and stay together.

The discussion at church wound down after more than an hour to an unedifying close. No decision had been reached, but that could wait. There would be another session at the same time next week. The minister, who had been quiet throughout the discussion, ended the meeting with a prayer and a request: "Thank you for your contributions this afternoon. I ask that you go home and think about your fellow congregants. Try before we meet again to think about things from their perspective."

His instruction reminded me of a technique from competitive debate: Side Switch.

Much of debate is an exercise in certainty. The moment one received a motion, one adopted the mindset of a person who was completely convinced of that point of view. One clung to this feeling of absolute conviction to make arguments, sink objections, and display passion. But there is also a window, between the end of prep and the start of a round, when one invited in the uncertainty:

Side Switch

In the last five minutes before the start of a debate, do
one or more of the following:

Brainstorm: Take out a new piece of paper. Imagine that
you are now on the other side of the motion. Brainstorm
the four best arguments in support of the position.

Stress-test: Review your arguments from the
perspective of an opponent. Think up the strongest
possible objections to each claim and write them in the
margins.

Loss ballot: Imagine that you have won the debate from
the opposing side. Write out the reason why you won,
including the mistakes made by the opposition.

Next steps varied. One could revise an argument to answer possible objections or plan rebuttal against opposing arguments. One
could strategize to block the other side's paths to victory. But the
basic idea was the same: set aside the certainty of one's convictions
and see things from another point of view, all *in order to* improve
one's chances of winning the debate.

Negotiation experts offered their own versions of Side Switch.
Getting to Yes coauthor William Ury dug out this rule from the Middle Ages: "One can speak only after one has repeated what the other
side has said to that person's satisfaction." The conflict scholar Anatol Rapoport urged people, before attacking an opposing argument,
to articulate its "region of validity"—that is, the conditions under

which the point might be true. To a person who insists "Black is white," respond "This is so, if one is interpreting a photographic negative."

But the problem with these tactics was that they maintained a strict separation between us and our opponents. Even in our most generous moment—straining, say, to find how black might be white—we remained apart from the rival position, as (benevolent) critics.

Side Switch was different because it forced us to actually adopt the opposing perspective. This gave us a firsthand experience of the subjective reasonableness of other beliefs. For a time, we felt what it was like to believe ideas that contradicted our own. We traced the steps of how a sensible person (us!) could arrive at conclusions that might otherwise have seemed alien.

From the switched position, we also saw ourselves in another light. We entertained the possibility that we might be the ones in error—that our beliefs were the results of certain choices and assumptions and not others; that we might be the ones who had to be tolerated, accommodated, or stopped; that opposition to us was natural and expected. The Scottish novelist Robert Louis Stevenson, describing the debates of his university years in the 1860s, made these same points with more exuberance:

> Now as the rule stands, you are saddled with the side
> you disapprove, and so you are forced, by regard for your
> own fame, to argue out—to feel with—to elaborate
> completely the case as it stands against yourself; and
> what a fund of wisdom do you not turn up in this idle
> digging of the vineyard! How many new difficulties take
> form before your eyes—how many superannuated

> arguments cripple finally into limbo, under the glance
> of your enforced eclecticism!

Together these aspects of Side Switch pointed to a certain way of thinking about empathy. Whereas most people viewed empathy as a spontaneous psychic connection, or a reflection of virtue, debaters knew it as an understanding achieved through a series of actions. This vision of empathy was unexciting. It called not for goodness or imagination, only paper and pen. But the upside was that it gave us something to do when our other faculties—imagination, virtue, emotion, intuition—had failed. It asked us to get to work precisely when we were stuck.

Of course, we would often misunderstand our opponents. But even then, the point of Side Switch was not to prejudge the other side, nor to excuse ourselves from listening to them. It was to unsettle us from complacency, so that we might engage with more openness and perspective.

In the *Pensées,* Blaise Pascal answered a question that has long bedeviled nonbelievers: What if one cannot bring oneself to believe in God? "Follow the way by which [others] began; by acting as if they believed, taking the holy water, having masses said." Faith, in other words, was less the precondition of religious practice than its consequence. Side Switch promised that empathy worked the same way: it arose out of ritualistic action. One needed only to follow the steps and let the rest follow.

The experience of seeing the world simultaneously through our eyes and those of another person was confusing, unsettling, enervating. It was also not the worst description of love.

In the days after the church forum, I used Side Switch on persistent arguments with my parents. I brainstormed the best case for thinking more seriously about dating and scrutinized my reasons for urging them to downsize their home. This helped to some extent. I was more patient and circumspect; I could understand where they were coming from. But as the conversation continued, this reservoir of reasonableness began to deplete. So I fell back into the dull and familiar grooves of bad argument.

Part of the issue seemed to be that Side Switch was short, whereas disagreements were long. The technique helped unsettle our assumptions and disrupt the cycle of bad argument—in the manner of a reset. But even as Side Switch pulled us away from our own perspective, powerful forces—pride, fear, identity—pushed in the opposite direction. Besides, in the heat of a dispute, cognitive dissonance was too much to handle. It was hard enough to advocate for oneself without also keeping the other side in mind.

Here again I realized that debate had something to teach me. Side Switch was one instantiation of a broader principle: that we should consider and even try on positions that are antithetical to our own. This idea not only recurred in competitive debate but was built into its structure.

In debate, one's personal views had no bearing on what one argued. The ways of assigning positions varied—coin toss, rock paper scissors, draw from a hat—but were invariably random. This had comic results. Debate might be the only setting in the world where a committed Marxist defends Amazon and a prolife advocate makes the case for stem cell research. Recordings of the Oxford Union debates came with the immortal disclaimer "The speaker in this video is a competitive debater, and therefore the views expressed may not necessarily represent their beliefs."

Some debate circuits actually required competitors to debate each motion from both sides—to affirm one week, then negate the following week. But even without this requirement, with enough time one argued both sides of most issues, and saw one's opponents do the same.

This aspect of debate has attracted serious criticism. Looking back on his university years, between 1876 and 1880, Theodore Roosevelt wrote that one thing he did not regret was avoiding the debate team. "Personally I have not the slightest sympathy with debating contests in which each side is arbitrarily assigned a given position," he wrote. "What we need is to turn out of our colleges young men with ardent convictions on the side of the right; not young men who can make a good argument for either right or wrong as their interest bids them."

Roosevelt's words rose back into the public consciousness during the Cold War. In 1954, the motion on the American college debate circuit was that the United States should extend diplomatic recognition to the communist government of China. The prospect of arguing against the policy of containment outraged some debaters and coaches. In fact, the U.S. Naval Academy (Annapolis) and Military Academy (West Point) banned students from partaking in the competition altogether, with the latter saying that "national policy has already been established."

The case raised a few hairy questions—about free speech, military codes, democratic citizenship. But it also thrust onto a national platform the ethics of competitive debate, including its insistence that debaters argue both sides of every issue. In an oft-cited article, professor and former debate coach Richard Murphy argued that public speech should be sincere. That is, a debater should figure out what he or she really believes and stick to that position. He borrowed this Rooseveltian line from the debate coach Brooks Quimby: "Our democracy needs men and women of principle . . . rather than men and women trained to take either side at the flip of a coin."

I found this argument persuasive. There came a time in the life of every debater—a quiet moment between rounds—when one wondered what one truly believed. For a bright young person trained to find the argument for any position, such introspection could be unsettling. The question seemed to call for a different set of skills than those at hand—not intelligence but judgment; not charisma but candor; not speed but consideration.

Besides, one saw the effects of this mercenary ethic in the public sphere. Silver-tongued politicians made an art of bending with the prevailing winds. Unscrupulous ad agencies honed the message of tobacco companies. If insincerity was ugly in politics and commerce, it was intolerable in our private lives. The idea that we could be embroiled in an argument with someone who did not believe what they were saying (rightly) drove us up the wall. This was trolling, the antithesis of good faith.

Most debaters never quite outgrew this concern. The novelist Sally Rooney wrote of her time on the university circuit, "I no longer found it fun to think of ways in which capitalism benefits the poor, or things oppressed people should do about their oppression. Actually I found it depressing and vaguely immoral." At various times in my debate career, I had felt the same pangs of apprehension.

So why, then, had I stuck around?

The answer lay inside the debate room. Before the start of a round, everyone—competitors and spectators—understood the conceit of the exercise. Those fifteen-year-olds did not really have strong opinions on the Iranian nuclear program. They were players in a game that for some bizarre reason required them to maintain that ruse.

But as the debate got underway, such awareness began to dissipate. At some point, we stopped noticing altogether that these were teenagers making arguments about nuclear disarmament. We just listened to the arguments about nuclear disarmament. Did that mean we no longer knew the speakers before us were teenagers? No. It was instead that we stopped caring so much about the nexus between the argument and the speaker's identity. As at a theater performance, our suspension of disbelief was willing.

Divorcing ideas from identity—the what from the who—was fraught. In some settings, such as courtrooms, it was obviously untenable. But in the debate room, it had three positive effects. First, the divorce gave speakers room to experiment. Free from the burden of being true to ourselves, we could flirt promiscuously with new ideas and ways of presenting ourselves. The conventional values of authenticity and consistency gave way to virtues such as adaptability and inventiveness.

Second, it gave listeners a chance to encounter ideas in a new light. In everyday life, we often used a person's identity as a shortcut for the credibility of their views. For the most part this was fine and efficient. But it also nudged us toward agreeing with people whom we liked and trusted. Debate broke these natural cycles of reinforcement by switching who said what. This gave us an opportunity to reconsider familiar ideas—not least through the experience of seeing an adversary advocate for our actual beliefs.

Third, the divorce gave opponents a better way to disagree. While we debaters took our rivals' case seriously, we seldom assumed that an argument was representative of their personality—that it defined or reflected who they were. Even as we shook our heads at the cruelty or stupidity of their ideas, we also whispered, "There but for the grace of God go I," knowing how close we had come to arguing for their position.

In the debate room, the result was a feeling of playfulness. None of us lost our egos—have you met a debater?—but we cut the ties between ego and specific beliefs. We put forward ideas without much regard for consistency with the past and our standing in the future. An important consequence was that it became easier to change our minds. One-eighty reversals were still rare. But many people left the debate room feeling that the issue was complicated; that the other side had some good arguments; that ambivalence could be a considered position.

Did that mean debate, in fact, undermined conviction? I didn't think so, but it did point to a different way of understanding that term. The conventional perspective saw conviction as something we brought into a discussion. An alternative was to view it as something we took out of spirited debate. In short, conviction was less an input than an output. The aim of a disagreement was not to safeguard our prior beliefs from outside attack but to play and experiment until we stumbled on ideas worthy of our commitment. We did not have to have things worked out in order to get started.

Such open-minded exploration might result in more moderate beliefs. But this was only a problem if one equated strength of conviction with the extremity of its content. Though dogmatic beliefs were seductive and all-consuming, they were also brittle. The more considered positions were cooler in temperature, but they tended to keep. As the University of Iowa debate coach, A. Craig Baird, wrote in 1955, *sound conviction* arose from *mature reflection*, and it was the role of debate to "facilitate the maturing of such reflective thinking and conviction."

Baird could have gone a step further. For the philosopher John Stuart Mill, who worked out many of his ideas with his lover and collaborator, Harriet Taylor, free debate was the *only thing* that could justify any sort of strong conviction. It alone gave us the assurance that our beliefs could have been refuted but were not. Where did Mill get this idea? One person whom he credited was Cicero and his secret to forensic success: "The greatest orator, save one, of antiquity, has left it on record that he always studied his adversary's case with as great, if not with still greater, intensity than even his own."

The most obvious way to harness the power of debate in our daily lives was to, well, debate. Though the prospect of formal rounds with random positions seemed awkward, it was starting to get some traction in workplaces. The investor Warren Buffett once floated the idea of hiring two advisers on any potential acquisition. One would advocate for the deal, while the other would oppose, and the winner would receive "say, 10 times a token sum paid to the loser." Even the U.S. intelligence community had embraced aspects of the idea. In the aftermath of the catastrophic intelligence failures of the early 2000s, the group sought to diversify viewpoints within its organization by, among other things, commissioning outside experts "to examine an alternative view or approach to an issue; to argue the pros and cons to a judgment involving uncertainty, ambiguity, or debate."

But we need not stage an entire debate to reap some of these benefits. In disagreements with my parents, the most surprising moments were those when they went off script: "I guess you might respond to that by saying . . ." or "But then again . . . ," Mum might begin, before proceeding to rebut her own ideas. This would prompt me to awkwardly defend her original claim, leading us to switch positions for a moment. "To play devil's advocate . . ." or "Just for the sake of argument . . . ," Dad might say to signal that he was not yet committed to a view but wanted to test out an argument.

Each of these gestures opened up a space between our ideas and egos. There, we could test and reform our beliefs. It was room in which to play—the rarest thing in high-conflict situations and, perhaps, the most necessary, too.

. . .

Lunch before the second debate at church had the usual hallmarks. In the dining room, a breezy and functional space reminiscent of a gymnasium, young men carried out the tables with studied insouciance; behind them, other adults followed with chairs and baby seats. An assembly line in the kitchen sent steaming plates of rice and soup to the pass-through, where another group stood ready to receive them. The older people gave instructions to the children as they laid out cutlery on the table.

No one at lunch discussed the upcoming meeting or the one from the previous week. People talked about the usual things—children, politics, work—and laughed at one another's jokes. But as lunch wound down, a realization seemed to blanket the room. Everyone appeared to be occupied with conversation and food, but their eyes revealed that their minds were elsewhere.

This time people did not amble into the room. Like jurors, they filed in with grim purpose. The minister prayed again for wisdom and kindness. He was a stoic man, but one wondered with every pause or stray syllable whether that was fear creeping into his voice.

The discussion was more substantial than the last one. No time was lost on platitudes. People understood one another's claims and responded directly to them; on the whole, the group had more things to say. In some respects, this made the debate more challenging. It revealed the differences between people and placed claims in contradiction with one another. There was simply a larger number of ideas—spanning theology, politics, personality—on which people could disagree. Soon tempers flared. Dad even left the room at one point to register a protest.

But in other respects the conversation was an improvement. No longer surprised by the mere existence of the disagreement, people arrived expecting a spirited argument. The speakers made few, if any, real concessions, but they acknowledged the points on which listeners might disagree and sought to preempt their concerns. There was even talk of a "middle ground" and "accommodations."

In the end, the group arrived at a rough consensus. Some people vigorously opposed the outcome, and many loose ends remained. As a competitive debater, I had been accustomed to rounds ending with one of two clear results: affirmative or negative. Ours had been a winner-take-all kind of game. So a partial and factious conclusion like this one was hard to stomach. However, the minister did not schedule another session. He prayed instead for the community and sent everyone on their way.

The meaning of this outcome became clear to me only several days later when I stumbled on an old memory. In January 2012, as part of a debate trip to South Africa, I had visited Robben Island. The place had been used as a prison since the end of the seventeenth century. But it was now best known as the jail that, starting in the 1960s, had housed opponents of the apartheid regime. To get there one had to take a forty-minute ferry ride. To board the ferry one passed through a gateway named after an inmate who had spent eighteen years on the island: Nelson Mandela.

Between the tour of Mandela's cell and the quarry where the prisoners would break limestone, the museum staff had prepared a video presentation. "I heard you are debaters," our guide said. "Did you know that Madiba was a debater? The prisoners on this island argued all day—about politics, philosophy, the future of this country. It was good practice."

In the video dated April 14, 1994, ten days before South Africa's first democratic election, Nelson Mandela prepared to debate the president of the apartheid government, F. W. de Klerk. He would be a formidable opponent: the Afrikaner lawyer was a seasoned and intelligent speaker. Mandela himself was a practiced debater, but his advisers worried that his equanimity would come across on television as passivity or lethargy.

The real difficulty of the task before Mandela, however, was not winning the debate. He was all but guaranteed to win the election. But de Klerk and his constituents, on account of their wealth and status, would have to play an important part in the country's reconstruction. So the two sides would have to make the transition overnight from opponents to partners.

Mandela's advisers must have been relieved. The candidate's performance was spirited and winning. As the challenger, Mandela pressed his case against de Klerk with prosecutorial zeal. He began his concluding remarks with such harsh criticism—"Where is their plan? With whom was it discussed?"—that some members of the audience groaned.

But then, within the space of one sentence, Mandela changed tack. "We are saying let us work together for reconciliation and nation building," he said. Then the candidate reached out his left hand and held, for a moment, his opponent's right hand. "I am proud to hold your hand. . . . Let us work together to end division and suspicion." The chapter on the 1994 debate in Mandela's autobiography ends: "Mr. de Klerk seemed surprised, but pleased."

Debate, however fierce, did not exclude the other ways we should respond to people with whom we disagree—among them negotiation, alliance building, and forgiveness. In fact, it could make these other interactions more durable and meaningful. What negotiated settlement or alliance could last, for example, without at least one thorough and critical exchange of views?

Yet for debate to serve such a positive role, it had to know its place. This seemed to me the last thing to remember about personal disagreements: we had to let arguments lapse and, on occasion, forgo them altogether in favor of other ways of working through our differences. Just as there was no additional barb in Mandela's remarks, there was no third forum at church, because debate had already served its role. Now the work of reconciliation and compromise had to begin.

◦ ◦ ◦

Near the end of November I got ready to start a new job. I had been offered, at the conclusion of a long recruitment process, a role as a cadet reporter at the nation's business daily, *The Australian Financial*

Review. The pay amounted to not much more than the minimum wage, but I was grateful to have gotten a start.

The night before my first day of work, I cooked dinner for my parents. The gesture was supposed to be a thank-you for the past five months and an apology for that same period. I realized, while accidentally burning some hazelnuts on the stove, that this was a lot of pressure to place on Sunday-night dinner.

While the whole fish roasted in the oven and the green beans blanched in boiling water, I replayed in my mind these months back at home. It had been an underwhelming start to adult life. The number of days for which I could not account was depressing. One could not imagine this time described in the "Where Are They Now?" feature of alumni magazines, let alone in a CV.

However, I had learned some things. Living with my parents reminded me that one could not avoid conflicts in personal relationships. To make a habit of argument aversion was to forever hold one's tongue or to hold people at arm's length. I had also learned that disagreements were at their best as discrete events rather than a permanent state of being. It was through the act of bringing our differences to a head that we exerted some control over them. A personal dispute was infinitely messier than a formal debate. One was life; the other was a game. But aspects of this game could help us navigate real challenges.

I carried the fish to the table, then the beans, the fennel, the potatoes, and the wine. Then I asked my parents to come join me. Hoping that tonight we would forgo disagreement in favor of other ways of getting along, I greeted them with two words that fell outside the natural vocabulary of debate: *thanks* and *sorry*.

9

TECHNOLOGY

How to debate in the future

On a Tuesday morning in February 2019, I set down a cup of lukewarm coffee on my desk in the buzzing Sydney bureau of the *Financial Review,* then went to the editors to pitch a story. It was a tough sell—an event in San Francisco with throngs of media stationed on the ground—and the editors looked unconvinced. "Shouldn't we run a wire?" one asked. Still at a phase of my career when I mistook instructions for questions, I began, "No, *we* shouldn't . . ."

In a moment of grace, the technology editor gave me a sympathetic hearing. He assigned the word count for a short column. I felt somewhat guilty on the walk back to my desk. I had not been entirely candid with him about my reasons for wanting to cover the event. But what could I have said? That I had to seize this chance to glimpse the future? That I needed to know whether the one thing I did best in the world—debate—could be better done by a machine? Come on.

I had been a reporter for less than three months. The newsroom was, for me, a humbling place. Journalism in Australia had historically been a trade—a vocation that one could enter with a high school education. Here, the many degrees I had spent years accumulating amounted to naught. The subeditors had discovered within days that, beneath the complex sentences and highfalutin language, I really had no idea how to write for a general audience. In my first week, an editor stumbled on me sweating through a stack of documents on rare-earth minerals and yelled, "If you don't know, *pick up the phone!*"

In many ways, I had become enamored of the work. News production was organized chaos. Each day was filled with errors and missed connections and the unrelenting thrum of deadlines, but somehow it ended with the miracle of a finished edition. On their best days, reporters helped inform and frame the public debate. They did so with humble tools: facts and ideas and stories—and words, always words. Plus, the fact that 2019 was an election year added to the work an immediate consequence. Not that I was doing cutting-edge work. For the first couple of months I had struggled to land a story at all, and I had since progressed to the pages near the magazine insert; yet the thrill, however vicarious, was real.

The business itself was obviously embattled. Inasmuch as one could blame the decline of an industry on a single source, the obvious candidate was technology. The loss of print advertising (including car, job, and real estate classifieds) to online rivals cratered revenue; big tech firms profited from news content shared on their platforms without adequately paying the publishers. Then there were the more diffuse harms of fake news, online trolling, and echo chambers, all of which hindered the work.

Technology also posed a more absurd threat to my career. For more than a decade, early adopters had been talking up the potential of artificial intelligence to automate aspects of journalism. The software that had since been deployed—Bloomberg's Cyborg, *The Washington Post*'s Heliograf, and *The Guardian* (Australia)'s ReporterMate—were mostly trained on simple, formulaic stories, such as company earnings and the results of sports games, but one could see the technology progressing.

Some of these things were on my mind as I tuned in, from my desk in Sydney, to the event in San Francisco. The stage at Think—the annual conference of tech company IBM—had been minimally set. Against a pristine backdrop of desktop blue, two lecterns stood at an equal distance from the center. In between was a black obelisk, tall and slick, a kind of enlarged thumb drive or human-sized e-cigarette. Some eight hundred people had gathered in the room for the debate. Many thousands more streamed online. And the debaters? In one corner, Harish Natarajan, a mild-mannered Cambridge graduate and an old rival of mine from the debate circuit (including in the grand final in Thessaloníki). In the other, Project Debater, an artificial intelligence system trained to engage, and possibly defeat, human beings in live argument.

I had heard whispers about Project Debater around the time of its debut, in June 2018, at a closed media event, also in San Francisco. The machine had taken on a couple of Israeli debaters on two separate motions: one about subsidizing space exploration and the other about increasing the use of telemedicine. The journalists in attendance wrote that Debater was "pretty convincing" and that, despite some missteps, the machine "more than held its own." They also remarked on its strong pedigree: IBM's previous grand challenges had resulted in the chess player Deep Blue, which famously beat the then World Champion Garry Kasparov in 1997, and the *Jeopardy!* player Watson, which beat two champions of the game, Brad Rutter and Ken Jennings, in 2011. At its debut, Debater recorded a draw, having been deemed less persuasive than its human opponent on space travel but more persuasive on telemedicine. The scoreboard was live: 1–1.

Despite this, I had not taken Project Debater seriously. Technology reporters tended to be breathless about such developments—but when was the last time I had been able to rely on Siri for anything? Besides, I belonged to a generation of nineties kids who were tech savvy but not of technology. We knew a time when tech was *bad* and had lived through the transition from dial-up to broadband, from Walkman to iPod, from Windows 2000 to XP to Vista. My own model for a debating machine was SmarterChild, a chatbot on AOL whom one could goad into anger, disappointment, and confusion with crude language and non sequiturs.

This morning in February, less than a year after its debut, the machine brought the fight to me. Harish was one of the best and most experienced debaters around. He had beaten me several times on the competitive circuit. So the transitive property gave me skin in the game.

In popular culture, malevolent robots were the silent types. Their muteness revealed a propensity for calculation over consultation; action over explanation. This was a virtue so long as machines remained subordinate to humans. Yet the silence became menacing when the robots made adverse or even homicidal resolutions. In a scene in Stanley Kubrick's *2001: A Space Odyssey*, the murderous AI system HAL 9000 rejects further dialogue:

> David Bowman: HAL, I won't argue with you anymore. Open the doors.
>
> HAL 9000: Dave, this conversation can serve no purpose anymore. Good-bye.

I wondered if a malevolent Project Debater, in the same situation as HAL 9000, would explain in great depth and eloquence its reasons for wanting to do us harm. Then I wondered whether we would be persuaded.

In San Francisco, the longtime host of the Intelligence Squared Debates, John Donvan, introduced the two speakers as the audience of tech geeks and nervous executives came to a reluctant hush. "First, arguing for the resolution tonight will be IBM Project Debater." A band of blue light appeared on the black obelisk. I had not known what Debater looked like and had assumed that it would be rolled onto the stage, so I was surprised to realize that it had been there all along. "Arguing against, representing the rest of us, please welcome to the stage Harish Natarajan." Harish, in a three-piece suit, walked on to some rock music.

The motion was "That we should subsidize preschool," and each side had fifteen minutes to prepare. I could remember those crowded minutes—the scribbling, subvocalizing, and cursing under the breath in search of a case that might not ever materialize. Harish had prepared backstage. The machine had been working in view of the whole world. And when its time came, Project Debater raised its elegant, feminine voice:

> Greetings, Harish. I have heard you hold the world
> record in debate competition wins against humans. But I
> suspect you've never debated a machine. Welcome to the
> future.

. . .

Eight years earlier, in February 2011, an Israeli computer scientist named Noam Slonim and his officemate met at the IBM research facility in Tel Aviv to brainstorm ideas. It had been a matter of weeks since Watson beat two (human) champions in the quiz game *Jeopardy!*. The company leadership was already on the search for the next grand challenge.

In some respects, Slonim fit the profile of a scientist who could lead such a project. He had graduated in 2002 with a PhD in machine learning (ML) from the Hebrew University; his specialty had been the application of ML to textual data—a field that had been integral to Watson's success. However, other aspects of his résumé were less obvious. As a doctoral student, Slonim had moonlighted as cocreator of a short-lived television sitcom called *Puzzle*. He had also spent several years after graduation as a biophysics researcher at Princeton before returning to Israel.

The idea that dawned on Slonim over the hour-long brainstorming session contained the signature of his disparate background. It combined human and machine language, entertainment, and science.

"The challenge: beat human expert debaters in competitive debates that are broadcasted on TV."

The initial proposal fit on a single PowerPoint slide. Slonim and his colleague wrote that the challenge would require "novel powerful methods for data mining, natural language understanding and generation, logical reasoning, intelligence capabilities, and more." Verifying success posed a particular challenge: unlike chess or *Jeopardy!*, disagreements had no objective results. Here, the tradition of competitive debate—with its "clear rules and a clear decision regarding the winner"—provided an answer. In an otherwise understated document, the authors indulged one strong prediction: "Accomplishing this challenge will undoubtedly be considered ground-breaking."

Not far from the research facility in Tel Aviv, a reckoning was underway. Israel borders four sovereign nations: Egypt, Jordan, Lebanon, and Syria. By the end of February, every one of these countries had experienced a mass-scale protest as part of a regional movement against sclerotic and corrupt regimes. The movement came to be known as the Arab Spring—more for the poetry than the seasonal description.

In the breathless coverage of these "prodemocratic" uprisings, the Western media appointed a new hero: technology. Journalists flashed screen grabs of social media pages used by protesters to organize gatherings and share information. They drew connections between a series of damaging disclosures about the Tunisian government on WikiLeaks and the antigovernment protests in that country. The phrase *social media revolution* soon became ubiquitous. In August, at the World Schools Debating Championships in Dundee, the topic was "This House believes that autocracy is doomed in the age of Facebook."

Such optimism lacked neither reason nor context. From its inception, the internet had inspired a healthy strain of utopian thinking. These theories, propagated by web pioneers and amplified in the mainstream media, held up the web as the ultimate commons, where people could meet and coexist without regard for borders or status. The risk, of course, was that such connectivity could lead as often to conflict as to cooperation. But early studies of internet forums marveled at the incidence of civil disagreement—in the words of one author, "the demonstrable faith of some sort in the power of argument and passionate advocacy amidst the flaming and the name-calling." They revived old anarchist notions of emancipation and drew comparisons between the internet and coffeehouses, salons, and public squares.

For founders in Silicon Valley, the currency of these ideas in the early months of the Arab Spring provided a boost in public relations. It made their mission statements seem credible, if not entirely convincing. It lent unicorns a scent of worldliness at a time when they were trying to expand overseas. At the annual G8 summit, French president Nicolas Sarkozy advocated further regulations on tech companies, and Facebook chief executive Mark Zuckerberg cashed in his chips. "People tell me: it's great you played such a big role in the Arab Spring, but it's also kind of scary because you enable all this sharing and collect information on people," he said. "But it's hard to have one without the other. You can't isolate some things you like about the internet, and control other things you don't."

Noam Slonim spent the rest of his year developing and refining the concept of a debating machine. The company leadership kept whittling down potential candidates. Slonim's idea kept progressing through more and more rigorous rounds of selection. At this early stage, the politics of the era was not much on his mind. The main motivation was for him "purely scientific," and the challenge from this perspective was formidable. As Slonim had told his colleague in their first meeting, the research on artificial intelligence and textual data had barely progressed since he had worked in the field eight years earlier: "They attack the same problems. This can go on forever. They can continue to do that for twenty more years, and I think it's boring. We really need to do something that is completely different."

In February 2012, Slonim received a message. Aya Soffer, vice president of AI technologies, asked whether he had heard the news (he had not) and informed him that debate had been selected as the next grand challenge. Slonim thanked Soffer for her support, then paused over her response: "Don't thank me yet . . ."

• • •

Seven years on, I watched this same machine speak in near-perfect sentences at the debate in San Francisco. The makers of Project Debater—a team co-led by Slonim and Ranit Aharonov—had given it two sources of content. One was a database of 400 million newspaper articles, or 10 billion sentences, from which Debater could "mine" claims and evidence. The other was a compendium of commonly occurring arguments, examples, quotes, analogies, and framing devices—for example, a point about the emergence of a black market applied to many debates about prohibition of goods and services.

Project Debater began by drawing on the latter. The machine

framed the debate in broad terms: "In the current status quo, we accept that the question of subsidies goes beyond money and touches on social, political, and moral issues." Then it proceeded on to a passable, if vague, principled argument: "When we subsidize preschools and the like, we are making good use of government money, because they carry benefits for society as a whole. It is our duty to support them. Subsidies are an important policy instrument."

None of this came easy. Even for humans, the work—parsing a topic, searching one's memory for relevant information, grouping and ordering ideas, editing the language for delivery—could take a lifetime to master. For a machine, each of these skills had to be coded.

Some ninety seconds into the opening speech, Project Debater revealed its biggest strength: a superhuman ability to marshal evidence. In a one-minute argument about poverty reduction, the machine had referenced the Organisation for Economic Co-operation and Development, the U.S. Centers for Disease Control and Prevention, a National Institute for Early Education Research (U.S.) metastudy spanning 1960 to 2013, and a 1973 speech by the Australian prime minister Gough Whitlam. The presentation felt rushed and confusing, but it was rarely glib.

I wondered how Harish would respond to this barrage of information. In debate, facts could be kryptonite to an ill-informed speaker. The machine had mined from its database no less than six unrelated studies. To quibble with each of these would have been useless. Even if one was immersed in the literature, the rebuttal would have taken a huge amount of time for, at best, a draw. So, what to do?

Harish began with an acknowledgment: "There was a lot of information in that speech, and lots of facts, and lots of figures." He spoke slowly and precisely, as if he were clearing up a misunderstanding. Then he serenely went on the attack. "Project Debater suggests something very intuitive: that if we believe preschools are good in principle, surely it is worth giving money to subsidize those. But I don't think that is ever enough of a justification for subsidies. . . . Because there are multiple things which are good for society." Harish listed health care and tertiary education as other priorities but did not commit to either of them. "My point here is not that all of those things are necessarily better than preschools, but simply that it cannot be, alone, a sufficient argument for Project Debater to claim that there are some benefits."

Then Harish went further. The problem with subsidizing preschool, in particular, was that a bunch of the money would go to middle- and upper-class families, who were most likely to enroll their children. Besides, the subsidy could be too small to make preschool affordable to the poorest families. In this case, the worst-off would be in the perverse position of subsidizing through their taxes a service that they themselves could not afford—"a double exclusion." And for what? "A politically motivated giveaway to members of the middle class."

Project Debater was unmoved. "For starters, I sometimes listen to opponents and wonder: What do they want? Would they want poor people on their doorsteps begging for money? Would they live well with poor people without heating or running water?" The words contained the hallmarks of demagogic speech—slander, hyperbole, inelegant repetition—but the voice remained as solicitous as that of a virtual assistant.

Next came the real test. Project Debater was designed to prepare its rebuttal in advance. So before Harish had even spoken, the machine had generated potential points for the other side, or "leads," and prepared counterarguments. What it had to do in the round was to identify which of these leads Harish had actually said, then slot in the appropriate response.

Here the machine seemed to falter. Project Debater asserted without evidence that the "state budget is a big one. . . . Therefore the idea that there are more important things to spend on is irrelevant, because the different subsidies are not mutually exclusive." It made the subtle observation that subsidies enabled parents to enter and remain in the workforce (a potential response to Harish's point about access to preschools). But without explaining this point, it moved on to another assertion: "We are talking about a limited, targeted, and helpful mechanism."

In his rebuttal speech, Harish assumed a conciliatory stance. "So I want to start by noting what Project Debater and I agree on. We agree that poverty is terrible. . . . Those are all things we need to address." Then he made a turn. "None of those [issues] are addressed just because you are going to subsidize preschool." Harish repeated his point about budgetary constraints. He added that even if the money was not scarce, political support for spending was. "I'm very happy to oppose," he concluded.

The speakers presented two-minute closing statements. Then the audience cast their votes. Prior to the debate, support for subsidizing preschool among the audience had the following breakdown:

79%   support

13%   oppose

8%   undecided

These numbers had shifted by the end of the round:

62%   support

30%   oppose

8%   undecided

Based on the measure of "stance change," Harish Natarajan was declared the winner.

The moderator had also asked the audience a second question: "Which of the two debaters better enriched your knowledge?" Here, Project Debater received 55 percent of the vote, against Harish's 22 percent (the remainder said it was a tie).

I punched out a comment piece for the newspaper. Then, over lunch at a banh mi place, I paused over the two measures that had been used to judge the round.

Project Debater had enriched our knowledge because doing so was integral to its strategy. The machine was programmed to believe in the persuasive force of facts and studies. As it said in summarizing its case: "I am convinced that in my speeches I've supplied *enough data* to justify support for preschools." If anything, the system seemed to overweight the importance of evidence—to its detriment. In a rush to squeeze in an additional study or quotation, Project Debater missed other opportunities: to unpack ideas, to connect with the audience, to be more responsive in rebuttal.

Harish had taken a different approach. He spoke in terms of trade-offs and budgetary constraints, and with these words, he drew a hard line between ideals and practical realities. This had seemed to me prudent—closer to how we do and should make decisions.

But now I wondered whether I had been too ready to accept the logic of scarcity. I had barely considered, for example, the costs of *not* improving access to education. Perhaps the machine had seen something that I had missed: the same societies that rationed learning on the basis of class had produced many papers about the irreversible harms of such an approach.

The other area where Harish had bested Debater was in forming connections with the audience. He emphasized "common ground" and projected concern; he smiled and frowned at the right moments. Against such a natural performer, the machine, with its computer screen body and efficient sense of humor, stood no chance. I had found this reassuring: that most humane competence—the ability to relate to other humans—remained exclusively ours. But now I thought of the ways that a preference for the messenger over the message, for like over unalike, could mislead us. What more elemental a form of homophily could there be than an inclination in favor of the human?

That raised for me one last question: Had Project Debater lost the round because it was inferior or superior to us in debate? As I wrapped up the rest of my sandwich and wandered back to the office, I settled on the answer: both.

. . .

The weeks after the San Francisco debate were busy. On the morning of April 11, the Australian prime minister advised the governor general to dissolve Parliament and set the election for the next month. An email went out to the newsroom. Though the thirty-eight-day campaign was modest by international standards, it would nonetheless be a "marathon" and the "biggest story of the year."

For me, the opportunity to cover an election was a dream. Here my romantic visions of journalism—of its service to democracy, of its necessity and consequence—seemed to more closely match reality. The hard part was finding an angle into the best-covered story in town. Most days I found myself scrolling through Twitter and other social media sites, where minor controversies, as raw and red as fresh wounds, opened every few minutes.

Part of me wanted to say, as in the meme, "This is fine." I had grown up with social media and relied on it to stay in touch with friends across three international moves. Besides, the debater in me welcomed the profusion of political disagreement online—a rare thing in times of self-segregation along class lines, echo chambers, unequal access to public platforms, and convergence of the major parties on matters of substance. I understood all this in the abstract. But the experience of spending an extended period on these sites was something else. In a word, it sucked, and I began to wonder if *anyone* disagreed well on the internet.

The existing research on online arguments kept directing me to this one forum on Reddit: Change My View (r/changemyview). Since its founding in 2013 by a seventeen-year-old Scottish musician named Kal Turnbull, the subreddit had grown to a community of 700,000 users, attracted the attention of a technology incubator inside Google, and been garlanded in *Wired* magazine as "our best hope for civil discourse online." The idea was simple: an original poster (OP) argued for a belief they held but were open to changing (for example, "gentrification is a difficult but necessary process"), then challenged others to "CMV" (change my view); the OP then debated responders and, if one of them managed to change his or her mind, awarded that person a delta symbol (Δ). Community members displayed next to their names the number of deltas they had won. The forum seemed to confirm two unlikely propositions: online disagreements could be civil, and they could change our view.

For scholars, user activity on CMV proved a rich source of data. It not only recorded the ways in which people disagreed but also identified which of these approaches were most likely to change someone else's mind—that is, earn the Δ. In the most robust of some half-dozen research papers based on CMV data, researchers from Cornell University studied eighteen thousand threads involving seventy thousand participants over a two-and-a-half-year span. The results seemed to provide the grounds for several rules of thumb:

Move fast: The likelihood of changing an original poster's mind diminished as delays in entry time increased. The first and second responders to an original post were three times more likely to succeed than the tenth responder.

Be honest: The more persuasive posts tended to acknowledge uncertainties and qualifications. Perhaps for similar reasons, effective arguments tended also to contain more "arguer-relevant personal pronouns" (e.g., I, you, us) to break up what might otherwise have been blanket and general statements.

Don't be (too) responsive: Successful arguments were more likely to provide "new information or new perspectives"—measured by differences in wording—than to respond using the same terms as the original post. The researchers also said the common practice of quoting one's opponent "does not seem to be a useful strategy" in rebuttal.

Show receipts: Persuasive posts tended to cite external evidence using hyperlinks and markers such as *for example* and *e.g.* A separate study by Arizona State University researchers in 2018 found that the persuasiveness of evidence was robust in both discussions about "sociomoral" issues and those on less charged topics.

Let go (after four): The likelihood of changing a view peaked at three back-and-forths between original poster and respondent, then plummeted after four such turns.

This all made good sense to me, but the more time I spent on CMV, the more unusual its denizens and environment began to seem. The users were earnest to an almost painful extent. Some original posts stretched to the length of op-eds. Others described minor personal crises—moments of frustration, doubt, or epiphany—that the author wanted to share with CMV users. The responders tended to be rigorous and, on occasion, harsh in their criticism. Just as often they asked questions and conceded parts of the argument.

These users seemed to me like refugees who had escaped perilous regions of the web and created a new world. This society was held together not only by underlying affinity or culture but also by laws and regulations. The "rules" tab of CMV contains more text than the U.S. Constitution. It spans the pedantic ("Titles are statements, not questions. For example, you should write 'CMV: Trix are just for kids,' not 'CMV: Are Trix just for kids?'") to the moralistic ("You are free to call the idea they present an offensive term—'That viewpoint is racist'—but you must stop short of saying anything about the person making the comment"). Each of these rules is enforced by a roving band of volunteer moderators who are empowered to remove posts and, in extreme circumstances, ban the user from the forum.

Through this combination of soft and hard power, CMV seemed to address three structural problems that gave rise to bad online debates:

Audience: One of the worst aspects of online disagreements was that participants seemed less interested in changing one another's minds, or even in discussing the question at hand, than in signaling to the crowd their virtues and affinities. CMV devised an elegant solution to this problem: the only way to "succeed" was to change someone else's mind.

Algorithm: Disputes on social media tended to be protracted and upsetting because the sites' algorithms selected for extreme content to drive engagement. CMV also relied on engagement, but promotion to the top of the thread was based on users "upvoting" the entire discussion thread, as opposed to individual comments.

Anonymity: Social media platforms have estimated that some 5 percent of the profiles on their websites were fake and that most of these were run by bots. This posed serious risks such as electoral interference and, on a smaller scale, cast suspicion on the identities and motivations of other netizens. CMV users were mostly anonymous (the founder posted as "Snorrrlax"), but they identified themselves through their Δ count, a signal of their long-term involvement with the community.

The result was a restoration of some of the background conditions for good disagreement—an acoustics that amplified arguments over slogans; listening over grandstanding; resolution over protraction. Some of that was due to self-selection, but a good deal of it was about design.

The idiosyncratic culture, rules, and enforcement required to sustain a discussion on CMV, however, exacted a cost. CMV remained, even within Reddit, a niche community. Its membership of 700,000 members was between twenty and twenty-five times less than those of subreddits such as r/gaming, r/todayilearned, and r/funny. To be honest, the rule-abiding earnestness of CMV was too much even for me. The disagreements, in their perfection, felt to me unnatural and prohibitive, as if the barrier to entry had been raised too high.

I left these browsing sessions with the same question: If this utopia was not to most people's liking (nor mine), what did a viable future for disagreement look like?

. . .

For some years I had been following the career of an unusual public servant in Taiwan named Audrey Tang. Born in 1981 to two journalists, Tang was a prodigy who started to learn computer programming at age eight and dropped out of school at age fourteen to pursue her own education ("I'm trained on Project Gutenberg and Arxiv .org"). She soon after founded her first company and embarked on a career as a tech entrepreneur and consultant.

In March 2014, at age thirty-three, Tang left her job in Silicon Valley to rush back home. In downtown Taipei, something major was afoot. The Kuomintang government had tried to pass, without review, a free-trade agreement with Beijing. On the evening of the eighteenth, a crowd of protesters, most of them students, broke into the legislature and began an occupation. Tang joined colleagues from g0v, a group of "civic hackers" working on solutions to social problems, and helped set up the technical infrastructure to help protesters communicate and organize. The so-called Sunflower Movement, which attracted more than 100,000 people at one rally, forced the legislature to make concessions. Tang retired from the business world and went full-time on the movement's broader mission to make the government more responsive to the people. In October 2016, at age thirty-five, Tang became digital minister of Taiwan.

Tang cut an unusual figure as a cabinet minister. She identified as a "conservative anarchist"—conservative in her desire to preserve cultures and traditions, anarchist in her opposition to coercion (as minister, she has vowed not to give or take orders, only suggestions). She wrote her job description in the form of a poem and ended most interviews with the Vulcan salute, "Live long and prosper." Tang had undergone hormone replacement in her twenties and identified as postgender (her preferred pronoun is "whatever"). Now in 2019, two years into her position, she was starting to publicize what Taiwan had done.

For me, one way to understand Tang's work was in contrast to Change My View. Whereas the subreddit thrived on regulation—the catchcry of most opponents of big tech—Tang and her team opted for a lighter touch. Their approach was not to take down objectionable content or antisocial platforms but to outcompete them.

First the government set up its own social platform, Join, to enable citizens to propose and debate petitions. The idea grew out of vTaiwan, an early g0v platform used to form "rough consensus"—a hacker's term for a solution one could live with—by visualizing points of agreement and disagreement between participants. Both websites were built on Polis—an open-source program that, among other things, dispensed with "replies" in favor of up- and downvotes to minimize trolling behavior. But whereas vTaiwan had attracted hundreds of thousands of people, Join had registered over five million users, or a quarter of the island's population. The uptake of Join seemed to indicate an underappreciated reason for the use of social media: citizens wanted influence over the policies that governed their lives.

Second, on platforms that it did not control, the government competed against misinformation and disinformation. Each ministry had a team that responded within sixty minutes to false and damaging information with an "equally or more convincing narrative." The measure of success was virality, so the teams' approach tended to make heavy use of jokes and memes (the Shiba Inu, of "doge" fame, is the spokesdog of the counterpandemic effort). Separately from the government, g0v and the messaging platform Line each maintained fact-checking bots that allowed users to check the veracity of certain claims.

To some extent these efforts were doomed from the start. There was plenty of evidence to suggest that lies spread faster than truth on social media, and that slander and misinformation, even when discredited, tended to stick in people's minds. The corrosive effects of distrust in expertise, concerted disinformation campaigns, and fake accounts only made the problem worse. But for Tang, the memes and fact-checks were aspects of a broader vision for a more accountable society. The latter also required public education in media competence and reforms to make governance more transparent. ("People get misinformation or rumors because they want to know what's happening and there's no complete context," Tang told a journalist in 2017.)

None of that seemed objectionable (who could oppose civic education?). But for me the most distinctive aspect of Tang's approach was an unwillingness to wait for ideal conditions before getting started. As minister, she published on the internet a transcript of every meeting she chaired—even though the information might be taken out of context or used against her. She held open hours every Wednesday and sorted through people's comments and feedback—even though some of these meetings were surely useless. "This needs to happen before asking people to trust the government," she told *Dumbo Feather* magazine. "Someone has to move first."

In many respects, Taiwan stands on its own. The island is the size of Lesotho or Belgium, and its 24 million residents are relatively wealthy, educated, and connected to the web. More to the point, Taiwan sits 180 kilometers away from the coast of mainland China. The Chinese government maintained that the island was a province and its leadership a regional authority. Only a dozen or so countries have official diplomatic ties with Taiwan, and nations such as the United States oppose its formal independence. Inasmuch as Taiwanese people closely engage with politics and democratic initiatives, some of that participation was due to the precariousness of their situation.

There is also the fact that democracy in Taiwan is a recent phenomenon. The island emerged in 1987 from almost forty years of martial law and held its first leadership ballot in 1996. As Audrey Tang has observed, the two dates happened to coincide, respectively, with the rollout in Taiwan of personal computers and the World Wide Web. "It's like internet and democracy is not two things. It's the same thing," she has said, cryptically, of the association.

Even within the Taiwanese government, Tang's position was highly unusual. Her commitment to transparency excluded her from top secrets and other highly sensitive discussions. Even as she refused to give or take orders, the Taiwanese cabinet had come under criticism for its more punitive attempts to address "fake news."

Listening to Tang's speeches and interviews, I experienced a kind of disorientation. She sounded at once like an anachronism—a techno-utopian from the earliest days of the internet—and a voice from the future. In each case, she was out of sync with a status quo in which confidence in technology seemed bound for disappointment, and faith in other netizens seemed a sure way to get burned.

However, on the night of the Australian federal election on May 18, as I maintained the newspaper's live blog, I found myself returning to two lines that Audrey Tang often quoted. They came from the Dao De Jing, a text from the sixth century BC credited to the philosopher Laozi:

To give no trust
is to get no trust.

. . .

By the time I met Noam Slonim in mid-2021, the world had been turned upside down by the COVID-19 pandemic. In Australia, the conservative government, reelected against extraordinary odds in 2019, now found itself on the back foot for a botched vaccine rollout. Audrey Tang and her colleagues were battling an online "infodemic" with real and immediate consequences for public health. Israel had endured three lockdowns and suffered thousands of deaths but appeared to have turned a corner. The world seemed to be teetering on the precipice of a new era.

I had last seen Slonim two years earlier on the livestream from

San Francisco. He had grown a beard since then. On video link, the blue light of the computer screen reflected off his glasses and made it hard to read his expression.

What I wanted to know from Slonim was how the debate had aged in his mind. This every debater knew: with time, one stopped ruing a high-profile loss. The memory mellowed and acquired new meanings. But for this process of maturation to begin, one had to first accept the defeat. So, had he?

"I think Harish was better at the live debate for the simple reason that he's really a stronger debater than Project Debater," Slonim began. "This is not to say that in any given debate that we would lose to him. But in most of the debates, he would do the better job.

"Now, I agree that if you listen to the debate again, and you think about it in a more rational way, the situation is more balanced. But this is not the way the competition is structured. You just listen to it live." Slonim reminded me that Project Debater had come out ahead on the measure of enriching the audience's knowledge. He explained that the initial distribution of opinion—80 percent in favor of subsidized preschools—had made it harder for the machine to win.

Then the man seemed to reset. "I can honestly say I don't care at all. To some extent I think it was serving us better that we lost. Maybe losing in a smaller margin could have been even better. But it was conveying the right message, and really I think it's a lesson." His team had labored for years under the weight of a singular ambition: to beat a champion debater in a live debate. Yet even in the immediate aftermath of the round, people focused less on the result than on the exchange. "When you look at it in retrospect, you realize this question was completely not important. So we were troubled by the wrong question."

But come on, I thought. In February 1996, Deep Blue had lost its first chess match against grand master Garry Kasparov, then had come back one year later to win the rematch. Sometimes the loss was a step toward a more meaningful win.

Slonim knew where the team would focus its energy in a rematch: reaching the "heart of the audience." They could program the machine to search for common ground instead of focusing only on rebuttal, and to more directly appeal to listeners. "Those things are not hard to do from a technological perspective," Slonim explained. His response contained a certain irony. This debating machine had been too, well, debate-y. If persuasion was the end, pure attack and logical reasoning were insufficient means. The softer skills of reassurance, sympathy, and compromise had to play their roles, too.

"Beyond that, can you really build stronger logic and stronger rebuttal and so on? Yes, these are things that are doable. You can work on that incrementally, and if you decide this is what you want to do, you can spend a few more years on that with a large enough team, and eventually we will win. This is my understanding."

For now, all this would remain speculation. IBM had decided not to further develop Project Debater as a live debate system and, instead, to focus on other uses of the technology. The initiatives unveiled thus far were about integrating the system's capabilities into a suite of enterprise AI products. But the company had also demonstrated some civic uses for the technology—such as parsing large volumes of public comments and presenting the key ideas to decision-makers.

The month before our conversation, Slonim and his team had published in *Nature* a complete description of Project Debater. Besides explaining how the system worked, the fifty-three coauthors sought also to define what kind of technology Debater represented. They observed that most AI research focused on completing a discrete, narrowly defined task using a monolithic system trained for that purpose. By contrast, Debater undertook a more complex job by breaking it down into smaller steps, then integrating the solutions. It was a "composite AI" system or, as Slonim put it to me, an "orchestrator" of many live components.

For the moment, Slonim reckoned that a single end-to-end system for debate—one that went straight from input to output without recourse to separately designed intermediate steps—was a distant prospect. Such a system would require enormous amounts of standardized data (the chess player Deep Blue chose its opening from a database of 700,000 grand master games). Moreover, the desired output in a debate round was so complicated that it was difficult to imagine how one might go about using the data. But that did not mean Slonim and his team had not thought about it.

One work-around to the data problem was an approach known as reinforcement learning. In October 2017, the Alphabet subsidiary DeepMind unveiled software that had mastered the game Go by playing against itself repeatedly. AlphaGo Zero started out knowing only the rules of the game. In three days, it played 4.9 million games and defeated an older version of AlphaGo that had beat the eighteen-time world champion, Lee Sedol. The system only kept improving from there. "A pure self-learning AlphaGo is the strongest. Humans seem redundant in front of its self-improvement," observed the Chinese player Ke Jie. In December of the same year, DeepMind introduced software that mastered chess, shogi, and Go using the same method.

Untethered to records of past performances, the system came up with strategies that had eluded the best players of these games. The resulting machine was, in the words of its makers, "no longer constrained by the limits of human knowledge."

Slonim said a version of this approach could theoretically apply to disagreements. His team had already built a "referee" capable of evaluating the strength of arguments. It was possible that a system arguing against itself and improving in response to feedback could "find patterns of persuasion that [humans] haven't thought about." But there was an important catch. Since the aim in a debate was to persuade a human to change his or her mind, a machine could not pull some incomprehensible, mind-boggling maneuver without losing the person. Whereas Go and chess players sought to transcend their opponents, debaters could not help but to bring them along.

"The human is inherently in the loop," Slonim said.

I found this idea comforting. Disagreement was such a human act that its boundaries traced those of our quirks and limitations. For better or worse, our capacity for reasoning, empathy, and judgment prescribed what debates could be. The machine that would ultimately defeat us in argument would arrive at this feat not by transcending our humanity but by embodying it instead.

In the days after my conversation with Noam Slonim, this same idea started to assume a more disquieting resonance. I imagined a system trained on millions of hours of human disagreements—from transcripts of parliamentary debates to logs of messages sent on social media. The machine would surely see that we had found ways to disagree well against improbable odds *and* that, on occasion, we had succumbed to the rhetoric of demagoguery, illogic, flattery, and hatred. It might even recognize that we built some technologies that enabled good arguments and others that hindered them.

A machine trained on such data would form a judgment about how we, as a species, had handled our disagreements. In response, the system would make the necessary adjustments to its performance. Whether such a machine would speak to our worse or better angels— in the language of eristic or debate, in the spirit of war or cooperation— remained, for the moment, in our hands.

CONCLUSION

This book, like a debate round, began with silence and will end with it, too.

In the wee hours of a Saturday in July 2021, I finished the first draft of my manuscript and, before the self-doubt could grip me, sent the document to a handful of friends. They were argumentative types who never struggled to form strong opinions, so I steeled myself for a lively response. What I got instead, for several, long weeks, was dead silence. Hundreds of pages and umpteen disclosures, and for what? "Talk to the hand."

Then, as I prepared to write off these so-called friends, their responses came one by one, in long email threads and intense phone conversations. The reaction fell short of universal admiration. Across the range of answers, one concern tended to predominate: "Good arguments are nice, but I wonder if the focus is too small-scale and individualized—concerned more with social niceties than structural reforms."

One friend, a start-up founder in Silicon Valley, told me to write four words on a sticky note—"How does debate scale?"—and to keep the note on my bathroom mirror until I had found an answer. Then minutes later he emailed me an image. In the small rectangle, an old man with a flowing beard and locks was lifting the globe on a lever. The quotation beneath read: "Give me a lever and a place to stand and I will move the earth." —Archimedes

I understood the impulse. The world seemed at this moment in the flux of great structural currents. From Australia I could see the shifts in geopolitical power in our region and felt the reverberations of the movement for racial justice in the United States. Then there was the pandemic, which seemed at once a disruption to and a reflection of the world that we had made.

The prevailing view of taking structures seriously posed a challenge to my argument: if the quality of our arguments was a *mere symptom* of broader social health, we should focus less on the debates themselves than on the institutional conditions that form their background. Perhaps we could start with the disparities in access to political representation or with the structure of our media organizations.

In the mornings, over my bathroom washbasin, I could not stop imagining the cursed sticky note—"How does debate scale?"—and, so, I resolved to answer the question. I eventually arrived at an agenda for imbuing public institutions with the spirit and practice of debate.

First, as a matter of design, public institutions should make more room for debate. We can achieve this through incremental reforms— say, to the rules of congressional and parliamentary procedure—or through the creation of new structures. One of the most promising examples of the latter is the citizens' assembly, a group of randomly selected citizens who are empowered to make binding or nonbinding policy recommendations.

Second, the state should provide citizens the education needed to participate in such forums. This means moving from basic civic awareness to what the scholar Meira Levinson calls the "knowledge, skills, attitudes, and habits of participation." Though we must begin this work at school, we should not foreclose possibilities for adult education—work hitherto shouldered by a small number of civil society organizations.

Third, after establishing these forums, public institutions— whether governments or public schools—should monitor and maintain their integrity. Debate relies on the existence of a level playing field, one that gives participants an opportunity to be heard and judged on the merits of their contributions. In our world such environments are rare. So we need to situate the effort to promote debate in a more substantive program for building more robust and equitable institutions.

Fourth, public institutions should be responsive to the outcomes of debates. Governments often use consultations as fig leaves to disguise inaction. However, a debate about protecting human rights is not the same as protecting human rights, and any forum that delivers only the former cannot long endure.

Though these ideas may seem abstract and quixotic, they have, in fact, already been implemented in many parts of the world. Citizens' assemblies have been formed in Canada, the United States, Ireland, the Netherlands, Belgium, Poland, and the UK within the last twenty years. When the Japanese government reintroduced the saiban-in system—a mandatory jury-like arrangement that invites citizens to deliberate with professional judges on criminal cases—they rolled out a massive public education campaign to teach citizens about legal arguments and deliberative procedures. (The minister of justice dressed as a parrot, the official mascot of the saiban-in system, to help promote the reforms.)

What's more, governments have shown they can quickly form ad hoc assemblies when it is in their interest to do so. For example, in response to the yellow-vest protests for economic reform, French president Emmanuel Macron in January 2019 began a massive public consultation exercise known as *Le Grand Débat National.* The process resulted, over two months, in "2 million online contributions, 10,000 local meetings, 16,000 complaint books, and a series of citizens' assemblies." The results of each of these experiments remain contested. Nonetheless, it would be folly to discount some of the most significant institutional reforms to democracy in the past one hundred years on account of their earliest iterations.

I believed in every item on this agenda, but as I rehearsed presenting them as a fully-integrated solution to the ailments of our public institutions, I could not shake the feeling that I had somehow missed the point.

• • •

How does debate scale? I felt an urgency to answer this question because I believed debate faced serious and even existential dangers. Observing the enraged arguments in the public square, I worried less for the participants' hurt feelings than for the great plurality of people who might be dissuaded from engaging at all. For I had known all my life that moment when one decided an argument was simply not worth it and that the best one could do was keep quiet.

Such silence had its temptations: it placed one at a distance from others and thus afforded safety, comfort, and feelings of superiority. However, as I had learned growing up in Australia, the decision to remove oneself from the conversation was a choice not only to walk away from other people but also to deny the self that exists in communion with the world. The motivations of such a move—frustration, boredom, hopelessness—could turn, over time, into the stickier substance of contempt.

In this respect, exhortations to tackle the structural bases of our social malaise could only be insufficient. Many of the problems in our public and private lives had institutional origins. However, the frustrations of bad disagreement—and the associated loss of faith in debate—could themselves drive social division and disfunction. Equally, no substantive reform could last in an environment where political adversaries lacked the will and ability to talk to one another. Institutional fixes could precede cultural change but could not outrun the need for it.

One afternoon, as I mulled over these ideas, my entrepreneur friend let me in on another secret about scaling: "The aim is not only to grow but to grow *disproportionately*, so that a small act on your part creates massive ripple effects," he said. "This is not about going door-to-door."

At that moment, the answer to his original question occurred to me: debate does not scale.

Whatever power debate has resides in the elemental magic of an encounter, face-to-face and one-to-one. Each disagreement requires care and attention on its own terms. In the flow of debate, there is no Archimedean lever: we can only ensure one good conversation, one sentence at a time.

Sometimes that can be enough. Good arguments generate new ideas and strengthen relationships. An education in debate makes people more immune to the slick manipulations of political opportunists. Though debate has trained many great individuals, its basic commitment is to dialog over monologue.

To change the world, debate has to first change the lives of debaters. In this book, I have told the story of how it changed mine. Debate gave me a voice when I had none. It taught me how to argue for my interests, respond to opponents, use words, lose with grace, and pick my battles. As far as transformations of the world go, this is minuscule but, for me, it was everything.

For a long time, I assumed that my interest in disagreement was rooted in the quirks and accidents of my biography. These days, I see debate in more universal terms. The writer Stan Grant likes to quote this line from Hegel: "Man is not at home in the world." As an Indigenous Australian who also has European ancestors, Grant places himself on both ends of the original encounter that created modern Australia: "I have lived between the ship and shore, trying to navigate the brackish waters of our troubled past." Grant argues, after Hegel, that liberation in such a circumstance must be found in dialectic: the process by which a point of view (thesis) clashes against another (antithesis), then, rather than defaulting to either one, gives rise to a third way that combines elements of both (synthesis).

Debate seems to me a response to the same challenge: humans disagree and are not at home in the world. That does not mean, however, that we need to choose between surrender and rejection, between subordinating ourselves to another person and standing so far apart that we cannot hear them at all.

Instead, debate asks us to remain open and susceptible to one another. A round that begins with the self—one's own position, arguments, ego—reaches inexorably toward the other.

This transition occurs, in the debate room, in the silence that follows after a speaker has finished his or her speech. Such a moment has neither the dullness of contempt nor the heaviness of avoidance. Instead, it teems with nervous anticipation of how one might be received and how the other side might respond.

For me, standing in this silence is one of the hardest moments in debate. It marks the time when you are most exposed, uncertain about the future, beholden to the grace of others. However, we debaters hand over the microphone because no dialogue can exist without this act of faith.

So that our arguments may live, we give them to someone else.

ACKNOWLEDGMENTS

I am grateful to the generations of debaters who built and maintained the tradition that gave me a home. I tried in these pages to give an account of their collective wisdom. I wrote with the voice they gave me. Special thanks to Fanele Mashwama for a now decade-long friendship—we ought to be grateful, indeed—and to Andrew Hood and Steve Hind for their wise guidance.

I acknowledge the faith and hard work of my publishing colleagues. Ben Ball at Scribner Australia was the first editor to take a chance on this book. He helped write the initial proposal (to himself) and has remained an indispensable guide through the journey's many twists and turns. My agents, Gail Ross and Dara Kaye, led me through eight iterations of the full proposal, then advocated for me with dazzling skill. William Heyward acquired the book for Penguin Press and became my main editor. His vision illuminated the path so that I could walk on.

Shoaib Rokadiya at William Collins inspired me with his grace and tenacity on long phone calls that crossed into the realm of friendship.

Any writer would be lucky to have one of these people in their corner. To have had all of them puts me in the unfortunate position of lacking any excuse.

Thanks to Ann Godoff, Scott Moyers, Arabella Pike, and Dan Ruffino, as well as their teams, for giving me a place on their storied lists. Natalie Coleman at Penguin Press and Amanda Zhang at Harvard College greatly eased the work of production with their acuity and good cheer. I am grateful to colleagues at, to date, Munhakdongne, Hayakawa, Beijing Xiron, Acme, Litera, as well as Abner Stein, Milkwood Agency, The English Agency, The Grayhawk Agency, and Livia Stoia Literary Agency, for bringing my book to a wider audience. For their work on this edition, I thank Sarah Hutson, Mollie Reid, Shina Patel, Meighan Cavanaugh, Nicole Celli, Tess Espinoza, Aly D'Amato, and Ryan Benitez.

This is a book about my education, so I have many teachers to thank. Judi Gilchrist showed me that words could change people's lives, not least by changing mine. Jamaica Kincaid remains for me the paragon of creativity and truth-telling. Elaine Scarry is the same for moral imagination and fortitude. Louis Menand taught me to be cool in judgment. Discussing politics and philosophy with Kevin Rudd, Wang Hui, Amartya Sen, Michael Rosen, and Roberto Unger was formative of my education. In journalism, Howard French, Richard McGregor, Julia Baird, Annabel Crabb, and many valued colleagues at the *Australian Financial Review* showed me how to ask good questions. In the law, I hope to walk in the footsteps of Michael Kirby, Gillian Triggs, Luis Moreno-Ocampo, Martha Minow, and Jeannie Suk Gersen. I am grateful to Steve Schwarzman and Bill Ackman for funding a part of my education. Thanks to Lissa Muscatine, Adam Grant, Robert Barnett, and Noam Slonim for their help.

I acknowledge the contributions of friends and family. Ceridwen Dovey took time away from her work as one of Australia's finest authors to coach me through every stage of this process. Jonah Hahn, Wynne Graham, Akshar Bonu, and Nathan Booth were the perfect interlocutors. I finished the manuscript in the home of my aunt, Mi Kyung Oh.

I dedicate this book to Jin Kyung Park and Won Kyo Seo, whom I love, for being on my side.

NOTES

INTRODUCTION

10 **In 2012, the Republican candidate:** David Corn, "Secret Video: Romney Tells Millionaire Donors What He REALLY Thinks of Obama Voters," *Mother Jones*, September 17, 2012, www.motherjones.com/politics/2012/09/secret-video-romney-private-fundraiser/.

10 **Four years later, the Democratic:** Amy Chozick, "Hillary Clinton Calls Many Trump Backers 'Deplorables,' and G.O.P. Pounces," *New York Times*, September 10, 2016, www.nytimes.com/2016/09/11/us/politics/hillary-clinton-basket-of-dep lorables.htm.

11 **University of California researchers found:** M. Keith Chen and Ryne Rohla, "The Effect of Partisanship and Political Advertising on Close Family Ties," *Science* 360, no. 6392 (2018): 1020–24.

12 **The collapse of the edifice:** Toni Morrison, "Nobel Lecture, 7 December 1993," *Georgia Review* 49, no. 1 (1995): 318–23.

CHAPTER ONE

42 **The term had been invoked:** Pauline Hanson, "Maiden Speech," Commonwealth of Australia, House Hansard, Appropriation Bill (No. 1), 1996–97, Second Reading, p. 3859.

43 **coined the phrase "new political correctness":** Mark Latham, "Politics: New Correctness," Commonwealth of Australia, House Hansard, Grievance Debate, 2002, p. 5624.

45 **"I have often felt"**: "House of Commons Rebuilding," Parl. Deb. H.C. (5th ser.) (1943) cols. 403–73, https://api.parliament.uk/historic-hansard/commons/1943/oct /28/house-of-commons-rebuilding.

45 **"We shape our buildings"**: "House of Commons Rebuilding."

CHAPTER TWO

55 **"I'm not a judge"**: *Scent of a Woman*, directed by Martin Brest (Universal Pictures, 1992).

56 **According to one poll**: "'Wingnuts' and President Obama," The Harris Poll, March 24, 2010, https://theharrispoll.com/wp-content/uploads/2017/12/Harris -Interactive-Poll-Research-Politics-Wingnuts-2010-03.pdf.

57 **"The facts are the facts"**: "Full Transcript: Obama Interview with NBC News," NBC News, Aug. 29, 2010, https://www.nbcnews.com/id/wbna38907780.

64 **the structure for the encomium**: "Encomium," Silva Rhetoricae, accessed February 9, 2022, http://rhetoric.byu.edu/Pedagogy/Progymnasmata/Encomium.htm.

65 **Some rhetoricians the progymnasmata**: Sharon Crowley and Debra Hawhee, *Ancient Rhetorics for Contemporary Students* (New York: Pearson/Longman, 2003), 385.

65 **"Just as it is no help"**: George Alexander Kennedy, *Progymnasmata: Greek Textbooks of Prose Composition and Rhetoric* (Leiden, Netherlands: Brill, 2003), 5–6.

66 **His editions of ancient**: David J. Fleming, "The Very Idea of a Progymnasmata," *Rhetoric Review* 22, no. 2 (2003): 116.

76 **Churchill was so turned off**: William H. Cropper, *Great Physicists: The Life and Times of Leading Physicists from Galileo to Hawking* (New York: Oxford University Press, 2004), 254–55.

77 **"One couldn't talk to him"**: John Horgan, *The End of Science: Facing the Limits of Knowledge in the Twilight of the Scientific Age* (New York: Basic Books, 2015), 29.

CHAPTER THREE

84 **"Silence is how you establish"**: Eugene Devaud, trans., "Teaching of Ptahhotep," 1916, www.ucl.ac.uk/museums-static/digitalegypt/literature/ptahhotep.html.

84 **"There is only one way"**: Dale Carnegie, *How to Win Friends and Influence People* (New York: Simon & Schuster, 2009), 122.

84 **"new trough in Australian politics"**: Paul Kelly, "Campaigns Characterised by Complacent Timidity," *The Australian*, July 28, 2010, https://www.theaustralian .com.au/subscribe/news/1/?sourceCode=TAWEB_WRE170_a_GGL&dest =https%3A%2F%2Fwww.theaustralian.com.au%2Fopinion%2Fcolumnists %2Fcampaigns-characterised-by-complacent-timidity%2Fnews-story

%2F4ae48b1667bbe66f4d63df9dd80b8f7e&memtype=anonymous&mode=premium&v2l=dynamic-hot-test-score&V21spcbehaviour=append.

85 **"repudiate[d] the destructive life"**: Norberto Bobbio, *In Praise of Meekness: Essays on Ethics and Politics* (Cambridge: Polity Press, 2000), 34.

91 **The Buddha warns Saccaka**: Bhikkhu Bodhi and Bhikkhu Ñanamoli, *The Middle Length Discourses of the Buddha: A Translation of the Majjhima Nikaya* (Somerville, MA: Wisdom, 2015), 326.

94 **In the second U.S. presidential debate**: David Jackson, "Study: Obama Wins 'Interruption Debate,'" *USA Today*, October 20, 2012, www.usatoday.com/story/theoval/2012/10/20/obama-romney-debate-interruptions-george-mason/1646127/.

94 **reward the decision**: "Obama Hits Back In Fiery Second Debate with Romney," BBC, October 17, 2012, https://www.bbc.com/news/world-us-canada-19976820.

94 **"and Rivals Bring Bare Fists"**: Jim Rutenberg and Jeff Zeleny, "Rivals Bring Bare Fists to Rematch," *New York Times*, October 16, 2012, https://www.nytimes.com/2012/10/17/us/politics/obama-and-romney-turn-up-the-temperature-at-their-second-debate.html.

94 **"President Obama may have benefited"**: Jackson, "Study: Obama Wins 'Interruption Debate.'"

103 **"spreads through the hearts of men"**: Aristotle and Jonathan Barnes, *The Complete Works of Aristotle: The Revised Oxford Translation, Vol. 2 (Bollingen Series LXXI-2)* (Princeton, NJ: Princeton University Press, 1984), 2195.

103 **For Aristotle, the opposite**: Aristotle, "Rhetoric," 350 BC, trans. W. Rhys Roberts, The Internet Classics Archive, http://classics.mit.edu/Aristotle/rhetoric.2.ii.html.

110 **"consistent program to be advocated"**: Jeremy Waldron, *Political Political Theory: Essays on Institutions* (Cambridge, MA and London, England: Harvard University Press, 2016), 102.

110 **"a body of men"**: Edmund Burke, "Thoughts on the Cause of the Present Discontents, 1770," in *Perspectives on Political Parties*, ed. Susan E. Scarrow (New York: Palgrave Macmillan, 2002), 40.

CHAPTER FOUR

113 **A thunderstorm derailed the ceremony**: Paul C. Nagel, *John Quincy Adams* (New York: Knopf Doubleday, 2012).

113 **At the revival:** John Quincy Adams and John Adams, *An Inaugural Oration: Delivered at the Author's Installation, as Boylston Professor of Rhetoric and Oratory, at Harvard University, in Cambridge, Massachusetts, on Thursday, June 12, 1806* (Boston: Munroe & Francis, 1806), 17.

115 **He castigated himself**: John Quincy Adams and Charles Francis Adams, *Memoirs of John Quincy Adams, Comprising Portions of His Diary from 1795 to 1848* (New York: AMS Press, 1970), 332.

115 **His father had once expressed:** K. H. Jamieson and D. Birdsell, "Characteristics of Prebroadcast Debates in America," in *Presidential Debates: The Challenge of Creating an Informed Electorate* (New York: Oxford University Press, 1988), 20.

115 **"Under governments purely republican":** Jamieson and Birdsell, "Characteristics of Prebroadcast Debates," 19.

115 **His final lecture filled:** Ralph Waldo Emerson, *The Works of Ralph Waldo Emerson Comprising His Essays, Lectures, Poems, and Orations* (London: Bell, 1882), 191.

123 **"Helen was not to blame":** Gorgias, *Encomium of Helen*, trans. Douglas M. MacDowell (Bristol, UK: Bristol Classical Press, 2005), 21.

123 **The philosopher put the question:** Plato, *The Dialogues of Plato*, vol. 1, trans. and with analyses by Benjamin Jowett (New York: Random House, 1936), 507.

125 **In the universities of medieval:** Encyclopedia Britannica Online, s.v. "Liberal Arts," August 10, 2010, www.britannica.com/topic/liberal-arts.

126 **the most popular classes:** Pooja Podugu, "CS50, Stat 110 See Continued Increases in Enrollment," *Harvard Crimson*, September 12, 2013, www.thecrimson.com/article/2013/9/12/course-enrollment-numbers-CS50/.

126 **two most recent Boylston:** For further reading, see: Jay Heinrichs, "How Harvard Destroyed Rhetoric," *Harvard Magazine* 97, no. 6, July–August 1995, 37–42.

126 **Though he made room:** Markku Peltonen, *The Cambridge Companion to Bacon* (Cambridge: Cambridge University Press, 1996), 224.

126 **"natural bent and peculiar quality":** Charles W. Eliot, "The New Education," *Atlantic Monthly*, February 1869.

126 **"rhetorical work spread over":** John C. Brereton, ed., *The Origins of Composition Studies in the American College, 1875–1925: A Documentary History* (Pittsburgh, PA: University of Pittsburgh Press, 1995), 13.

127 **newly founded British Broadcasting Company:** British Broadcasting Company, "History of the BBC: 1920s," accessed February 9, 2022, www.bbc.com/historyofthebbc/timelines/1920s.

127 **"descending tricolon with anaphora":** Boris Johnson, "Boris Johnson explains how to speak like Winston Churchill," *The Telegraph*, November 3, 2014, YouTube video, 2:31, https://www.youtube.com/watch?v=FLak2IzIv7U.

129 **"Every year, tens of billions":** People for the Ethical Treatment of Animals, "Debate Kit: Is It Ethical to Eat Animals?" accessed February 9, 2022, www.peta.org/teachkind/lesson-plans-activities/eating-animals-ethical-debate-kit/.

143 **He argued that whereas:** Edward T. Channing, *Lectures Read to the Seniors in Harvard College [with a Biographical Notice of the Author, by R. H. Dana the Younger]* (Boston: Ticknor & Fields, 1856), 7.

144 **"No Westerner, Southerner, Jew"**: William Bentinck-Smith, *The Harvard Book: Selections from Three Centuries* (Cambridge, MA: Harvard University Press, 1986), 254.

144 **They elected as their speaker**: Bruce A. Kimball, "'This Pitiable Rejection of a Great Opportunity': W. E. B. Du Bois, Clement G. Morgan, and the Harvard University Graduation of 1890," *Journal of African American History* 94, no. 1 (2009): 5–20.

145 **Law professor James Thayer resigned**: Kimball, "'This Pitiable Rejection of a Great Opportunity,'" 13.

145 **Clement Morgan had entitled**: Philip S. Foner and Robert James Branham, *Lift Every Voice: African American Oratory, 1787–1900* (Tuscaloosa: University of Alabama Press, 1998), 731.

146 **He had chosen as the subject**: W. E. B. Du Bois and David Levering Lewis, *W. E. B. Du Bois: A Reader* (New York: H. Holt, 1995), 18.

147 **"Du Bois, the colored orator"**: W. E. B. Du Bois, "Harvard in the Last Decades of the Nineteenth Century, May 1960," W. E. B. Du Bois Papers (MS 312), Special Collections and University Archives, University of Massachusetts Amherst Libraries.

148 **Her speech, a tribute**: Sarah Abushaar, "Undergraduate Speaker Sarah Abushaar— Harvard Commencement 2014," Harvard University, May 29, 2014, YouTube video, 9:41, www.youtube.com/watch?v=AiGdwqdpPKE.

CHAPTER FIVE

150 **the National Speech & Debate Association served**: National Speech & Debate Association, "The National Speech & Debate Association Announces 2018 National High School Champions," July 2, 2018, www.globenewswire.com/en/news-release/2018/07/02/1532485/0/en/The-National-Speech-Debate-Association-announces-2018-National-High-School-Champions.html.

151 **The term *spreading* refers**: Peter Rosen, "Policy Debaters Argue at the Speed of Cattle Auctioneers," KSLTV, March 9, 2019, https://ksltv.com/409597/policy-debaters-argue-speed-cattle-auctioneers/.

151 **Such speed is not**: Guinness World Records, s.v. "Fastest Talker (English)," August 30, 1995, www.guinnessworldrecords.com/world-records/358936-fastest-talker.

151 **(636 wpm, 1990)**: "UK: World's Fastest Talker Speaks," AP Archive, July 27, 1998, www.aparchive.com/metadata/youtube/46e1d010e07752b77b4a7b86ec67e2cc.

151 **"Practice holding your breath"**: Rachel Swatman, "Can You Recite Hamlet's 'To Be or Not to Be' Soliloquy Quicker Than the Fastest Talker?" Guinness

World Records, www.guinnessworldrecords.com/news/2018/1/can-you-recite-hamlets-to-be-or-not-to-be-soliloquy-quicker-than-the-fastest-t-509944.

151 **"You will hurt your voice"**: Princeton Debate, "Speaking Drills," accessed February 9, 2022, https://sites.google.com/site/princetonpolicydebate/home/debaters/speaking-drills.

151 **Some people traced**: Jay Caspian Kang, "High School Debate at 350 WPM," *Wired*, January 20, 2012, www.wired.com/2012/01/ff-debateteam/.

152 **"When I was involved"**: Debra Tolchinsky, "Fast-Talk Debate in an Accelerated World," *Chronicle of Higher Education*, July 22, 2020, www.chronicle.com/article/fast-talk-debate-in-an-accelerated-world/.

152 **"We often competed against"**: Tim Allis, "Education: The Bloody World of High School Debate," *D Magazine*, May 1986, www.dmagazine.com/publications/d-magazine/1986/may/education-the-bloody-world-of-high-school-debate/.

152 **the spread had been**: A work that is thoughtful on the spread: Ben Lerner, *The Topeka School* (New York: Farrar, Straus and Giroux, 2019).

152 **"A billion seconds ago"**: Tom Pollard, "Lincoln-Douglas Debate: Theory and Practice" (Lawrence: University of Kansas, 1981), 7.

153 **"One thing about speech"**: Pollard, "Lincoln-Douglas Debate," 7.

153 **They had to avoid**: Pollard, "Lincoln-Douglas Debate," vi.

153 **The billionaire founder**: Jack McCordick, "The Corrosion of High School Debate—and How It Mirrors American Politics," *America Magazine*, September 26, 2017, www.americamagazine.org/arts-culture/2017/09/26/corrosion-high-school-debate-and-how-it-mirrors-american-politics.

154 **"Debate needs to be like"**: *Resolved*, directed by Greg Whiteley (One Potato Productions, 1992).

155 **In a 2012 article for *Wired* magazine**: Kang, "High School Debate at 350 WPM."

155 **What began in the 1600s**: UK Parliament, "Origins of Parliament," accessed February 9, 2022, www.parliament.uk/about/living-heritage/transformingsociety/electionsvoting/chartists/overview/originsofparliament/.

155 **In Britain, students formed**: Taru Haapala, "Debating Societies, the Art of Rhetoric and the British House of Commons: Parliamentary Culture of Debate Before and After the 1832 Reform Act," *Res Publica* 27 (2012): 25–36.

156 **Across the pond, a group**: American Whig-Cliosophic Society, "Who We Are," accessed February 9, 2022, https://whigclio.princeton.edu/.

170 **"I will be the greatest"**: "Donald Trump: 'I Will Be Greatest Jobs President God Ever Created'—Video," *The Guardian*, June 16, 2015, https://www.theguardian.com/us-news/video/2015/jun/16/donald-trump-us-president-republicans-video.

170 **"Nobody builds walls better"**: Glenn Kessler, "A History of Trump's Promises

That Mexico Would Pay for the Wall, Which It Refuses to Do," *Washington Post*, January 8, 2019, https://www.washingtonpost.com/politics/2019/live-updates /trump-white-house/live-fact-checking-and-analysis-of-president-trumps -immigration-speech/a-history-of-trumps-promises-that-mexico-would-pay -for-the-wall-which-it-refuses-to-do/.

170 **"They're bringing drugs":** "Donald Trump Announces a Presidential Bid," *Washington Post*, June 16, 2015, https://www.washingtonpost.com/news/post -politics/wp/2015/06/16/full-text-donald-trump-announces-a-presidential-bid/.

171 **"What was initially intended":** Staff, "Ayaan Hirsi Ali Responds to Brandeis University," *Time*, April 9, 2014, https://time.com/56111/ayaan-hirsi-ali-they -simply-wanted-me-to-be-silenced/.

172 **"As I look ahead":** Samuel Earle, "'Rivers of Blood': The Legacy of a Speech That Divided Britain," *Atlantic*, April 20, 2018, www.theatlantic.com/international /archive/2018/04/enoch-powell-rivers-of-blood/558344/.

172 **At the 1969 local elections:** Martin Walker and Don Bateman, *The National Front* (London: Fontana, 1978).

172 **"I'm going to make a speech":** Camilla Schofield, *Enoch Powell and the Making of Postcolonial Britain* (Cambridge, UK: Cambridge University Press, 2013), 209.

172 **As the historian Evan Smith:** Evan Smith, *No Platform: A History of Anti-Fascism, Universities and the Limits of Free Speech* (Oxford and New York: Routledge, 2020), 28.

173 **"no platform" policy:** Smith, *No Platform*, 93.

173 **"individuals known to espouse":** NUS, April Conference: Minutes and Summary of Proceedings (London: NUS, 1974), 79.

173 **For example, in the 1980s:** 99 Parl. Deb. H.C. (6th ser.) (1986) cols. 182–277, https://api.parliament.uk/historic-hansard/commons/1986/jun/10/education -bill-lords.

173 **Nowadays, the NUS:** "NUS' No Platform Policy," NUS Connect, February 13, 2017, https://www.nusconnect.org.uk/resources/nus-no-platform-policy-f22f.

174 **"Debate or deliberation may not":** Joseph Russomanno, *Speech Freedom on Campus: Past, Present, and Future* (Lanham, MD: Lexington Books, 2021), 11.

174 **"Anybody who comes to speak":** Janell Ross, "Obama Says Liberal College Students Should Not Be 'Coddled.' Are We Really Surprised?" *Washington Post*, April 26, 2019, www.washingtonpost.com/news/the-fix/wp/2015/09/15/ obama-says-liberal-college-students-should-not-be-coddled-are-we-really-surprised/.

175 **"mere act of disagreement":** Richard Tuck and Michael Silverthorne, eds., *Hobbes: On the Citizen* (Cambridge, UK: Cambridge University Press, 1998) 26.

176 **termed "civil silence":** Teresa M. Bejan, *Mere Civility* (Cambridge: Harvard University Press, 2017), 11.

CHAPTER SIX

188 **"Countless tribes of men"**: Roger Gottlieb, *The Oxford Handbook of Religion and Ecology* (New York: Oxford University Press, 2011), 316.

188 **While arguing with Glaucon**: S. Marc Cohen, Patricia Curd, and C. D. C. Reeve, *Readings in Ancient Greek Philosophy: From Thales to Aristotle* (Indianapolis: Hackett, 2016), 315.

191 **"Our goal for this evening"**: *Washington Post* Staff, "Wednesday's GOP Debate Transcript, Annotated," *Washington Post*, April 26, 2019, www.washingtonpost .com/news/the-fix/wp/2015/09/16/annotated-transcript-september-16-gop -debate/.

191 **"How are you, Donald?"**: Commission on Presidential Debates, "September 26, 2016 Debate Transcript," September 26, 2016, www.debates.org/voter-education /debate-transcripts/september-26-2016-debate-transcript/.

192 **"For thirty years you've been"**: Commission on Presidential Debates, "September 26, 2016 Debate Transcript."

194 **As a young academic**: Martin Cohen, *Philosophical Tales: Being an Alternative History Revealing the Characters, the Plots, and the Hidden Scenes That Make Up the True Story of Philosophy* (Malden, MA: Blackwell, 2008), 172.

194 **The book starts with**: Arthur Schopenhauer, *The Art of Controversy: And Other Posthumous Papers*, ed. and trans. T. Bailey Saunders (London: Swan Sonnenschein, 1896), 4.

195 **"This world cannot be"**: Robert Wicks, *The Oxford Handbook of Schopenhauer* (New York: Oxford University Press, 2020), 98.

195 **"natural baseness of human nature"**: Schopenhauer, *Art of Controversy*, 5.

195 **"loquacity and innate dishonesty"**: Schopenhauer, *Art of Controversy*, 5.

195 **"Put objective truth aside"**: Schopenhauer, *Art of Controversy*, 10.

195 **"thrust and parry"**: Schopenhauer, *Art of Controversy*, 11.

195 **"Even when a man"**: Schopenhauer, *Art of Controversy*, 10.

196 **"what counter-trick"**: Schopenhauer, *Art of Controversy*, 46.

199 **The concept of wrangling**: Keith Lloyd, "Rethinking Rhetoric from an Indian Perspective: Implications in the 'Nyaya Sutra,'" *Rhetoric Review* 26, no. 4 (2007).

200 **"The very serious function"**: Portland State University, Toni Morrison, Primus St. John, John Callahan, Judy Callahan, and Lloyd Baker, "Black Studies Center Public Dialogue. Pt. 2" (1975). Special Collections: Oregon Public Speakers, 90. http://archives.pdx.edu/ds/psu/11309.

202 **"It takes 30 seconds"**: George Monbiot, "This Professor Of Denial Can't Even Answer His Own Questions on Climate Change," *The Guardian*, September 14, 2009, https://www.theguardian.com/commentisfree/cif-green/2009/sep/14 /climate-change-denial.

204 **"If we set those goals":** Commission on Presidential Debates, "October 9, 2016 Debate Transcript," October 9, 2016, www.debates.org/voter-education/debate-transcripts/october-9-2016-debate-transcript/.

205 **The percentage of respondents:** Anna Palmer and Jake Sherman, "Poll: Hillary Clinton Won the Second Debate," *Politico*, October 11, 2016, www.politico.com/story/2016/10/clinton-trump-debate-poll-229581.

209 **"What are you showing us":** Nikita Sergeevich Khrushchev, *Memoirs of Nikita Khrushchev*, vol. 3, ed. Sergei Khrushchev (University Park: Pennsylvania State University Press, 2007), 183.

210 **"Speaking is a conversation":** Jonathan Aitken, *Nixon: A Life* (Washington, DC: Regnery, 1993), 27.

216 **After I disembarked from the plane:** "Live Presidential Forecast," *New York Times*, November 9, 2016, www.nytimes.com/elections/2016/forecast/president.

216 **"Bad hombres":** Commission on Presidential Debates, "October 19, 2016 Debate Transcript."

216 **"A mélange of showmanship":** Bonnie Kristian, "America's Presidential Debates Are Broken. Here's How to Fix Them," *The Week*, September 7, 2016, https://theweek.com/articles/646203/americas-presidential-debates-are-broken-heres-how-fix.

216 **televised "crisis simulations":** Lee Drutman, "The Presidential Debate Format Stinks. We Should Run Crisis Simulations Instead," *Vox*, September 23, 2016, https://www.vox.com/polyarchy/2016/9/21/13006732/presidential-debate-format-bad.

217 **In 1851, he wrote:** Arthur Schopenhauer, *Parerga and Paralipomena* (Oxford: Clarendon Press, 2000), 26.

217 **He said he would not revisit:** Schopenhauer, *Parerga and Paralipomena*, 31.

218 **Whereas one brought wars:** "Hesiod: Works and Days," trans. Hugh G. Evelyn-White, 1914, https://people.sc.fsu.edu/~dduke/lectures/hesiod1.pdf.

CHAPTER SEVEN

219 **"Mathematics leaves no room":** Malcolm X, *Autobiography of Malcolm X*, 43.

220 **"Malcolm, you ought to":** Malcolm X, *Autobiography of Malcolm X*, 43.

220 **"I was smarter than":** Malcolm X, *Autobiography of Malcolm X*, 44.

221 **"never used a foul word":** Malcolm X, *Autobiography of Malcolm X*, 178.

221 **"steam under pressure":** Malcolm X, *Autobiography of Malcolm X*, 212.

222 **"But I will tell you that":** Malcolm X, *Autobiography of Malcolm X*, 212.

222 **"They're extraordinarily good":** "Education: Oxford v. Norfolk," *Time*, December 31, 1951, http://content.time.com/time/subscriber/article/0,33009,821992,00.html.

223 **Malcolm nearly always:** Peter Louis Goldman, *The Death and Life of Malcolm X* (Urbana and Chicago: University of Illinois Press, 1979), 16.

223 **"This is a humanizing event":** Natasha Haverty, "After Half A Century, In mates Resurrect The Norfolk Prison Debating Society," NPR's *Morning Edition*, December 27, 2016 https://www.npr.org/2016/12/27/506314053/after-half-a -century-inmates-resurrect-the-norfolk-prison-debating-society.

223 **"It had really begun":** Malcolm X, *Autobiography of Malcolm X*, 198.

227 **For example, a decade-long study:** Susannah Anderson and Briana Mezuk, "Participating in a Policy Debate Program and Academic Achievement Among at-Risk Adolescents in an Urban Public School District: 1997–2007," *Journal of Adolescence* 35, no. 5 (2012): 1225–35.

227 **Since 2013, Broward:** Scott Travis, "Broward Schools Make the Case for Debate Classes," *South Florida Sun-Sentinel*, June 18, 2018, www.sun-sentinel.com/local /broward/fl-broward-debate-classes-20141222-story.html.

229 **"I'm glad to know":** Farmer, *Lay Bare the Heart*, 117.

229 **But competitive debate, which pitted:** Michael D. Bartanen and Robert S. Littlefield, "Competitive Speech and Debate: How Play Influenced American Educational Practice," *American Journal of Play* 7, no. 2 (2015): 155–73, https://doi .org/ISSN-1938-0399.

230 **"deep-seated disgust":** David Gold, *Rhetoric at the Margins: Revising the History of Writing Instruction in American Colleges, 1873–1947* (Carbondale: Southern Illinois University Press, 2008), 41.

230 **"Almost every debater":** Robert Littlefield, *Forensics in America: A History* (Lanham, MD: Rowman & Littlefield, 2013), 254.

231 **"My boy, it is customary":** James Farmer, *Lay Bare the Heart: An Autobiography of the Civil Rights Movement* (Fort Worth: Texas Christian University Press, 1998), 121.

231 **"You've got to put something":** Douglas Martin, "Henrietta Bell Wells, a Pioneering Debater, Dies at 96," *New York Times*, March 12, 2008, https://www .nytimes.com/2008/03/12/us/12wells.html.

231 **"international shipment of arms and munitions":** Gail K. Beil, "Wiley College: The Great Debaters," *East Texas Historical Journal* 46, no. 1 (2008): 18–26, https://scholarworks.sfasu.edu/cgi/viewcontent.cgi?referer=&httpsredir=1 &article=2530&context=ethj.

232 **"thrill of seeing beyond":** Beil, "Wiley College."

232 **"Many folk have asked me":** Hobart Jarrett, "Adventures in Interracial Debate," *The Crisis* 42, no. 8 (August 1935): 240.

232 **under his direction, the Wiley:** Linda Green, "Excitement Builds for Washington-Winfrey Debate Movie," *Global Debate*, October 19, 2007, https:// globaldebateblog.blogspot.com/2007/10/excitement-builds-for-washington.html.

237 **The linguist Deborah Tannen:** Deborah Tannen, *The Argument Culture* (New York: Ballantine Books, 1999), 3, 134.

238 **"I was saved":** Farmer, *Lay Bare the Heart*, 224.

238 **"what is thy cure":** Farmer, *Lay Bare the Heart*, 225.

238 **"searching for a speech":** Farmer, *Lay Bare the Heart*, 225.

238 **He regained his footing:** Robert James Branham, "'I Was Gone on Debating': Malcolm X's Prison Debates and Public Confrontations," *Argumentation and Advocacy* 31, no. 3 (1995): 117–37, https://doi.org/10.1080/00028533.1995.11951606.

238 **"Mr. X, you have":** Ben Voth, *James Farmer Jr.: The Great Debater* (Lanham: Lexington Books, 2017), 167.

239 **Perhaps the best of these:** The Open Mind, "Malcolm X, Wyatt Tee Walker, Alan Morrison, and James Farmer," PBS, aired June 11, 1963, https://www.njtvonline.org/programs/the-open-mind/the-open-mind-open-mind-special-race-relations-in-crisis-61263.

240 **"Come off it, Malcolm":** Beil, "Wiley College."

241 **"It's time now for you":** Malcolm X, "The Ballot or the Bullet" (speech, Cleveland, Ohio, April 3, 1964), www.edchange.org/multicultural/speeches/malcolm_x_ballot.html.

241 **For example, he advocated:** Leilah Danielson, "The 'Two-ness' of the Movement: James Farmer, Nonviolence, and Black Nationalism," *Peace & Change* 29, no. 3–4 (2004): 431–52, https://doi.org/10.1111/j.0149-0508.2004.00298.x.

241 **"And we may well":** James Farmer, *Freedom—When?* (New York: Random House, 1966; 1965), 92, 95.

241 **In 2006, a professor of organizational:** Christina Ting Fong, "The Effects of Emotional Ambivalence on Creativity," *The Academy of Management Journal* 49, no. 5 (2006): 1016–30.

CHAPTER EIGHT

250 **"Do we think so little":** "Malcolm Turnbull Takes Question from Reporters On Postal Plebiscite Decision," *Sydney Morning Herald*, August 8, 2017, https://www.smh.com.au/politics/federal/transcript-malcolm-turnbull-takes-question-from-reporters-on-postal-plebiscite-decision-20170808-gxrwp7.html.

252 **"The plumb line":** Justin Welby, "Archbishop Delivers Presidential Address to General Synod," The Archbishop of Canterbury, November 24, 2015, https://www.archbishopofcanterbury.org/speaking-and-writing/speeches/archbishop-delivers-presidential-address-general-synod.

253 **The manufacturers of the laundry:** Finish, "Finish Launches #Skiptherinse: A Movement to Help End Wasteful Dishwashing Habits and Conserve Water," Cision PR Newswire, July 28, 2020, www.prnewswire.com/news-releases/finish

-launches-skiptherinse-a-movement-to-help-end-wasteful-dishwashing-habits
-and-conserve-water-301101054.html.

258 **In 2010, cognitive scientists:** Hugo Mercier and Dan Sperber, "Why Do Humans Reason? Arguments for an Argumentative Theory," *Behavioral and Brain Sciences* 34, no. 2 (2011): 57–74, doi:10.1017/S0140525X10000968.

258 **"[Reasoning] was a purely social":** Patricia Cohen, "Reason Seen More as Weapon Than Path to Truth," *New York Times*, June 14, 2011, www.nytimes.com/2011/06/15/arts/people-argue-just-to-win-scholars-assert.html.

260 **"One can speak only after":** William Ury, *Getting to Peace: Transforming Conflict at Home, at Work, and in the World* (New York: Viking, 1999), 148.

260 **The conflict scholar Anatol:** Anatol Rapoport, "Three Modes of Conflict," *Management Science* 7, no. 3 (1961): 210–18, www.jstor.org/stable/2627528.

261 **"Now as the rule stands":** Robert Louis Stevenson, *Lay Morals and Other Papers* (New York: Scribner, 1911), 137.

262 **"Follow the way by which":** Blaise Pascal, *Pensées*, trans. A. Krailsheimer (London: Penguin, 2003), 68.

264 **"The speaker in this video":** Chris Zabilowicz, "The West Treats Russia Unfairly | Chris Zabilowicz | Part 1 of 6," Oxford Union, posted March 28, 2017, YouTube video, 18:06, www.youtube.com/watch?v=Ufb0ClkQY7U.

264 **"Personally I have not":** Theodore Roosevelt, *Autobiography* (New York: Macmillan, 1913), 28.

264 **In fact, the U.S. Naval Academy:** "Fearful Colleges Ban Debate on Recognition of Red China," *The Harvard Crimson*, June 17, 1955, www.thecrimson.com/article/1955/6/17/fearful-colleges-ban-debate-on-recognition/.

265 **"Our democracy needs men":** William M. Keith, *Democracy as Discussion: Civic Education and the American Forum Movement* (Lanham, MD: Lexington Books, 2007), 197.

265 **"I no longer found":** Sally Rooney, "Even If You Beat Me," *The Dublin Review*, Spring 2015, https://thedublinreview.com/article/even-if-you-beat-me.

268 **"facilitate the maturing":** A. Craig Baird, "The College Debater: 1955," *Southern Speech Journal* 20, no. 3 (1955): 204–11, https://doi.org/10.1080/10417945509371360.

268 **"The greatest orator":** Robert M. Martin and Andrew Bailey, *First Philosophy: Fundamental Problems and Readings in Philosophy* (Peterborough, ON: Broadview Press, 2012), 598.

268 **One would advocate for:** "Warren Buffett Has a Problem with 'Independent' Directors," *New York Times*, February 24, 2020, www.nytimes.com/2020/02/24/business/dealbook/warren-buffett-deals.html.

268 **In the aftermath of the catastrophic:** Gordon R. Gordon, "Switch-Side Debating Meets Demand-Driven Rhetoric of Science," *Rhetoric & Public Affairs* 13, no. 1 (2010): 95–120, https://doi.org/10.1353/rap.0.0134.

271 **Mandela himself was a practiced:** Nelson Mandela, *Long Walk to Freedom: The Autobiography of Nelson Mandela* (New York: Back Bay Books, 1995), 616.

272 **with such harsh criticism:** SABC News, "De Klerk, Mandela Pre-election Debate Rebroadcast, 14 April, 1994," streamed live on April 14, 2019, YouTube video, 1:57:47, www.youtube.com/watch?v=oTIeqLem67Q.

272 **"We are saying let us":** Stanley B. Greenberg, *Dispatches from the War Room: In the Trenches with Five Extraordinary Leaders* (New York: Thomas Dunne Books/St. Martin's Press, 2009), 145.

272 **"Mr. de Klerk seemed surprised":** Mandela, *Long Walk to Freedom*, 617.

CHAPTER NINE

277 **I had heard whispers:** N. Slonim et al., "An Autonomous Debating System," *Nature* 591 (2021): 379–84, https://doi.org/10.1038/s41586-021-03215-w.

278 **Debater was "pretty convincing":** Dave Lee, "IBM's Machine Argues, Pretty Convincingly, with Humans," BBC News, June 19, 2018, www.bbc.com/news/technology-44531132.

278 **"more than held its own":** Edward C. Baig and Ryan Suppe, "IBM Shows Off an Artificial Intelligence That Can Debate a Human—and Do Pretty Well," *USA Today*, June 20, 2018, www.usatoday.com/story/tech/2018/06/18/ibms-project-debater-uses-artificial-intelligence-debate-human/712353002/.

279 **"HAL, I won't argue":** *2001: A Space Odyssey*, directed by Stanley Kubrick (Metro-Goldwyn-Mayer, 1968).

279 **"First, arguing for the resolution":** Intelligence Squared Debates, "IBM Project Debater," February 26, 2019, YouTube video, 46:48, www.youtube.com/watch?v=3_yy0dnIc58&t=1275s.

281 **"The challenge: beat":** IBM Research, "What Happens When AI Stops Playing Games," June 22, 2020, YouTube video, 25:48, www.youtube.com/watch?v=NSxVEaWEUjk&t=483s.

281 **Slonim and his colleague wrote:** IBM Research, "What Happens When AI Stops Playing Games."

282 **But early studies of internet:** T. W. Benson, "Rhetoric, Civility, and Community: Political Debate on Computer Bulletin Boards," *Communication Quarterly* 44, no. 3 (1996): 359–78.

282 **"People tell me":** Patrick Winter, "Facebook Founder Zuckerberg Tells G8 Summit: Don't Regulate the Web," *The Guardian*, May 26, 2011, www.theguardian.com/technology/2011/may/26/facebook-google-internet-regulation-g8.

283 **"They attack the same problems":** Noam Slonim and Chris Sciacca, interview with the author, April 14, 2021. Quotes from Slonim are from this interview, unless otherwise noted.

283 **"Don't thank me yet"**: IBM Research, "What Happens When AI Stops Playing Games."

283 **The makers of Project Debater**: Nick Petrić Howe and Shamini Bundell, "The AI That Argues Back," *Nature*, March 17, 2021, www.nature.com/articles/d41586 -021-00720-w?proof=t.

283 **compendium of commonly**: For a detailed description of Project Debater's internal operations see: "An Autonomous Debating System—Supplementary Material," *Nature*, March 17, 2021, https://static-content.springer.com/esm/art%3A10.1038 %2Fs41586-021-03215-w/MediaObjects/41586_2021_3215_MOESM1_ESM.pdf.

285 **So before Harish had even**: Howe and Bundell, "AI That Argues Back."

289 **"our best hope for civil"**: Virginia Heffernan, "Our Best Hope for Civil Discourse on the Internet Is on . . . Reddit," *Wired*, January 16, 2018, www.wired .com/story/free-speech-issue-reddit-change-my-view/.

290 **In the most robust**: Chenhao Tan et al., "Winning Arguments," in *Proceedings of the 25th International Conference on World Wide Web* (Geneva: International World Wide Web Conferences Steering Committee, 2016), 613–24, https://doi.org/10.1 145/2872427.2883081.

291 **A separate study**: John Hunter Priniski and Zachary Horne, "Attitude Change on Reddit's Change My View," in *Proceedings of the 40th Annual Conference of the Cognitive Science Society*, eds. T. T. Rogers, M. Rau, X. Zhu, and C. W. Kalish. (Austin, TX: Cognitive Science Society, 2018), 2276–281.

291 **The "rules" tab of CMV**: "Change My View (CMV)," Reddit, accessed October 21, 2021, www.reddit.com/r/changemyview/wiki/rules#wiki_rule_a.

292 **Social media platforms**: Jack Nicas, "Why Can't the Social Networks Stop Fake Accounts?" *New York Times*, December 8, 2020, https://www.nytimes.com/2020/ 12/08/technology/why-cant-the-social-networks-stop-fake-accounts.html.

293 **"I'm trained on Project Gutenberg"**: Audrey Tang, "Meeting with Dr. Todd Lowary," *SayIt*, September 18, 2019, https://sayit.pdis.nat.gov.tw/2019-09-18-mee ting-with-dr-todd-lowary#s328598.

294 **In October 2016, at age thirty-five**: "Taiwan's Digital Minister Audrey Tang Highlights Opportunities in Social Innovation," *Asia Society*, March 26, 2021, https://asiasociety.org/texas/taiwans-digital-minister-audrey-tang-highlights -opportunities-social-innovation.

294 **She identified as**: Audrey Tang, "Interview with Cindy Yang Fiel," *SayIt*, January 7, 2021, https://sayit.pdis.nat.gov.tw/2021-01-07-interview-with-cindy-yang -field#s453187.

294 **Tang had undergone**: Audrey Tang, "Nancy Lin Visit," *SayIt*, April 17, 2019, https://sayit.pdis.nat.gov.tw/2019-04-17-nancy-lin-visit#s287792.

294 **First the government set up**: Andrew Leonard, "How Taiwan's Unlikely Digital Minister Hacked the Pandemic," *Wired*, July 23, 2020, www.wired.com/story /how-taiwans-unlikely-digital-minister-hacked-the-pandemic/.

295 **Both websites were built:** Leonard, "How Taiwan's Unlikely Digital Minister Hacked the Pandemic."

295 **Join had registered over:** Audrey Tang, "Conversation with Alexander Lewis," *SayIt*, January 7, 2019, https://sayit.pdis.nat.gov.tw/speech/266922.

295 **Each ministry had a team:** Tang, "Conversation with Alexander Lewis."

295 **"People get misinformation or rumors":** Audrey Tang, "Interview with Felix Lill," *SayIt*, November 7, 2017, https://sayit.pdis.nat.gov.tw/2017-11-07-interview -with-felix-lill#s111583.

296 **"This needs to happen":** Audrey Tang and Mele-Ane Havea, "Audrey Tang Is Radically Transparent," *Dumbo Feather*, December 7, 2017, www.dumbofeather .com/conversations/audrey-tang/.

297 **"It's like internet and democracy":** Audrey Tang, "Media Training with Joe Dolce," *SayIt*, October 10, 2017, https://sayit.pdis.nat.gov.tw/2017-10-10-media -training-with-joe-dolce#s99991.

297 **Even as she refused:** Matthew Strong, "Taiwan Plans to Punish Fake News About Coronavirus with Three Years in Prison," *Taiwan News*, February 19, 2020, www.taiwannews.com.tw/en/news/3878324.

297 **"To give no trust":** Audrey Tang, "Conversation with German Interviewers," *SayIt*, October 22, 2020, https://sayit.pdis.nat.gov.tw/2020-10-22-conversation -with-german-interviewers#s438054.

300 **"A pure self-learning AlphaGo":** Guo Meiping, "New Version of AlphaGo Can Master Weiqi Without Human Help," CGTN, October 19, 2017, https:// news.cgtn.com/news/314d444d31597a6333566d54/share_p.html.

301 **The resulting machine was:** David Silver and Demis Hassabis, "AlphaGo Zero: Starting from Scratch," *DeepMind* (blog), October 18, 2017, https://deepmind .com/blog/article/alphago-zero-starting-scratch.

CONCLUSION

305 **This means moving from:** Meira Levinson, *No Citizen Left Behind* (Cambridge, MA: Harvard University Press, 2014), 42.

306 **The minister of justice dressed:** Colin P. A. Jones, "Mascots on a Mission to Explain the Mundane," *Japan Times*, March 11, 2019, www.japantimes.co.jp /community/2011/08/30/general/mascots-on-a-mission-to-explain-the -mundane/.

306 **The process resulted:** Renaud Thillaye, "Is Macron's Grand Débat a Democratic Dawn for France?" *Carnegie Europe*, April 26, 2019, https://carnegieeurope .eu/2019/04/26/is-macron-s-grand-d-bat-democratic-dawn-for-france-pub -79010.

308 **"I have lived between":** Stan Grant, "Between the Ship and the Shore: The Captain James Cook I Know," *Sydney Morning Herald*, April 28, 2020.

INDEX

BPP University, 159–60
brainstorming, 260
Brandeis University, 171
brawler, 207–8, 210–13
British Broadcasting Company
    (BBC), 127
British Parliament, 44–45, 93, 110–11,
    155–56
"broke into the outrounds," 105
Brown University, 132
Bruce
    at New South Wales Debating Union,
        59–62, 71–72, 73–74
    at World Schools Debating, 78–82,
        85–87, 89, 98, 102–3, 106–7, 108,
        110, 182, 196
Buddhism (Buddha), 8, 91, 195
Buffett, Warren, 268
bullies (bullying), 187–218
    author's experience of, 196–98, 206–7
    the Brawler, 207–8, 210
    the Dodger, 198, 202
    the Liar, 200–202
    Nixon and Khrushchev, 207–8, 210
    personas, 198–203
    Schopenhauer and *Eristic Dialectic,*
        194–96
    Trump and presidential debate of 2016,
        190–94, 203–5, 207–8, 216–17
    the Twister, 199, 202
    the Wrangler, 199–200, 202
burden push, 202
burdens of proof. *See* "two burdens of proof"
buried ledes, 94–95, 137
Burke, Edmund, 110–11
Burr, Aaron, 156
Bush School, 2–4, 15, 20–21, 116–18
Butt Off the Couch threshold, 142–43
Byzantine Empire, 180

caesura, 137
"calling bullshit," 79, 81, 82, 85, 86, 96, 101–2
calmness, 103–4
Cambridge Debate Union, 128, 155–56, 181
Cambridge Rindge and Latin School,
    149–50, 155
Canada, 87, 88, 105, 305
cancel culture. *See* deplatforming
caprice, 142

Carnegie, Dale, 84
Cassandra, 62
Celebrity Apprentice (TV show), 171
Channing, Edward Tyrrel, 143
Charlestown Prison, 220–21, 223
Charlie Hebdo shooting, 163
chess, 16–17, 23, 278, 299, 300–301
Chicago Urban Debate League, 227
China, 242–49, 264
    author's Schwarzman Scholarship in,
        215–16, 242–46
Chiron, 187
Chris, 81
Chronicle of Higher Education, 152
Churchill, Winston, 44–45, 76, 127
Cicero, 114, 125, 268
Cincinnati Enquirer, 153
citizens' assemblies, 305–6
citizenship, 24, 65–66
Civil Rights Movement, 232, 240–41
"civil silence," 175–77
Class Day at Harvard, 144–48
climate change, 32–34, 202
Clinton, Bill, 204
Clinton, Hillary
    presidential debates of 2016, 190–94,
        203–5, 207–8, 216–17
    presidential election of 2016, 10, 170–71,
        215–17
"clogging," 178–79
CNN, 153, 191
codes duello, 178
code-switching, 16
Cohen, Leonard, 223
Cold War, 208–14, 264
Columbia University, 130–31
common ground, 253–54, 288, 299
"comparative advantage," 63
competitive debates, 8–9, 23, 38, 70, 155,
        229–30, 281. *See also* World Schools
        Debating
    ethics of, 264–65
    policy debate", 151
    topic analysis, 27–29
complaisance, 84
conclusion of argument, 59–63
Confederate States of America, 146–47
confirmation bias, 259
conflict aversion, 82–84, 86–87, 103